A Quintet of Cuisines

LIFE WORLD LIBRARY
LIFE NATURE LIBRARY
TIME READING PROGRAM
THE LIFE HISTORY OF THE UNITED STATES
LIFE SCIENCE LIBRARY
GREAT AGES OF MAN
TIME-LIFE LIBRARY OF ART
TIME-LIFE LIBRARY OF AMERICA
FOODS OF THE WORLD
THIS FABULOUS CENTURY
LIFE LIBRARY OF PHOTOGRAPHY

Foods of the World

A Quintet of Cuisines

by

Michael and Frances Field

and the Editors of

TIME-LIFE BOOKS

photographed by

Sheldon Cotler and Richard Jeffery

photography in Poland by Eliot Elisofon

TIME-LIFE BOOKS, NEW YORK

THE AUTHORS: Michael and Frances Field traveled on three continents—counting a research trip to the Polish Embassy in Washington, D.C., for an ambassadorial dinner party—gathering material for this book. Mr. Field is the consulting editor for this library; he teaches and lectures on cooking, has appeared on television and radio and has contributed to numerous national magazines. His books include *Michael Field's Cooking School, Michael Field's Culinary Classics and Improvisations* and *All Manner of Food*. Mrs. Field's short stories have appeared in *Esquire* and *Story*. For the Ford Foundation, she wrote a teacher's manual for the publication *Looking at Modern Painting*. Her own paintings have appeared in eight one-man shows and a number of group shows, and are included in the collections of five galleries and museums. The Fields live in New York City and Provincetown, Massachusetts.

THE FIELD PHOTOGRAPHERS: Sheldon Cotler *(far left)* photographed in all but one of the countries pictured in this book. He is art director of TIME-LIFE BOOKS, and his design awards include one from the American Institute of Graphic Arts and the Gold Medal of the Art Directors Club.

Eliot Elisofon, who took the pictures in Poland, has fulfilled more assignments than any other photographer for FOODS OF THE WORLD volumes. He is author of a cookbook of his own, and his more recent books include *Hollywood Style* and *Java Diary*.

THE TEST KITCHEN PHOTOGRAPHER: Richard Jeffery *(left)* is a New York freelance photographer. Other volumes to which he has contributed in this series include *Russian Cooking, African Cooking* and *American Cooking: New England*. Still-life materials for his pictures were chosen by Yvonne McHarg.

THE COVER: A still life represents the book's five cuisines: cheese from Switzerland, herring and mussels from the Low Countries, dried mushrooms from Poland, peppers from Bulgaria and Romania, *couscous* from North Africa.

TIME-LIFE BOOKS

EDITOR: Jerry Korn
Executive Editor: A. B. C. Whipple
Text Director: Martin Mann
Art Director: Sheldon Cotler
Chief of Research: Beatrice T. Dobie
Picture Editor: Robert G. Mason
Assistant Text Directors: Ogden Tanner, Diana Hirsh
Assistant Art Director: Arnold C. Holeywell
Assistant Chief of Research: Martha T. Goolrick
Assistant Picture Editor: Melvin L. Scott

PUBLISHER: Walter C. Rohrer
General Manager: John D. McSweeney
Business Manager: John Steven Maxwell
Production Manager: Louis Bronzo

Sales Director: Joan D. Manley
Promotion Director: Beatrice K. Tolleris
Public Relations Director: Nicholas Benton

FOODS OF THE WORLD

SERIES EDITOR: Richard L. Williams
EDITORIAL STAFF FOR A QUINTET OF CUISINES:
Associate Editor: Harvey B. Loomis
Picture Editor: Kaye Neil
Designer: Albert Sherman
Assistant to Designer: Elise Hilpert
Staff Writer: Helen I. Barer
Chief Researcher: Sarah Brash
Researchers: Joan Chambers, Rhea Finkelstein, David L. Harrison
Test Kitchen Chef: John W. Clancy
Test Kitchen Staff: Fifi Bergman, Sally Darr, Leola Spencer

EDITORIAL PRODUCTION
Production Editor: Douglas B. Graham
Color Director: Robert L. Young
Assistant: James J. Cox
Copy Staff: Rosalind Stubenberg, Eleanore W. Karsten, Florence Keith
Picture Department: Dolores A. Littles, Joan Lynch
Traffic: Arthur A. Goldberger

The text for this book was written by Michael and Frances Field, the recipe instructions by Michael Field assisted by Helen I. Barer, and other material by members of the staff. Valuable assistance was provided by the following individuals and departments of Time Inc.: Editorial Production, Robert W. Boyd Jr., Margaret T. Fischer; Editorial Reference, Peter Draz; Picture Collection, Doris O'Neil; Photographic Labtoratory, George Karas; TIME-LIFE News Service, Murray J. Gart; Correspondents Maria Vincenza Aloisi (Paris); Alex des Fontaines (Geneva); Friso Endt (Amsterdam); Andrzej Glowacz (Cracow); Stephen Hughes (Rabat); Elisabeth Kraemer (Bonn); Ann Natanson (Rome); Antoine Yared (Brussels).

Contents

The Recipe Booklet that accompanies this volume has been designed for use in the kitchen. It contains all of the 60 recipes printed in this book plus 91 more. It has a wipe-clean cover and a spiral binding so that it can either stand up or lie flat when open.

40163

Introduction: A Handful of Gastronomic Gems

The title of this book, *A Quintet of Cuisines,* requires some explanation. It refers to the cooking of five regions that include 10 countries: Switzerland, the Low Countries (Belgium-Luxembourg-Netherlands), Poland, Bulgaria and Romania, North Africa (Tunisia-Algeria-Morocco). In all candor, it should be said that they have little in common except, perhaps, that they are all members of the United Nations. But they all have fascinating foods—and for purposes of exploring their styles of cooking they are all gathered in one kitchen, as it were, in this book.

Before the words mini, midi and maxi became fatigued, the editors even considered the title *Mini-Cuisines.* It would not have been unapt, for none of these countries has what could be described as a large or infinitely varied repertoire of food. They did not exactly cry out to be dealt with in five or ten separate books. But in planning the library that we have called FOODS OF THE WORLD, we have felt free to construct our own, sometimes arbitrary culinary world. To all of South America, for example, we assigned one volume, while to France, which is gastronomically more complex, we allotted two, one on provincial cooking and one on the classic cuisine. From this subjective world of food we consigned to oblivion such potential titles as *The Cooking of Antarctica.* But we also felt that a few specialized parts of the world were too fascinating to leave out of account. Five of these small yet valuable gems of cuisines are spread out before you in this book, along with a look at the peoples who have fashioned them and live by them.

Finding an author who could function gracefully as ringmaster of such a gastronomic circus might have seemed impossible, except that he was right in our midst. Michael Field has been consulting editor for this series since its inception. It has not been a dull or easy job. He has had to write or edit thousands of recipes assembled from dozens of countries and regions, has tasted the end products of most of them as re-created in our test kitchen, and has had to put his knowledge and judgment to the test every time: is this dish really good, bad or indifferent, and are the techniques it requires understandable and workable or not?

Mr. Field is a member in good standing of what has been appropriately called the Food Establishment. At no time did the term mean a corporate establishment, like General Mills and General Foods. At one time it meant simply those helpful household oracles, Fannie Farmer and Irma Rombauer; now it denotes a growing coterie of professional people of all ages and both sexes who devote their working lives to investigating food, writing about it, and teaching people what to do with it.

They are a fractious faculty, at least as deeply involved in philosophical controversy and personality shoot-outs as are the members of the elites in economics, ecology, the space sciences and the fine arts. (No two of them agree in every detail on how one cooks an omelet.) Many of them, including Julia Child, James A. Beard, Craig Claiborne, M. F. K. Fisher and Joseph Wechsberg, have been enlisted as consultants or authors to enlighten and enliven FOODS OF THE WORLD.

In this small and seething population of culinary experts Michael Field is unique. He is the only member of the Food Establishment to enter it from a career in the performing arts. As the Field of the two-piano team of (Vera) Appleton and Field, he spent 20 years playing concerts in thousands of communities in America and abroad. All the while he was studying food and making himself adept in the field, preparing for a second career that would not entail a life of one-night stands.

Like his wife Frances, the co-author of this book, Mr. Field is a person of taste, charm and wit, and strong opinions. He is not alone among the Establishment in being a good showman, although in that department he probably has more experience than all the others put together. He may be alone, though, in loathing the term gourmet as intensely as he does, out of a feeling that it is pretentious. He likes to say that he is a teacher and writer about food, period. He is helped in both activities by a palate that is as discerning as a bloodhound's nose, and by a compulsively passionate desire to get accuracy and precision into recipes while keeping phoniness out. He is not against kitchen short cuts by any means, but is dead set against the ersatz ingredient or procedure that may bring an unpredictable or incorrect result.

As you read the book, we think you will agree that the Fields have done their field work and their home work well. Their text evokes visual delights as well as scents and flavors, for everywhere they went, Frances Field saw things with an artist's eye and recorded them with a writer's touch. The interesting differences between a *hutspot* and a *hochepot,* a *ghiveciu* and a *ghivetch,* a *brik* and a *bastila* are explored here, along with more significant attributes of the regions and their cooking. Most important, perhaps, can be your discovery that the foods throughout this quintet of cuisines are delightful to cook and eat.

—*Richard L. Williams, Editor,* FOODS OF THE WORLD

I Switzerland

A Small Treasury
of Alpine Pleasures

On a whirlwind trip we took through Switzerland when this book was a gleam in the editor's eye, my wife and I were struck, as we had been before, by the excellence and variety of traditional Swiss food. The country's cooking does, of course, reflect the lavish culinary influences of its many neighbors. But at the heart of Switzerland's international cuisine is a veritable treasure of purely Swiss dishes. It was these that Frances and I sought and rediscovered on a journey that took us from Zurich in the north to Bern in the west and ended in Lugano in the extreme south.

Once again we marveled at the complexity of this tiny republic and the distracting diversity of its five languages—German, French, Italian, Schwyzerdütsch and Romansch, a dialect descended from Latin. As if for the first time, we were enchanted by the terrain: sky-piercing mountains, placid rich plateaus, shimmering fish-filled lakes. The kaleidoscopic shift from wintry austerity in the north to balmy luxuriance in the south makes it, I thought, almost a microcosm of our own vast land.

Switzerland is a checkerboard of a country, a federation of 25 sovereign areas called cantons; they exist in a state of not-so-friendly rivalry that can erupt into outright animosity on the subject of food. What is the right way to prepare a cheese fondue? What do you drink with it? What should come before or after it? Or should it be served alone? These and similar gastronomic controversies can raise Swiss temperatures well above the boiling point.

Of course, when threatened by the outside world, the Swiss rise above their regional chauvinism. They have somehow managed to maintain a

Tucked into the Alps in the canton of Fribourg, the town of Gruyères gave its name to one of Switzerland's best-loved cheeses. But a lunch-time favorite there, as throughout the country, are the *Wähen,* or large tarts. The variety opposite is filled with fresh local apricots and topped with whipped cream. *Wähen* also are made with other fruit, cheese or vegetables and are eaten communally, like outsized pizzas.

Paul Spuhler, chef of Zurich's Dolder Grand Hotel, displays an assortment of Switzerland's prized cured meats, mostly from the canton of Grisons. Next to some sliced raw bacon are *(from right)* cuts of dark red air-dried beef called *viande des Grisons* or *Bündnerfleisch;* smoked ham from Valle Mesolcina in the Italian part of the Grisons; *jambon des Grisons (top),* another variety of Grisons ham; and *coppa,* a hard, thick sausage from the canton of Ticino. The sliced meats are Mesolcina ham *(in front of the bacon)* and, moving clockwise, two rows of *jambon des Grisons, coppa,* and *Bündnerfleisch.* At bottom is a heap of *salsiz,* a very dry small sausage also from the Grisons.

virtually indestructible democratic unity, even if they sometimes ruefully describe their country as "our land of brotherly hate." Yet this hate—a mask, I am convinced, for its opposite—has enabled Switzerland to resist political thrusts and invasions from France, Germany, Austria and Italy, the imposing neighbors that surround it. No European country similarly enclosed has withstood such challenges so effectively.

Food is another matter, however, and the Swiss, shrewd as they are, have opened their arms wide to receive a great culinary bounty from their neighbors. It is this willingness to assimilate that has produced Switzerland's international cuisine. But it has not discouraged the country's indigenous cooking, which appears in fine restaurants alongside a French *coq au vin,* a German schnitzel and an Italian *cannellone.* Admittedly, purely Swiss cooking is rather limited. Many food historians do not even consider it a "cuisine"—at least as the term is applied to the varied cooking of Germany, Austria and Italy, let alone the structured cuisine of France. But food historians notwithstanding, I think of Swiss cooking in different terms and call it a small *gem* of a cuisine.

Switzerland is mostly mountainous and is therefore poor in natural foodstuffs. But one can only admire the way the Swiss use to best advantage that which they do have—cattle, for example. It is from their seemingly endless supply of rich milk that the incomparable Swiss cheeses are made, and it is these same cows that provide much of the cured meats and varieties of sausages that are now famous throughout the world. The thrifty Swiss, mountaineers and city dwellers alike, are accustomed to plain, hearty food. They eat simply if copiously of heavy and filling soups, cheese dishes, vegetables, sausages, and a wide range of breads, cakes, fruit tarts and desserts, for the most part bakery-made.

The awesome Alpine regions, if they give the herdsman and his family little to subsist on, are the prime attraction for one of Switzerland's main sources of wealth—tourists. And with the influx of affluent visitors who demand the best and are willing to pay for it, Swiss cooking has gradually taken on international and more refined dimensions. Hotels with their own excellent restaurants have sprung up all over the country, and the Swiss, perfectionists in everything they do, have established hotel schools for training the personnel to run them.

The great hotel schools in Lausanne, Lucerne and Montreux are better organized and staffed and more demanding of their students than similar institutions in other countries. As a result, hoteliers trained in such schools boast an elegance of style and service and a dedication to the meticulous preparation of international food that are unsurpassed. A hotel manager or chef trained in a Swiss hotel school is instantly assured a job wherever important hotels exist.

In Zurich Frances and I stayed at that paragon of hotels, the Dolder Grand. After a turbulent night flight from New York, we were entranced by our luxurious suite overlooking the Lake of Zurich. In anticipation of our arrival, the rooms had been decked with flowers, dazzling baskets of fruit, and dishes heaped with exquisite Swiss chocolates. Without wasting a moment I telephoned the manager, introduced myself, thanked him for his thoughtfulness, and came right to the point: could we see the hotel's kitchen? The manager was most obliging and assented immediately.

Following him and Frances down the plush-lined stairs, I picked up snatches of his conversation: "Our recent innovation . . . brunch!" He said "brunch" with such contempt that it sounded like an epithet; my heart warmed to him at once. "When I was a boy," he went on, as if the noxious word had triggered nostalgia for his past, "breakfast was not such nonsense. Porridge of cornmeal, smoked bacon, 'coffee-milk,' the fried potatoes we call *Rösti (Recipe Index). That* was a *breakfast!*" I glanced at Frances to see how she was bearing up; both of us had spurned the airline's food and as yet had had no breakfast at all. "In those days when I lived on my family's farm," the manager was saying, "no one had a plate of his own; we each had a fork, and took what we wanted from a big platter of hot *Rösti* in the center of the table. If we wanted bacon, my mother cut a slice from a piece hanging in the chimney."

Then he opened a door and his nostalgia was instantly erased by managerial austerity. The kitchen we entered was the most formidable one of its type I had ever seen. As I walked from refrigerator to refrigerator and from room to room, I boggled at the neatly trimmed carcasses of beef, lamb and veal, the immaculately dressed birds of all varieties, the crates of freshest vegetables, the trays of intricately constructed pastries, crusty rolls, burnished brioches and freshly baked breads. My eye, wandering clinically over the kitchen, caught sight of a white-coated young man bent over what looked like a sculpture. And, indeed, that is just what it was—a butter sculpture, and by far the best example of its type I had ever seen. It was a composition of a Roman youth in a two-wheeled chariot, drawn by four prancing horses with tossing manes and streaming tails. Having been a sculptor herself, Frances was soon engaged in a technical discussion. She was amazed to learn that no armature had been used to build the figure on; I was equally amazed to find out that it had been carved from real butter (which is very expensive in Switzerland) and not from lamb's fat, as most "butter" sculptures are.

But impressed as I was by all this, my heart was still in the hinterlands with the manager's. *Rösti* potatoes, I thought with longing. Sausages, smoked bacon, and above all *Bündnerfleisch,* that incredible beef dried in mountain air—these were the tastes I really hankered for. Frances helped. "Would it be possible," she asked, as if reading my thoughts, "to see some *Bündnerfleisch?*"

A flick of the manager's finger, and a youngster—a recent graduate, most likely, from one of the hotel schools—appeared, and in seconds reappeared with not one but several types of *Bündnerfleisch.* While we tasted the dark-red, paper-thin slices of meat, the manager discoursed patiently on how it had been made—"spiced, brined, then dried for months in the mountain air." Interesting as the facts were, I was more immediately involved with the texture and flavor of the *Bündnerfleisch* I was then ravenously eating. Paradoxically, it was moist and dry at the same time, and its flavor was of the very essence of beef. In fact, one thin sliver had more impact on my palate than a thick slice of the finest American steak would have.

"Where does this one come from?" I asked. His answer—"From the

Protected by mountain ramparts and peopled by stubborn individualists, Switzerland has resisted the advances of its powerful neighbors for centuries. The Swiss have been adaptable enough, however, to absorb the culinary influences of these nations while preserving the character of their own cuisine. The cantons (in capital letters) and cities on the map offered the author choice examples of Swiss cooking.

Continued on page 14

11

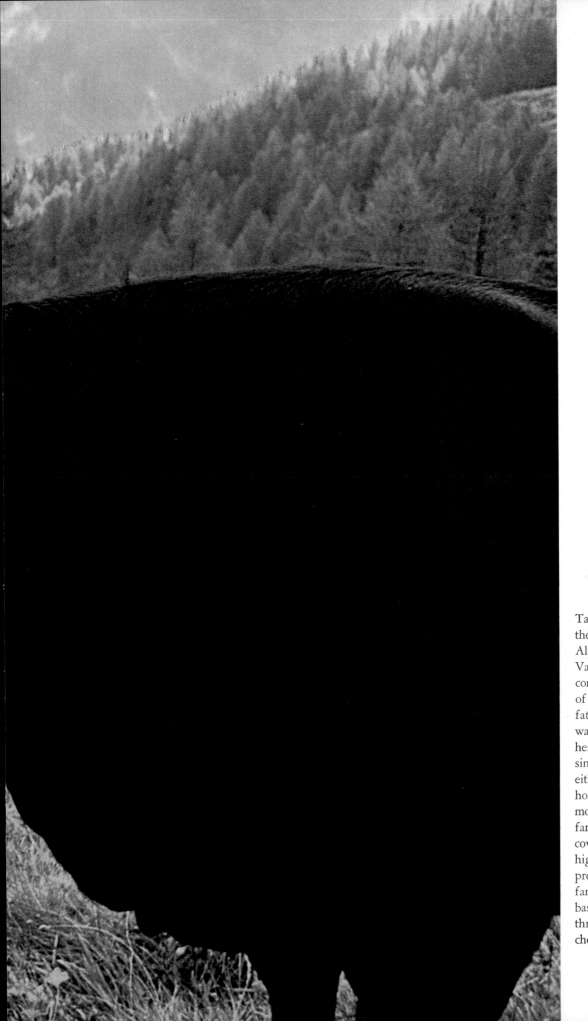

Taking his turn tending the family cows in an Alpine meadow in the Valais, a Swiss farm boy communes with the "queen of the herd." Like his father before him, he has watched and milked the herd practically every day since he was old enough, either down in his valley home or here in the mountains where the family moves with the cows during summer. The high quality of the milk produced by such small family-owned herds is the basis for Switzerland's thriving cheese and milk-chocolate industries.

canton of the Grisons"—I should have known. The Grisons, Switzerland's easternmost canton, is the source of the very best of all *Bündnerfleisch,* notwithstanding some stubborn claims of the Swiss in other cantons to the contrary. Frances, meanwhile, had been nibbling a slice from another platter. Because the meat had a translucence and a light pink cast, I commented that it looked much like an Italian prosciutto from Parma. "No, not from Parma," the manager said, almost indignantly; but I had come close. It was ham, to be sure, but rubbed with a soupçon of garlic, lightly smoked and *then* air-cured. Not surprisingly, it had an Italian name, Mesolcina, indicating that it came from a valley connecting the Grisons with Ticino—the Swiss canton that dips deep into Italy. Zigzagging my way from *Bündnerfleisch* to *Bündnerfleisch,* I thought wistfully that if only the Swiss would export as much of this remarkable meat as they do their equally remarkable cheese it would drive from the market forever the dreadful chipped dried beef sold in our own country, which bears as little resemblance to Swiss dried beef as cardboard does to damask.

Back in our room, I regretted not having asked the chef to show me his technique for making *Rösti* potatoes. Frances, again sensing my thoughts, said, "Thank heavens, it didn't occur to you—or did it?—to put another Swiss chef to the *Rösti* test." What she was alluding to was an experience I had had some years ago in another Swiss hotel kitchen with an inordinately self-confident young chef.

The Swiss are famous for meats, sausages and an unlimited capacity to consume them. They make the most of all this in a *Berneplatte,* a meal-sized platter of simmered meats—smoked pork chops, slices of fresh brisket, smoked bacon, knackwurst and other kinds of sausage—flanked by boiled potatoes and spread on a bed of buttery garlic-flavored string beans.

Rösti potatoes are as indigenous to Swiss country cooking as hashed brown potatoes are to the United States. Cold cooked potatoes are coarsely shredded on a special *Rösti* grater with tear-shaped openings (they can be bought in the United States, although our four-sided, stand-up graters do the job quite as well). Then they are packed down in a pan filled with sputtering butter, crisply fried on one side, turned over, and fried on the other. The result is a crusty potato cake with a basket-weave pattern on both sides. The particular chef Frances mentioned had boasted to me that he could make his *Rösti* turn over like a pancake in mid-air. His demonstration had been an embarrassing fiasco. Again and again, he had tossed the potatoes into the air, but each time they landed with a plop in the pan and promptly fell apart. Then, with an arrogance as Swisslike as his, I had the audacity to demonstrate to him how *Rösti* should be made.

Ideally—that is, when the grated potatoes are of the type (baking potatoes, we would call them) that contain enough starch to make the shreds adhere—it is indeed possible to flip *Rösti* like a flapjack. I have seen this maneuver executed skillfully, although I consider it not only exhibitionist but decidedly unpredictable, even when performed by an expert chef, which this young man clearly was not. That day I showed him a method I had learned from a more modest Swiss chef. Grating a fresh batch of potatoes, I patted them into the pan and browned them carefully. I set a platter over the pan, inverted the potatoes onto it, then simply slid them back into the pan and browned the other side. The poor fellow watched this

simple operation wide-eyed; evidently it had never occurred to him to try it. My wife's reminder recalled the painful scene and I was glad I had resisted the impulse to put the Dolder Grand's chef to the test, although no doubt he would have passed it brilliantly.

That night we went to the Kronenhalle, a restaurant Frances particularly loves because of its collection of modern art. As usual, I had my eye on the menu while she gazed with delight at the impressive array of paintings on the walls. As I exclaimed, *"éminçé de veau,"* Frances simultaneously cried, "Bonnard." It turned out for both our sakes that the *éminçé de veau (Recipe Index)* was as ravishing as the painting. The pale, delicate strips of veal were, for once, literally bathed in cream—not what we call heavy cream, but as thick and buttery as the cream I used to steal as a child from the top of a bottle of nonhomogenized milk. These veal strips had been sautéed with loving care, and had that lightly glistening glaze that only the hand of a master sauté chef can achieve. Nor, thankfully, was there any flour in the sauce. I did detect a faint undertone of white wine—not obtrusive in the least, but like an echo of a flowery Swiss mountain wine's bouquet faintly recalled. I happily ordered an Amigne, and as I sipped it, silently offered a compassionate toast to stay-at-home American wine lovers who, unfortunately, would never taste it; the fragility of this *vin du pays* couldn't possibly survive the rigors of travel as Frances and I, at that moment at least, seemed to be doing so well.

The next morning I did much less well. We set off for Bern, and on the way to the train I felt as fragile as the wine of the night before and as little fit for travel. Frances, who had been abstemious as always, was as pink as a freshly cut rose. She had feasted headily on the paintings as I had, too greedily, on the wine and the *éminçé de veau.* But our breakfast on the train transformed misery to euphoria: steaming coffee in shining silver pots; jugs of hot milk; crusty rolls; tiny jars of honey and confitures. Never had I had, even in France, *croissants* of such ephemeral flakiness. The scrambled eggs were properly creamy, and I understood at that moment why the great chef Escoffier preferred eggs scrambled to those prepared in any other way.

No trains in the world can compare with those of Switzerland. Like the finest Swiss watches they are always on time, and so noiselessly and smoothly do they move that only by seeing the landscape go by are you aware that they are moving at all. The dining car at this early hour was almost surreal. While hovering waiters poured the coffee, Sunday-best-dressed country folk at neighboring tables breakfasted abundantly on large open-faced sandwiches of ham, plates of sausages, eggs, bottle after bottle of various beers and wines. The time passed so swiftly that it seemed we arrived in Bern in only minutes, although the trip actually takes one and a half hours. It was the first time since our last visit to Switzerland that I was reluctant to leave a train.

To our delight, Heinz Hofer and Willi Bühlmann were at the station to meet us. Heinz and Willi head the Switzerland Cheese Association and are responsible for exporting the great cheeses we are able to buy now in such profusion almost everywhere in America. In typical Swiss fashion they took us in hand; before we knew it we were seated between

 Continued on page 22

Following an age-old practice, a Swiss farm boy and his dog make their twice-a-day delivery of fresh milk to the local cheese maker.

To the Swiss "the Cheese Stands Alone," but only After Much Loving Toil

Cheese, perhaps more than mountains, watches or even Heidi, is Switzerland's trademark. Made from the milk of cows nourished by clean mountain water and rich Alpine grasses, more than 100 varieties of cheese *(page 22)* are produced in the country's 2,000 family-owned dairies. By far the most famous variety is Emmentaler—the cheese with the big holes that is imitated and called Swiss cheese the world over. Anybody can make cheese with holes—a natural result of fermentation—but no one makes it as the Swiss do. Though their cheese-making equipment is modern and efficient, the Swiss have not given in to mass-production methods. In an average day, a small dairy turns out only two wheels of Emmentaler—and they must be aged at least six months before they are deemed fit for market.

In the first step in the painstaking process of making Emmentaler, or Switzerland Swiss cheese, dairy workers in the town of Krauchthal pour milk into a copper vat *(above)*. All cheese is made from curd —the solid protein-rich part of milk that is separated from the liquid whey. But the end result varies with certain vital factors in the process: the freshness of the milk; the length of time it is heated and at what temperature; the kinds of bacteria in the milk and the bacterial cultures that are added to aid curdling or for flavor; and the fermenting and aging time. The formula for Emmentaler starts with a combination of fresh milk and precured milk, from which some cream has been removed. The mixture is heated to about 80°, stirred, and mixed with rennet, a natural coagulant used to hasten curdling. As the milk curdles, it is "combed" with a cheese harp *(right)*, which begins the process of separating the whey from the curd.

When the mixture reaches the right consistency, a cheesecloth bag is lowered into the vat and raised, with a block and tackle, to scoop up the curd *(left)*. As the whey pours through the cheesecloth (the fabric got its name from its use in this process) a worker gathers up leftover curd by hand. Then the bag is lowered into a stainless-steel hoop and pressure is applied to squeeze out more whey and to shape the curd into wheels about three feet in diameter and seven inches thick. The pressure eventually reaches 3,300 pounds per square inch and, when the press is opened 24 hours later, what was 2,120 pounds of milk (265 gallons) the day before has been reduced to a firm 190-pound wheel of Emmentaler-to-be.

After a brief soaking in brine and a few days in a cool cellar, newly formed wheels begin the fermenting process that will turn them into fine cheese. This transformation takes place in a warm cellar *(left)* where the cheese rests at 70° for at least two months. Three times a week the wheels are turned, washed and salted to aid preserving and aging. The natural rind on the cheese thickens, protecting the cheese while letting it breathe; at the same time gases form in the cheese, producing holes and causing the wheels to expand slightly. Finally the wheels are removed to a storage room *(right)* where they age for a minimum of four months. (In the United States, minimum aging time for "Swiss cheese" is 60 days.) The big wheel cut open for display is an Emmentaler. The cheese on the top shelf (also made at the Krauchthal dairy) is Gruyère, which has smaller and fewer holes than Emmentaler and a more pungent taste.

them in a streetcar. Most high officials in this capital city—even the President of Switzerland himself—travel by streetcar instead of private car, which would be considered ostentatious. The trolley, in this case, was the quickest way to get to Willi's car parked on the outskirts of Bern.

Willi and Heinz had decided that before anything else, we simply had to taste the white asparagus that had just reached its peak of flavor in Fribourg, a town whose asparagus is renowned for its delicacy and flavor. We were told that the first seeds of asparagus had been planted there by a priest in 1907 and were nurtured throughout his life by him alone; even now, because fertile land is so scarce, this cloistered queen of asparagus is grown in only limited amounts. For the few weeks in May when it is available, Swiss come from all over to feast on it. We were now headed, at breakneck speed, for the Löwen, a rustic eating place in Kerzers, a small town near Fribourg; if we were late, Willi warned, the morning's crop might well be gone.

I have been on some pretty dizzying drives in my day, but this one was especially harrowing. It had begun to rain. We were skidding through tunnels, swerving around corners and into narrow lanes that, Willi explained, were short cuts. Frances, sometimes given to back-seat driving, was surprisingly silent at my side, transfixed by the spring landscape while I wondered if asparagus—or anything else, for that matter—could be worth it after all.

Like most of the American cooking fraternity, I am obsessed with food. Sometimes this obsession gets the better of me, to a degree that, recalled in more lucid moments, I think verges on insanity. Usually, though, I am sensible and objective about the food I eat—but not that hour we spent at the Löwen Restaurant in Kerzers. There, what I had come to rely on as a built-in ability to distinguish between eating and gluttony went completely awry. Frances, eating her asparagus in ladylike fashion, seemed embarrassed by the rapidity with which I was consuming mine, then alarmed by the number of my reorders. The asparagus was served simply, but almost reverently, as it deserved—a dozen or so spears all by themselves, with only a dish of melted butter as a sauce.

I have a vague recollection of looking at guests at the other tables —they were reordering too—and telling Willi and Heinz that the only other vegetable I could consume in such prodigious quantities was freshly picked American corn. One of the advantages here, I said, was that I was spared the embarrassment of denuded corncobs piling up grossly on my plate. This usually has the effect of stopping me cold in my tracks. Fortunately, or perhaps not, the asparagus was so tender that I could eat it stalks and all; no one could prove that I had eaten as many of them as I had. But my haze of bliss evaporated at once when I heard Willi say to Frances, "Michael is certainly enjoying his first course." I could scarcely believe it. Willi's and Heinz's plan, which at this point I could only think a malevolent one (they hadn't said a word about it before), was that we would proceed from Kerzers back to Bern to another restaurant for the main course.

In the car the coming challenge seemed so overwhelming that I promptly fell asleep. Frances, reluctant to wake me up, told me later what I had missed: transporting views of Neuchâtel—its castles, steep hills and high walled-in gardens reminiscent of Monte Carlo. When we passed through Gruyères there had been talk about little wooden pots filled with strawberries and covered with double cream; poetic adjectives about its air-cured country hams, excellent butter, and its world-famous cheese. To top it off—and I wished Frances hadn't mentioned it—along the way there had been a wine tasting in a cellar filled with ceiling-high casks of lively white Shaffiser wine. I had slept soundly through it all.

In any case, Frances did wake me on our arrival at the Grosser Kornhauskeller in Bern. The size of this restaurant and the staircase leading down to it put New York's Grand Central Station to shame. Used in the 18th Century as a granary and wine cellar, and converted to a banqueting hall in the 19th Century, it is now a colossus of a restaurant divided into seating areas by shoulder-high wooden enclosures that make for convivial dining. An antique bar in one vast corner has a Dr. Seuss-like array of winding tubes connected to beer barrels deep in the Kornhauskeller's cellars. From great brass spouts lined up in a row the beer gushed foaming into mugs for the buxom waitresses to add to their heavily laden trays. A gargantuan setting for gargantuan appetites, it seemed to me. Overstuffed though I was, the obvious choice for a main course here had to be *Berneplatte (Recipe Index)*. I ordered one.

Berneplatte, as its name indicates, is a specialty of Bern, and it is not for anyone with a delicate appetite. It combines a massive assortment of meats and sausages served with boiled potatoes. The *Berneplatte* set before me I thought was especially notable. Instead of using the juniper-flavored Alsatian sauerkraut base popular in Bern, the chef had arranged the boiled beef, tongue, bacon, sausage and smoked pork chops so that they reposed on a bed of the freshest of young string beans, which shone with a delicately seasoned garlic sauce. I was enchanted with such inventiveness. One could drink wine with this *Berneplatte*—inconceivable with a sauerkraut-laden version, which calls for beer.

Throughout the meal, Willi and Heinz were busy planning the evening's gastronomic activities. We would have a "typical light Swiss supper," Willi said, at which his wife would join us, at the Hirschon, a local—and very good—restaurant featuring those most Swiss of all Swiss specialties, *raclette* and fondue. From there, Frances and I would rush to make the train to Lugano.

Thankful that there would be two hours before dinner, I suggested that a rest in a hotel seemed sensible, pointing out that my nap in the car and the wine I had drunk seemed to have compounded my need for more sleep. Willi said he would gladly drive us to a hotel but, he added, with an impish inflection that I in my drowsy state missed entirely, why go to an expensive one just for a two-hour nap? Ordinarily, I would have insisted that the hotel be the best in town, but shamed by his Swiss good sense, to say nothing of his sobriety, I agreed to go to a small place where he could also park his car and later pick us up.

Willi deposited us on a busy arcaded street and, with a drowsy *à bientôt* to him, I groped my way down the long, dismal hallway of his sensibly cheap hotel. After negotiating with a curiously suspicious concierge, Fran-

Switzerland's best-known cheese dishes are fondue and *raclette* (*Recipe Index*). The boy on the opposite page is about to devour a piece of bread that has been dunked in a fondue, a dish originated by the frugal Swiss as an appetizing way of using up stale bread and hard cheese during the long winters. *Raclette,* taken from the French word *râcler,* meaning to scrape, is prepared traditionally by exposing a section of cheese to an open fire and then scraping the melted cheese onto a heated plate; a boiled potato is added to the plate, and the dish is often accompanied, as here, by pickles and pickled onions.

ces and I followed a chambermaid up three flights of dusty stairs and ensconced ourselves in a room with a sagging bed and depressingly faded yellow walls. "What an ugly place," Frances exclaimed, but I was too tired to care. "Let's sleep," I said; "it will probably cost us 50 cents instead of 50 dollars." I dropped off into the deepest of sleeps, but Frances told me later that the sound of people passing back and forth in the hall had been loud enough to wake the dead. She complained she hadn't been able to sleep a wink.

On our way downstairs we passed what I thought was an oddly matched pair on their way up—a citified woman with bleached hair and a young man, perhaps a farmer, clumping after her in heavy shoes. At the desk we paid our bill, but since I don't and probably never will know the value of a Swiss franc I didn't think about it until we were outside. Willi showed up, prompt as a Swiss train, and as we were getting into his car Frances informed me in a testy whisper that the room had been as expensive as the one at the Dolder Grand. Suddenly I got the point: a typical Swiss joke. "Extraordinary place," I said to Willi and Heinz meaningfully. They both turned around, smiling broadly. We laughed all the way to the Hirschon.

There I got down at once to the serious business of *raclette* and fondue. Instead of settling at the table with the others I watched the chef in his small enclave, going through the ritual of making *raclette (Recipe Index)*. The last time Frances and I had eaten it had been at the home of friends in Basel, in northern Switzerland, during Carnival. The cut edge of a half wheel of Bagne cheese had been exposed to the heat of the fire roaring in their fireplace. The surface of the cheese was allowed to melt, then was quickly scraped off with a large knife onto a hot serving plate. A small boiled potato was set on one side of it, and a gherkin cut into the shape of a fan on the other. Prosaic as this may sound, it has remained an unforgettable gastronomic experience. Possibly the confluence of cultivated people, the softly falling snow and the expectation of Carnival festivities made that *raclette* so memorable. I was curious to see whether a *raclette* without the ambiance of that night would still measure up as the important dish the Swiss feel it is.

Now, in the Hirschon, all was speed and modern efficiency. There were two half wheels of Valais cheese in front of a radiant stove (several kinds of semisoft cheeses are used to make *raclette* in Switzerland, but only a cheese exported under the name *raclette* is easily available in the United States). As the cheese melted to just the proper degree of softness, the chef deftly scraped it onto a waiting hot plate. He then placed a small boiled potato and gherkins alongside the cheese, and handed the plate to the waitress. As I watched this mechanical performance disenchantment set in, and my earlier enthusiasm deflated. However, at the first taste I knew that *raclette* can stand honestly on its own. It was even better than the one I had remembered so passionately. The cheese was creamy, mild yet distinctive, and the mealy texture of the perfectly cooked potato, sharpened by the accent of the gherkin, gave the melted cheese another dimension altogether. Frances matched me *raclette* for *raclette,* as did our three companions. Finally, however, I called a halt, because I was

determined to find out what the Hirschon did with its renowned fondue.

No Swiss in his right mind would order a fondue after eating four *raclettes* any more than he would drink cold water, chilled wine or beer with any hot cheese dish; he thinks it more sensible to drink a glass of kirsch or a cup of hot tea. There is a persistent myth in Switzerland that if you drink cold liquid with hot melted cheese you do so at your peril, at the very least inviting violent indigestion. How this singular notion arose defies investigation. At any rate, to compound my heretical behavior in ordering a *fondue neuchâteloise (Recipe Index)* after the *raclettes*, I ordered a wine I especially like, a Fendant, and insisted that it be well chilled. The waitress looked predictably appalled; but in due course the fondue appeared. When I dipped a speared bread cube into it, I quickly realized that here was a superior fondue indeed. There was not the slightest edge of the acidity or stringiness I so dislike in poorly made fondues.

Frances tasted it at my insistence, and not only agreed with my opinion of it but began a monologue of recollections of her stay in the Swiss Alps a long time before we met each other. We all, even Willi, his wife and Heinz who knew their country so well, listened enthralled. For her, this one taste of fondue summed up a whole phase of Swiss life: its mountain dairy-farm culture, an almost mystical reverence for cows, tinkling cowbells echoing in the mountain air, reverberating yodels and the melancholy lowing of the alpenhorn.

"Isn't it true, Heinz," she asked, "that whole communities move up the mountainsides to higher and higher plateaus so that their cattle can graze?" "Yes," Heinz said with a misty look, "and some dairymen live in huts, away from their families for months at a time." Frances, picking up from there, tapped the edge of the now empty casserole and said, "Just to produce the cheese for this superb fondue." Then Willi recalled how his mother used to make *riebeles* for any meal of the day: she would cook cornmeal with water until it was a thick porridge, let it cool until it was firm, then slice it into cubes and fry them in butter *(Recipe Index)*.

All of this proved to me once again that the phrase, "It's not the food, it's the people," so often uttered by nervous American hostesses before dinner parties, is a defensive cliché devised to divert attention from badly prepared meals. As I have staunchly maintained for years, it's the food *and* the people that make for civilized communication.

Our repast—and the visit to Bern—ended antiphonally. We remained seated silently while a group of Salvation Army women who had just come in sang hymns to an audience who forsook their food and listened respectfully. It couldn't have been a more bizarre though curiously touching finale to our adventures in Bern.

Traveling from Switzerland's north to its south is always a dramatic experience; there are sudden and startling changes in the landscape, the climate and the temperament of its people. We passed through barricading black, snow-ridged mountains and through seemingly endless tunnels.

At a sidewalk stall in Lugano—largest city in Ticino, one of the Swiss cantons next to northern Italy—strollers pick out snacks of ham sandwiches, precooked lasagne wrapped in tinfoil and other delicacies the Ticinese have adapted from their Italian neighbors. On permanent display in the archways are papier-mâché replicas—complete with bands bearing the Italian tricolor—of three-and-a-half-foot sausages the Ticinese import from across the border.

We emerged into brilliant shafts of sunlight flashing on church spires far down in the valley where tiny houses clustered, their rooftops rising in golden layers. Between mountainsides again, foaming waterfalls cascaded in crooked patterns into hidden trenches beside the road. And when we arrived in Lugano, that most Mediterranean of Ticinese cities, everything and everyone appeared to be Italian. The air was soft, the talk loud, and foodstuffs burgeoned among the arcades on the wide cobblestoned back streets of the town.

Basking in the warm sunshine, we window-shopped among the arcades. Here was a profusion of food with an Italianate vengeance, and gaily dressed crowds swarmed everywhere. Our eyes were caught from afar by the monster sausages hanging in front of one of the famous Lugano *salumerias,* or sausage shops. It was amusing to see how artfully these pale green sausages were displayed, dangling like enormous chimes from the arch of the arcade to the pavement. Like a child, I was tempted to push them against each other, convinced they would give off a clanging sound. What was even more amusing was to learn that they were not sausages at all, but wonderfully lifelike papier-mâché copies that hang outside the shop day and night, in good weather and bad. The Italians might have hung real sausages and taken them down at night. The Swiss, combining their usual inventiveness with their usual caution, had found a safe way to advertise their wares around the clock.

That night we dined at the restaurant La Tinèra where, without preliminaries, we were immediately served a rough red Nostrano wine in thick ceramic mugs. We began our dinner with *busecca (Recipe Index).* Now, Ticinese *busecca* may look like an ordinary Italian *minestrone,* but there the resemblance ends. We read its contents like an alphabet soup—tomato, spinach, cabbage, beans, celery, potatoes, carrots, leeks—and then discovered the element that distinguishes it from its Italian cousin: tripe. We were delighted. Tripe—an innard not to everyone's taste, I'll admit, but definitely to ours—is gelatinous in texture, and not only flavors the soup distinctively but also gives it a density that Italians achieve with pasta, very often vermicelli. A subtle departure such as the use of tripe is a perfect example of the way in which the Swiss, while absorbing the important dishes of their neighbors, so often impose upon them their own unmistakable imprint.

After downing a tomato-sauced *pollo alla campagna (Recipe Index)* accompanied by a mushroom *risotto,* we sensibly finished with fruit and cheese—not a cheese the Ticinese themselves are proudest of, Piora for example, but my own favorite, Sbrinz. A three-year-old Sbrinz, not yet hardened into a granitic block, closely resembles a young crumbly Italian Parmesan, and is to my mind the aristocrat of Swiss dessert cheeses.

So absorbed were we in savoring each morsel that it was a few seconds before we heard the sound of my name ricocheting from wall to wall of the *taverna.* There stood René Kramer, a Lugano friend whom I had seen on and off over the years in many parts of the world. The bond between René and me is, not surprisingly, food—he is a cookbook publisher and one of the best in Europe.

When he learned that we were leaving Lugano in the morning, René in-

At Zurich's elegant Kronenhalle Restaurant, a waiter prepares an order of *éminçé de veau (center)*. *Emincé,* a Swiss specialty that has achieved international status, is a delicate dish of veal strips sautéed in butter and cooked in a white wine and cream sauce *(recipe, page 30)*. Also on the table is a chafing dish of flamed veal kidneys. Both entrées are accompanied by *Rösti,* the crusty potato cake at right *(page 30)*.

sisted, despite the lateness of the hour, that we return with him to his château overlooking Lake Lugano. He waved away our pleas of fatigue with every ruse he could think of: we must meet his cat and dog; we must see his grape arbor in the moonlight; inspect his new cookbooks; have a pousse-café; anything we wished. He was impossible to resist.

Inside his charming château, René served us coffee and for a pousse-café —literally, a "coffee pusher," a term used for such after-dinner drinks as liqueurs or brandy—he offered us a *grappa,* a fiery brandy that he had distilled from the pressings of his own grapes. As it turned out, the *grappa* was not only strong enough to push the coffee down but so potent that Frances confessed that her mind was suddenly dizzy with the thoughts of all the food she had eaten on this whirlwind trip. As for me, the drink instantly restored my energy. In fact it set me afire; I sat down at René's Bechstein and tossed off a Chopin étude—wrong notes and all—with all the aplomb I had had in my concert-playing days.

Playing the piano was not exactly the note I had intended as a finale to our jaunt through Switzerland. Yet, inspired as it was by a Ticinese *grappa,* it may in fact have had a culinary logic of its own.

Fondue Neuchâteloise

In a large bowl, toss together the cheeses and cornstarch until thoroughly combined. Pour the wine into a 2-quart fondue dish (or any 2-quart flame-proof enameled casserole), drop in the garlic, and bring to a boil over high heat. Let the wine boil briskly for 1 or 2 minutes, then with a slotted spoon remove and discard the garlic. Lower the heat so that the wine barely simmers. Stirring constantly with a table fork, add the cheese mixture a handful at a time, letting each handful melt before adding another. When the fondue is creamy and smooth, stir in the kirsch, nutmeg, salt and a few grindings of black pepper, and taste for seasoning.

To serve, place the fondue dish or casserole over an alcohol or gas table burner in the center of the dining table, regulating the heat so that the fondue barely simmers. Set a basketful of the bread cubes alongside the fondue. Traditionally, each diner spears a cube of bread on a fork (preferably a long-handled fondue fork), swirls the bread about in the fondue until it is thoroughly coated, then eats it immediately.

Zürcher Leberspiessli
SKEWERED CALF'S LIVER AND BACON

Wash the fresh spinach under cold running water. Drain, then strip the leaves from the stems and discard the stems and any discolored leaves. In a heavy 2- to 3-quart saucepan, bring ½ cup of water to a boil. Add the spinach, lower the heat, and simmer tightly covered for about 3 minutes. Drain the spinach in a sieve, cool, and squeeze it completely dry. Chop it as fine as possible. (Frozen spinach needs only to be drained, squeezed dry, then finely chopped.) Set the spinach aside.

Press a small sage leaf on each piece of liver and wrap each piece of liver in a strip of bacon. Thread 5 squares of liver apiece on four 6- to 8-inch-long thin metal skewers, pressing the pieces tightly together. In a heavy 12-inch skillet, melt 3 tablespoons of the butter with the oil over moderate heat. When the fat begins to color very lightly, arrange the skewers side by side in the skillet. Fry uncovered, turning the skewers occasionally, for 10 to 15 minutes, or until the bacon is brown and crisp. Regulate the heat if necessary to prevent the bacon from burning.

Meanwhile, in a heavy 8- to 10-inch skillet, melt the remaining butter over moderate heat. When the foam subsides, add the onions and garlic and, stirring frequently, cook for 2 or 3 minutes, until they are soft and transparent. Drop in the spinach, add the salt and a few grindings of pepper, and stir for a few minutes longer, until the ingredients are thoroughly combined and the spinach is heated through.

Spread the spinach on a heated platter and arrange the skewers of liver side by side on top. Then, working quickly, discard the fat remaining in the skillet in which the liver was fried. Pour in the wine and bring to a boil over high heat, stirring constantly and scraping in the brown particles clinging to the bottom and sides of the pan. Let the sauce boil for a moment or so, then pour it evenly over the liver and serve at once.

To serve 4 to 6

½ pound imported Swiss Gruyère cheese, coarsely grated (about 2 cups)
½ pound imported Swiss Emmentaler cheese, coarsely grated (about 2 cups)
1 tablespoon cornstarch
2 cups dry white wine, preferably Neuchâtel
1 medium-sized garlic clove, peeled and bruised with the flat of a knife
2 tablespoons imported kirsch
⅛ teaspoon nutmeg, preferably freshly grated
⅛ teaspoon salt
Freshly ground black pepper
1 large loaf French or Italian bread with the crust left on, cut into 1-inch cubes

To serve 4

1½ pounds fresh spinach, or substitute two 10-ounce packages frozen chopped spinach, thoroughly defrosted
20 dried sage leaves
1½ pounds calf's liver, sliced ¾ inch thick, then cut in 1-inch squares
10 lean bacon slices, cut crosswise into halves
7 tablespoons butter
¼ cup vegetable oil
2 tablespoons finely chopped onions
¼ teaspoon finely chopped garlic
½ teaspoon salt
Freshly ground black pepper
¼ cup Neuchâtel or other dry white wine

Rösti
FRIED SHREDDED POTATO CAKE

To serve 4 to 6

9 medium-sized baking potatoes
  (about 3 pounds)
½ teaspoon salt
¼ cup vegetable oil
2 tablespoons butter

Drop the potatoes into enough boiling water to cover them completely and cook briskly for about 10 minutes, or until the point of a knife can be inserted about 1 inch into a potato before meeting any resistance. Drain the potatoes. When cool enough to handle, peel them with a small, sharp knife, cover with plastic wrap, and refrigerate for at least an hour. Just before frying the potatoes grate them into long strips on the tear-shaped side of a four-sided stand-up grater. Toss lightly with the salt.

In a heavy 10-inch slope-sided skillet (preferably one with a nonstick cooking surface), heat the oil and butter over moderate heat until a drop of water flicked over them splutters and evaporates instantly. Drop in the potatoes and, with a spatula, spread them evenly in the pan. Fry uncovered for 8 to 10 minutes, using a spatula to gently lift up a side of the potatoes to check their color as they brown. When the underside of the potato cake is as brown as you can get it without letting it burn, place a plate upside down over the skillet. Grasping the skillet and plate firmly together, invert them quickly. Then carefully slide the potato cake, browned side up, back into the skillet. (If you are not using a pan with a nonstick surface, add more butter and oil before returning the potatoes to the pan.) Fry for 6 to 8 minutes, or until the bottom side of the potatoes is as evenly browned as the top and the edges are crisp.

Slide the potato cake onto a heated platter and serve at once.

NOTE: *Rösti* potatoes are often made with onions or bacon. Sauté ½ cup of finely chopped onions in 3 tablespoons of butter until they are soft and transparent. Drop half the shredded potatoes into the skillet, pat them flat and smooth and spread the onions evenly over them before adding the remaining potatoes, patting them down as before. Or fry ½ cup of finely diced bacon until the bits are crisp, drain on paper towels and spread the bacon over half of the potatoes as described for the onions.

Émincé de Veau
VEAL STRIPS IN WHITE WINE AND CREAM SAUCE

To serve 4

5 tablespoons butter
3 tablespoons vegetable oil
1½ pounds veal scallops, sliced
  ¼ inch thick and cut into strips
  about 2 inches long and ¼ inch
  wide
1 tablespoon finely chopped
  shallots, or substitute 1
  tablespoon finely chopped
  scallions, using only the white
  parts
⅓ cup Neuchâtel, Fendant or other
  dry white wine
1 cup heavy cream
Salt
White pepper

In a heavy 10- to 12-inch skillet, melt 2 tablespoons of the butter with the oil over high heat. When the foam subsides, drop in half the veal and, tossing the strips about constantly with a fork, fry for about 2 minutes. When the veal is delicately colored, transfer it to a large sieve set over a bowl. Melt 2 more tablespoons of butter in the pan, then drop in the remaining veal and cook as before. Add the veal and its juices to the veal in the sieve. Add the remaining butter to the pan and melt it over moderate heat. Then stir in the shallots and cook for about 2 minutes before pouring in the wine. Raise the heat to high and stir until the liquid comes to a boil. Immediately add the cream and all the drained veal juices. Stirring constantly, boil briskly for 8 to 10 minutes, or until the sauce has reduced to about half its original volume and thickened lightly. Taste for seasoning. Return the veal to the skillet and turn it about until it is thoroughly coated with the sauce. Simmer over low heat for 2 or 3 minutes until the veal is heated through. Serve at once, accompanied, if you like, by *Rösti (above)*.

The Ubiquitous "Rösti": Switzerland's Fried Potato Cake

Rösti, shredded potatoes fried into a neat golden cake, appears on restaurant and household menus throughout Switzerland. (In the picture above, it accompanies a Zurich favorite: *Leberspiessli,* skewered liver-and-bacon on a bed of spinach, *Recipe Index.*) The parboiled potatoes are grated *(top left)* on the tear-shaped holes of a stand-up grater. Next they are tossed with salt and then dropped into fat sizzling in a slope-sided skillet. With a spatula the potatoes are flattened and spread out in the pan, then fried until golden brown. The potato cake is inverted onto a flat plate, more butter and oil is added to the skillet, then the cake is returned to the skillet to brown on the other side. The completed *Rösti (bottom)* is then slid onto a heated plate.

To serve 4

½ pound imported Swiss *raclette*
    cheese, cut into 16 slices, each
    approximately ⅛ inch thick, 5
    inches long and 2 inches wide
4 freshly boiled small new potatoes,
    peeled and kept hot
4 to 8 small sour gherkins,
    preferably imported *cornichons*
4 to 8 pickled onions

Raclette
MELTED CHEESE WITH POTATOES AND PICKLES

Preheat the oven to 500° for at least 15 minutes. Heat four 10-inch oven-proof dinner plates in the oven for 3 to 5 minutes. To ensure the success of the *raclettes,* the plates must be very hot.

When ready to serve, remove the plates from the oven, grasping them with potholders, and, as quickly as you can, arrange four slices of the cheese in the center of each plate, overlapping them slightly. The cheese should begin to sizzle as soon as it comes in contact with the plate. At once, place the four plates on the floor of the oven (if you are using an electric oven, place the plates on a rack set in the first slot above the source of heat). In about 2 minutes (5 to 6 minutes in an electric oven) the cheese should melt to a creamy, bubbly mass; do not let it turn the slightest bit brown. Remove from the oven, place a potato and one or two gherkins and pickled onions on the side of each plate and serve at once, setting each plate on a service plate to prevent it from scorching the table.

NOTE: Swiss diners often consume at least 2 or 3 plates of *raclettes* in succession at one sitting. Should you want to do the same, double or triple all the ingredients and have two or three sets of dinner plates heating in the oven while the first batch of *raclettes* is being eaten.

To serve 8 to 10

2 pounds fresh lean brisket of beef,
    trimmed of excess fat
2½ to 3 pounds uncooked smoked
    pork loin, cut into 1-inch-thick
    chops (about 10 chops)
1 pound slab bacon, preferably
    double smoked, with rind
    removed, cut into slices ¼ inch
    thick and about 4 inches long
8 to 10 knackwurst
8 to 10 uncooked pork sausages
8 to 10 small frankfurters or Vienna
    sausages
2 quarts lightly salted boiling water
2 pounds trimmed fresh green
    string beans
4 tablespoons butter
4 tablespoons flour
½ teaspoon finely chopped garlic
⅛ teaspoon ground nutmeg,
    preferably freshly grated
½ teaspoon salt
10 to 12 boiling potatoes (about 4
    pounds), peeled and boiled in
    salted water until tender

Berneplatte
SIMMERED MIXED MEATS WITH STRING BEANS AND POTATOES

Place the brisket in a 5- to 6-quart heavy pot and pour in enough cold water to cover it by at least 2 inches. Bring to a boil over high heat, skimming off the foam and scum as they rise to the surface. Reduce the heat to low and simmer partially covered for 1½ hours. Add the smoked pork loin and bacon, partially cover the pot, and simmer for 15 minutes longer. Add the knackwurst and pork sausages and cook for 10 minutes. Then drop in the small frankfurters or Vienna sausages and let them simmer slowly for about 5 minutes. (All the meats should be completely covered with water throughout the cooking period; replenish the pot with boiling water whenever necessary.)

Meanwhile prepare the green beans. Bring 2 quarts of lightly salted water to a boil in a 3- to 4-quart saucepan. Drop in the beans and cook briskly, uncovered, for 10 to 15 minutes, until they are tender but still slightly crisp. Drain the beans in a sieve set over a bowl and set aside the cooking liquid. Run cold water over the beans, and set aside.

In a heavy 8- to 10-inch skillet, melt the butter over moderate heat. When the foam subsides, stir in the flour and continue to stir until the mixture is smooth. Pour in 2 cups of the string bean liquid and, stirring constantly, cook over high heat until the sauce comes to a boil and thickens heavily. Reduce the heat to low, add the garlic, nutmeg and salt, and simmer for about 5 minutes, stirring occasionally. Add the beans to the sauce and simmer only long enough to heat them through. To serve, carve the brisket into slices ¼ inch thick. Slice the knackwurst or the pork sausage into serving pieces if you like or serve them whole. Spread the string beans and their sauce on a large heated serving platter. Arrange the meats attractively over the beans, surround with the potatoes, and serve at once.

Zwiebelwähe
ONION-AND-CHEESE TART

In a large chilled bowl, combine the flour, salt, chilled butter and the lard or vegetable shortening. With your fingertips, rub the flour and fat together until they look like flakes of coarse meal. Be careful not to let the mixture become oily.

Pour 3 tablespoons of ice water over the mixture all at once, toss together lightly, and gather the dough into a ball. If the dough crumbles, add up to 2 tablespoons more ice water by drops until the particles adhere. Dust the pastry with a little flour and wrap it in wax paper. Refrigerate for at least 1 hour before using.

To prepare a baked but unfilled, or "blind," pastry shell, use a pastry brush to spread the tablespoon of softened butter over the bottom and sides of a 9-inch false-bottom fluted quiche pan, 1 inch deep.

On a lightly floured surface, pat the dough into a rough circle about 1 inch thick. Dust a little flour over and under it and roll it out, from the center to within an inch of the far edge of the pastry. Lift the dough and turn it clockwise about 2 inches; roll again from the center to within an inch or so of the far edge. Repeat—lifting, turning, rolling—until the circle is about ⅛ inch thick and 13 to 14 inches in diameter.

Drape the dough over the rolling pin, lift it up, and unroll it slackly over the quiche pan. Gently press it into the bottom and around the sides of the pan, being careful not to stretch the dough. Roll the pin over the rim of the pan, pressing down hard to trim off the excess dough.

Preheat the oven to 400°. Spread a sheet of buttered aluminum foil across the tin and press it gently against the bottom and sides to support the pastry as it bakes. Bake on the middle shelf of the oven for 10 minutes, then remove the foil.

With the point of a small knife prick the pastry where it has puffed up. Then return it to the oven for 10 minutes, or until it begins to brown. Remove it from the oven and cool before using.

To make the filling: Preheat the oven to 350°. In a heavy 6- to 8-inch skillet, heat the oil over moderate heat until a light haze forms above it. Add the onions and, stirring frequently, cook for about 5 minutes, or until they are soft and transparent but not brown. Watch carefully for any sign of burning and regulate the heat accordingly. Stir in the paprika and set aside off the heat.

Place the Gruyère and Emmentaler cheese in a bowl and toss together until they are thoroughly combined.

Spread half of the cheese evenly in the baked pastry shell and scatter the onions over it. Then cover them with the remaining cheese. Beat the eggs, cream, milk, salt and nutmeg together with a wire whisk, and pour the mixture slowly and evenly over the cheese. Bake in the upper third of the oven for 10 minutes, then increase the heat to 425° and bake for 15 minutes longer, or until the filling has puffed and browned and a knife inserted in the center comes out clean.

To remove the tart from the pan, set it on a large jar or coffee can and slip down the outside rim. Run a long metal spatula under the pie to loosen the bottom, then slide the pie off onto a heated platter. Serve hot or at room temperature as a first or main course.

To serve 6

PASTRY SHELL
1½ cups all-purpose flour
¼ teaspoon salt
6 tablespoons unsalted butter, chilled and cut into ¼-inch bits
2 tablespoons lard or vegetable shortening, chilled and cut into ¼-inch bits
3 to 5 tablespoons ice water
1 tablespoon butter, softened

FILLING
2 tablespoons vegetable oil
½ cup finely chopped onions
⅛ teaspoon paprika
¼ pound imported Swiss Gruyère cheese, coarsely grated (about 1 cup)
¼ pound imported Swiss Emmentaler cheese, coarsely grated (about 1 cup)
2 eggs
½ cup light cream
½ cup milk
¼ teaspoon salt
⅛ teaspoon ground nutmeg, preferably freshly grated

Hot chocolate complements a slightly tart Swiss teatime favorite, *Birnbrot*—pear bread made with a mixture of dried fruits.

To make 1 loaf

BREAD
1 package active dry yeast
1 teaspoon plus ¼ cup sugar
½ cup lukewarm milk (110° to
  115°)
2 to 2½ cups all-purpose flour
¼ cup vegetable shortening
1 egg
⅛ teaspoon salt
1 teaspoon butter, softened

Birnbrot
PEAR BREAD

In a deep mixing bowl, sprinkle the yeast and 1 teaspoon of sugar over the lukewarm milk. Let the mixture stand for 2 or 3 minutes, then stir well. Set the bowl in a warm, draft-free place such as an unlighted oven for about 5 minutes, or until the yeast bubbles up and the mixture almost doubles in bulk.

Stirring constantly, slowly add ½ cup of the flour. Beat in the vegetable shortening and then add the egg, the remaining ¼ cup of sugar and the salt. Beating well after each addition, stir in up to 2 cups more flour, adding it ½ cup at a time and using only as much as necessary to make a dough that can be gathered into a compact ball. If the dough becomes difficult to stir, work in the flour with your fingers.

On a lightly floured surface, knead the dough by folding it end to end, then pressing it down and pushing it forward several times with the heel of your hand. Sprinkle the dough with a little extra flour when necessary to prevent it from sticking. Repeat for about 10 minutes, or until the dough is smooth and elastic.

Shape the dough into a ball and place it in a large bowl coated with 1 teaspoon of butter. Dust the top with a little flour, drape a kitchen towel over the bowl, and set in a warm, draft-free spot for 45 minutes to an hour, until the dough doubles in bulk.

Meanwhile prepare the filling in the following fashion: Bring the water to a boil in a small enameled or stainless-steel saucepan. Add the pears, prunes, raisins and lemon juice and, stirring frequently, simmer over low heat for 10 minutes, or until the fruit is tender and can easily be mashed with the back of the spoon.

Drain the fruit thoroughly, then purée it through a food mill or use the back of a spoon to rub it through a sieve set over a bowl. Add the walnuts, sugar, kirsch, lemon peel, cinnamon and nutmeg. When all the ingredients are well mixed, stir in 2 tablespoons of the red wine. The filling should be thick enough to hold its shape almost solidly in a spoon. If it seems too firm, stir in up to 2 tablespoons more wine, a teaspoon or so at a time.

With a pastry brush coat a large baking sheet or jelly-roll pan evenly with the tablespoon of softened butter. Punch the dough down with a single blow of your fist. Transfer it to a lightly floured surface and roll it into a 15-inch square no more than ¼ inch thick.

With a spatula, spread the filling over the dough, covering it smoothly to within 1 inch of the edges. Fold the edges over the filling to make a perfect 13-inch square, then roll the dough jelly-roll fashion into a tight cylinder 12 inches long and about 3 inches in diameter.

Transfer the roll to the buttered baking sheet and lightly prick the outside surface all over with the tines of a fork. Set the roll aside to rise for about 1 hour.

Preheat the oven to 350°. Brush the top, sides and ends of the bread with the egg-and-milk mixture and bake in the middle of the oven for 30 to 35 minutes, or until the bread is golden brown and crisp. Transfer to a wire cake rack to cool. Serve the pear bread warm or at room temperature.

Veal Cordon Bleu
BREADED VEAL SCALLOPS

With a pastry brush, coat one side of each veal scallop lightly with the egg-and-milk mixture and sprinkle with a light dusting of the flour. Wrap each strip of cheese in a slice of ham and place it lengthwise in the center of the coated side of a scallop. Fold the scallop in half lengthwise to make a 6-inch-long packet enclosing the ham and cheese completely, and press the edges firmly together to seal them tightly. One at a time, coat the scallops with the remaining flour and shake them free of any excess. Then dip them first in the remaining egg-and-milk mixture and then in the bread crumbs, making sure each scallop is thoroughly coated with crumbs. Set the scallops side by side on a plate or wax paper and refrigerate for at least 1 hour.

In a heavy 12-inch skillet, melt the butter with the oil over moderate heat until the foam subsides and the fat colors lightly. Add the scallops, turning them occasionally with tongs or a slotted spoon, and fry for 15 to 20 minutes, or until they are golden brown and crisp on both sides. Drain on paper towels and serve at once from a heated platter. Top each scallop with a slice of lemon sprinkled lightly with paprika.

FILLING

1½ cups water
1½ cups coarsely chopped dried pears (about ½ pound)
½ cup coarsely chopped, pitted dried prunes (about ¼ pound)
½ cup seedless raisins
2 tablespoons strained fresh lemon juice
½ cup finely chopped walnuts
6 tablespoons sugar
2 tablespoons imported kirsch
1 teaspoon finely grated fresh lemon peel
¼ teaspoon ground cinnamon
¼ teaspoon ground nutmeg
2 to 4 tablespoons dry red wine
1 tablespoon butter, softened
1 egg beaten lightly with 1 tablespoon milk

To serve 4

Four 6-by-4-inch veal scallops (about 4 ounces each), cut about ⅜ inch thick and pounded ¼ inch thick
2 eggs, lightly beaten with 2 tablespoons milk
½ cup flour
¼ pound imported Swiss Gruyère cheese, cut into 4 strips, each 3 inches long, 1 inch wide and ¼ inch thick
4 slices boiled ham, each 3 inches square and ⅛ inch thick
1 cup fine dry bread crumbs
4 tablespoons butter
1 cup vegetable oil
4 thin lemon slices
Paprika

II Belgium—Luxembourg—Netherlands

The Intermingling of Proud Styles

A bemused Belgian girl has her hands full with a freshly made waffle, or *gaufre*. Waffles are eaten in great quantities by Belgians of all ages, and they come with various elaborate trimmings. Many people like them topped with whipped cream, fresh fruit or caramelized sugar, but some, like this young lady, prefer them simply with butter and sugar.

Twenty-odd years ago, on our honeymoon, Frances and I spent nine days and nights crossing a rough Atlantic aboard an old reconverted freighter, our destination Antwerp. Our first view of Belgium was through a porthole. As the ship moved slowly through a narrow canal, we saw, to our astonishment, what appeared to be Holland: first a windmill, then a little girl in wooden shoes keeping pace with the ship as she walked along the grassy bank. The landscape, or what we could see of it, was as flat as the palm of my hand. We knew, of course, that we were in Belgium, but throughout our stay in Antwerp, the feeling that we were in the Netherlands persisted—particularly since, except for a smattering of French, everyone spoke what sounded to us like Dutch.

Our confusion was understandable. Belgium, we soon discovered, is a patchwork quilt of differing terrains, religious divisions, two languages (each a dialect of the language of a neighboring country) and Gothic, Baroque and Renaissance architectural influences. Typical not only of Belgium but also of the Netherlands and Luxembourg, the many disparate elements stand as reminders of the royal marauders from France, Austria and Spain who once ruled the Low Countries.

Had we approached Belgium from the south we would have been just as confused as we were in Antwerp; in southern Belgium, where French is spoken, we might well have thought ourselves in France. On the other hand, we might have thought ourselves in Luxembourg, since Luxembourg is also the name of one of Belgium's own southern provinces adjoining the grand duchy. And, to confound one further, the capital city of the grand duchy of Luxembourg is also called Luxembourg.

But to try to put it as simply as possible, Belgium consists of nine provinces. Those in the north share a border with the Netherlands and are occupied by Catholic, Dutch-speaking Flemings. Those in the southern half share a border with France, and their inhabitants are anticlerical, French-speaking Walloons. One province, Flemish Brabant, has no foreign borders at all; in it is Brussels, the capital of Belgium and, as it were, its heart. Brussels, a densely populated city of over one million, is the seat of Belgium's constitutional monarchy and host to representatives of the Low Countries' economic union called Benelux, an acronym that is derived from the first letters of the names of its three members—Belgium, the Netherlands and Luxembourg.

Benelux represents the three countries' determination to keep pace with today's industrial world, but the Belgians, Dutch and Luxembourgers seem equally determined to retain their separate identities. Intensifying this division is a stubbornness characteristic of them all, an unyielding attitude apparent not only in politics and religion but in cooking as well.

The Dutch, for example, enjoy the food of Indonesia, their former colony, but have clung to their own simple cooking so steadfastly that their native dishes are still basically the same as they have been for hundreds of years. The Flemings in the north of Belgium have developed a culinary style of their own that is closer, not surprisingly, to that of Holland than that of southern Belgium. And the people of little Luxembourg, even more chauvinistic than the Dutch and Flemings, have the most limited cuisine of them all. From my point of view, southern Belgium's cooking, essentially French-oriented but also to some extent influenced by the Spaniards who ruled the region from 1556 to 1713, is the richest and most varied in the Low Countries.

Yet the cuisines of these nations are errant by nature. They cross borders freely, intermingle with one another and exchange identities; ironically, the inhabitants of each Low Country end up obstinately claiming various dishes as their own. Isolating the culinary sources of each country is, if for this reason alone, a formidable task indeed.

To unravel these polymorphous cuisines I began with the cooking of Belgium—and soon encountered an example of the complexities involved. The famous Flemish dish, *hochepot,* a mélange of meats, vegetables and herbs poached in a broth, has a near facsimile in the Netherlands, where it is called *hutspot (Recipe Index).* The only significant difference between them is that the Dutch usually mash the vegetables and the Flemings use them whole.

In many other dishes, however, the Flemings reveal an identifiable culinary style of some distinction. Eels are plentiful in both Holland and the north of Belgium and common to their cuisines, yet they are prepared by the Flemings in more imaginative and original ways than by the Dutch. While the Dutch simply fry, smoke, or stew their eels, the Flemings go much further, and have created a masterpiece, *paling in 't groen,* or eels with potherbs, also known throughout Belgium by its French name, *anguilles au vert (Recipe Index).* This sophisticated dish is made of eels slowly simmered in butter and white wine (or, on occasion, Belgian beer) and combined with as many green herbs as a Flemish cook can get her hands on: chervil, sorrel, tarragon and more. The fragrant herbal sauce is then thickened suavely with egg yolks and seasoned with lemon juice. The result—usually served cold, but occasionally lukewarm or hot—bears not the slightest resemblance to eel dishes I have encountered anywhere else in the world.

Frances, like many Americans, had always taken a dim view of eels in any form until, with a Machiavellian ploy, I introduced her to *anguilles au vert* in a seaside restaurant in Ostend. I whisked her from the bracing North Sea air straight to the restaurant's kitchen, determined to shame her into at least tasting this extraordinary dish. Once informed of my mission, the chef, Josef Minsen, got to work and promptly cut up the freshest of eels. Frances, mesmerized by the speed with which the dish was being made (it seemed to take him only minutes), and lulled into a sense of security by the familiarity of the chopped green herbs that soon entirely masked the eels, was taken unawares when Josef offered her a forkful —suddenly she had tasted eels, and not only that but had admitted that she actually liked them.

Her resistance overcome, it was a simple matter for me next to have her taste *anguilles au vert* the way I really prefer them—cold. Because eels contain natural gelatin, the dish's green sauce, when chilled, thickens to a glutinous consistency, and the flavor of the herbs—especially the tart sorrel—becomes subtly muted. To this day, Frances is as ardent about this Flemish dish as I am, and always orders it in New York at the restaurant Quo Vadis, whose chef makes *anguilles au vert* as well as my friend in Ostend, if not better, with an interesting additional touch, fresh mint.

But when it comes to the dish known as fish *waterzooi (Recipe Index)*, Josef has no peers. Truly indigenous to the Flemish part of Belgium, this creation is rarely found anywhere else. Other Belgians, for some reason, prefer chicken *waterzooi (Recipe Index)*: a poached chicken, its broth thickened with egg yolks and cream, served as a one-dish meal—a fricassee, in fact—often garnished with thin slices of lemon. But I prefer the fish *waterzooi,* especially as Josef prepared it for us in Ostend. First he flavored some boiling water in the Flemish way with white wine, celery, parsley, onions and bay leaf, then added a variety of North Sea fish that naturally included eels. Some Flemings give their *waterzooi* a Dutch overtone: Holland rusks are, on occasion, crumbled into the fish broth in order to thicken it. But fortunately for me, because the rusks are too sweet for my taste, Josef omitted them.

Since fish *waterzooi* is, to my knowledge, never available in American restaurants I often make it at home, following Josef's method almost to the letter. Our fish, on the whole, are more fragile than those of the North Sea; therefore I remove them from the pot before they disintegrate, and boil the broth rapidly until it reaches the density I like. When I set a tureen of fragrant *waterzooi* before Frances and our guests, we frequently speak of Josef and his resturant that faces the busy, boat-filled North Sea harbor; the savory scent of *waterzooi* recalls for us that colorful seascape, with masts tipping in the wind and ships sailing slowly by, their names in gold letters glittering in Ostend's cold Flemish light.

Though linked by an economic union, Benelux, and by a shared history as pawns in the war games of Europe's kings, each of the three Low Countries maintains a rugged individualism that is expressed in everything from politics to food. There are even strong differences within Belgium, whose Flemings, living in the north, have their own cooking style that is related to but distinct from that of the Dutch.

Belgium is so small that it is possible to drive from Ostend to Brussels, or from Brussels to any of the country's borders—France, the Netherlands, Germany, the North Sea or the grand duchy of Luxembourg—in two or three hours at the most. As a consequence the fish, fowl, game, vegetables and fruits that Belgium produces in such profusion reach Brussels' marketplaces within hours.

For Belgians, "seasonal" vegetables and fruits mean something quite different from what they mean in America, where on endless acres of mostly mechanically tended farmland the goal, I feel, is size rather than quality. Belgian farming is mostly small truck farming, carried on by individual farmers with intense devotion and ingenuity. Vegetables—accurately called *primeurs* (in their prime)—are started in hothouses, transplanted outdoors, then hand-picked before maturing, when they are small and at the peak of their flavor. In this way, Belgian farmers not only raise exquisite vegetables but can reseed their small plots and thus often gain two crops a season. Many of these vegetables, bottled attractively, are exported to America and can be bought in our more sophisticated shops, but they have nothing in common with the *primeurs* of Belgium in their pristine state. However, one Belgian specialty, endive, as we know it *(witloof* in Flemish, and *chicorée de Bruxelle* in French), tastes the same here as it does there—crisp and slightly but pleasantly bitter. But why don't we stop using endive only in salads? If we would stuff, braise and sauce it in the Belgian fashion, we would consume far more of it than we do. I have re-created many of Belgium's delicate endive dishes, such as cream of endive soup and braised endive stuffed with chicken *(Recipe Index),* and there is no reason why any enterprising American cook can't do the same.

In Hoeilaart and Overijse, only a few miles outside cosmopolitan Brussels, thousands of gleaming glass hothouses grow the world's most sumptuous clusters of tear- and ball-shaped grapes, ranging in color from green to blackish purple. By a process called *égrainage*—the removal of smaller grapes to allow the others to grow larger—each grape at maturity is perfect in size and shape. The ripened clusters, with their silvery bloom intact (and woe to the worker who carelessly rubs it off), are tied with colorful ribbons, then nestled seductively on beds of soft cotton. They have the appearance of rare Belgian jewels, and are, in fact, almost as formidably expensive.

Not long ago, discussing Belgian food with some friends in Brussels, we learned to our dismay that the precious grapes were being slowly and insidiously supplanted by cheaper and inferior varieties from Belgium's Common Market partners. Soon, our friends said, hothouse Belgian grapes may be no more. But, happily, this sad news was tempered with good; when I asked about another star in the diadem of Belgium's cuisine, *rognons de veau à la liégeoise (Recipe Index),* a sautéed kidney dish made with juniper berries and gin, our knowing friends instantly suggested L'Abreuvoir, "an unpretentious restaurant" on the outskirts of Brussels. There, they were certain, we would have *rognons liégeoise* every bit as good as anything we could find in Liège itself.

Enthusiastic as our friends were about the food—as well they might have been—they had neglected to add that L'Abreuvoir was also an en-

Continued on page 44

In the Flemish town of Wingene, crowds assemble along the banner-bedecked streets for the biennial Bruegel *Feest*.

"Peasant" Pieter Bruegel Gets His Due at an All-Out Flemish Feast

Every other year on the second Sunday in September, the town of Wingene in western Belgium turns the clock back more than four centuries to honor Pieter Bruegel the Elder, Flanders' most famous artist. Known as "Peasant" Bruegel, he was a master of the colloquial Dutch scene, and 20th Century citizens get into the spirit by wearing the costumes of Bruegel's time and creating tableaux of his works, such as *Netherlandish Proverbs* and *Peasant Wedding*. Thousands of tourists flock to Wingene—a town Bruegel himself probably never visited—to watch the parade and banquet that highlight the holiday's festivities. In one part of the parade, a procession of men representing guilds of butchers and cheese makers carry great quantities of their local products to the main square. There, the townsfolk set upon the food with lusty Bruegelian appetite, wolfing down sausages, salami and cheese by the ton, pancakes by the thousands, and countless barrels of beer.

At the post-parade banquet, revelers heed a Low Countries proverb: "Forget ye not to eat plenty and drink ye merrily."

A pert parader keeps her dinner discreetly in her lap, while a fellow participant approaches his sausage less delicately.

Three draped sausage strings add the perfect touch to this diner's apt personification of a Bruegelian peasant butcher.

chanting place. At one time it had been a farmhouse, and Monsieur and Madame Redemans, the proprietors, told us that the rough walls still contained the original straw and earth with which the building was constructed three hundred years ago. But there the restaurant solidly stood, its sloping floors supporting crowds of serious Belgian diners in three good-sized rooms on different levels.

What struck us when we entered was the huge, ceiling-high fireplace where a whole lamb, pierced from snout to tail, was roasting over a smoldering wood fire. The chef and his assistants were in full view near a serving table laden with bread, fruits and heavy crocks of mustard. The walls were covered with unframed portraits, landscapes and still lifes painted in the manner of the old Flemish masters. Although haphazardly hung, the paintings glowed as if lit from within under the soft light cast by glass-bowled kerosene lamps of gemlike colors—sapphire, ruby and amethyst. Our table was small and quite close to the next one—a restaurant practice I deplore and have often attacked in my own country; but here it didn't bother me at all. I was pleased, in fact, when the gentleman on my right handed me his card and shyly introduced himself and his wife. In a few moments we were all deeply engaged in a discussion of the menu, and our neighbor was delighted to learn that we had come for the *rognons liégeoise*—for he and his wife had come for it too.

As a habitué of L'Abreuvoir, he told us that there were other dishes on the menu almost if not quite as good as the famed *rognons*—and suggested that I start with a *mousse au truite,* and Frances with the *écrevisses au gratin.* I was surprised. A mousse of trout and gratinéed crayfish are representative of the classic cooking of France; what were they doing in this rustic restaurant?

I recalled experiencing this culinary confusion in Belgium before and reminded myself that southern Belgians have for centuries been absorbing as if by osmosis the French cuisine and translating it into Belgian terms. Needless to say, neither of these dishes resembled its French prototype in the least. Each was richer and more solid, more definitely seasoned, and had a robustness that elegant French cooking seldom has. The *écrevisses* were served in the traditional way, in an oval copper dish, but instead of crayfish masked with a subtle French sauce, the Belgian version that was set before me had a lightly browned crust, and the *écrevisses* underneath it were swimming in butter and cream. And the mousse, rather than being airy and velvety, was dense in texture and had a surprisingly lively lemony flavor.

After the *écrevisses* and mousse came the *rognons liégeoise,* perfectly sautéed and redolent of juniper berries—a superb example of Belgian cooking at its best. It was accompanied not by *pommes frites* (which Belgians consume in prodigious quantities on every possible occasion, heaven knows why), but by a baked potato the likes of which I had never eaten before nor have forgotten since. It had been baked *au cindre*—in ashes—then gently split apart to receive a few tablespoons of sauce poured into its steaming center. The sauce looked like a simple mixture of oil, vinegar and herbs—a vinaigrette, in fact—but upon tasting it I discovered it was far more interesting than that; it had been made of bruised juniper

Opposite: Belgian desserts are not for weight watchers. This lavish temptation, illuminated by a shaft of sunlight in L'Abreuvoir near Brussels, is a *café liégeois.* Its preparation is a simple matter: *sirop de café* (a coffee-flavored syrup) is poured generously over mocha ice cream, which is then embellished with liberal dollops of *crème chantilly*—sweetened whipped cream flavored with vanilla.

Impeccable service and table settings as well as excellent food are the hallmarks of Brussels' Villa Lorraine Restaurant, where these diners have ordered *écrevisses Villa Lorraine.* A house specialty, the dish consists of Belgium's delicate crayfish simmered gently in a mild white wine and cream sauce.

berries and chopped shallots and garlic, moistened with a touch of fresh lemon juice *(Recipe Index).* Such piquancy combined with the texture of the potato was a joy, and I would not have traded this potato at that moment for one prepared in any other way.

During the lively conversation that went with this memorable meal, our newly found companions told us that in the early 1900s the restaurant had been a village café, and a favorite haunt of Brussels residents who would stroll out from the city on Sundays to indulge in a now forgotten sport: hunting *cockschafers,* a species of beetle—a rollicking game such as chasing and netting butterflies might have been for our forebears. Fatigued, apparently, by this arduous play, the ladies and gentlemen of Brussels would refresh themselves from time to time in true Belgian fashion with tankard after tankard of beer in the nearby café. When our friends suggested that we conclude dinner with a similar refreshment, I agreed despite the fact that neither Frances nor I was, at that moment, in need of refreshment of any kind.

What swayed me was professional curiosity to see what L'Abreuvoir had to offer in the way of Belgian beer. I knew that Belgians never export their beer, and I had tasted many local types distinctive for their extraordinary lightness. Nevertheless on this occasion, after an hour of Bruegelian swilling (I'm ashamed to admit now) I emerged from a foamy sea of malt and hops with something significant to add to my knowledge of beer; I had for the first time tasted a five-year-old brew called Geuse-Kriek, which was at once briskly effervescent and dense, with as notably lively a character as that of a fine French champagne. I can only hope that fellow Americans don't have to drink themselves so deeply into the ground as I did that night to unearth a treasure so rare.

After this indulgent repast, Frances and I decided to walk back to the center of Brussels as a restorative and to look once again at the Grand' Place—so gay during spring and summer with crates of fresh flowers under red, white and green umbrellas, and at night so overpowering, in truth, a Grand'Place. Disconcertingly, as we approached it, the names of the streets recapitulated, note by note, what it would have been more comfortable to forget: Rue au Beurre (Butter Street), Rue Chair et Pain (Meat and Bread Street) and like an accusation, one we should have tried to avoid—Rue de l'Abondance. From these dimly lit streets, to come upon the Grand'Place—the vast square lined with Baroque and Gothic buildings, their ornamented façades gilded and softly illumined —was to be uplifted at once to the sublime. There are many cafés on the square, yet for us, at least, gaiety was subdued by grandeur.

It was difficult to believe while gazing at the domes, sculptures, and sparkling mullioned windows that peace had not always reigned here. But for centuries Brussels was the center of the Low Countries battleground fought over by the kings of Europe, and this very square had rung to the boots of many foreign armies—most especially those of the soldiers, generals and grandees of Spain who had ruled what is now Belgium for almost two hundred years. This long vassalage left many scars, but it also left some reminders of a more pleasant nature, as we were to see firsthand the very next day.

Our friends who had sent us to L'Abreuvoir had also suggested that we go to Binche, a small town farther south in Belgium, where the Mardi Gras was about to begin. In Binche, Carnival festivities include an ancient celebration of Spain's conquest of Mexico in the 16th Century, and it offered us an opportunity to learn about the Spanish influence on Belgian cooking, since the Spanish-oriented dishes are always served at their best during Carnival. It was obviously a culinary experience I couldn't resist.

At a restaurant in Binche we had a choice of many traditional Belgian dishes, but I was interested only in those made à l'escavêche—that is, meat, fish or fowl first fried, then pickled in the Spanish fashion in a highly acidulated, vegetable-laden marinade and served cold. On the menu there were three different kinds of these dishes made with pork, eels and fish. I ordered them all, and discovered that they tasted almost as they had in Spain except for the fact that the marinade had been thickened quite pleasantly, to my surprise, with flour. In addition, we had a rice torte, its Spanish ancestry evident in the recognizable flavor of saffron and its pale orange hue. And if I needed any further confirmation of the Spanish imprint on Belgian food, it was provided by our dessert: innumerable chewy macaroons that were composed almost wholly of delicious Spanish almonds.

It was later that day, at the height of Carnival, that I had a signif-

Continued on page 54

47

Riding in the dawn mist, Armand Vanbillemont trawls for shrimp near the Belgian beach resort of Oostduinkerke.

A Belgian Shrimp Fisherman Who Goes Down to the Sea on Horseback

On mornings when the tide is low along the North Sea coast of Belgium, Armand Vanbillemont dons his oilskin coat, wading boots and fisherman's hat, leaves his home in Oostduinkerke and drives his horse to the beach to catch shrimp. The shrimp, small and sweet, are a delicacy much admired by local citizens and resort tourists; M. Vanbillemont is a *pêcheur de crevettes à cheval,* a mounted shrimp fisherman. Shrimp boats have almost eliminated his picturesque calling, but a few horsemen keep the custom alive. Summer and winter, on a quiet beach not far from the scene of the British evacuation at Dunkirk in World War II, M. Vanbillemont plows the sea bottom, dragging a trawl to scoop up shrimp. The trawling done, he hauls his catch home, with the work of sorting, cooking and selling the shrimp still to be done.

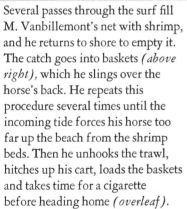

Several passes through the surf fill
M. Vanbillemont's net with shrimp,
and he returns to shore to empty it.
The catch goes into baskets *(above
right)*, which he slings over the
horse's back. He repeats this
procedure several times until the
incoming tide forces his horse too
far up the beach from the shrimp
beds. Then he unhooks the trawl,
hitches up his cart, loads the baskets
and takes time for a cigarette
before heading home *(overleaf)*.

In his back yard, M. Vanbillemont empties the baskets onto a large wire screen *(above)* that lets the shrimp fall through, leaving crabs, also caught in the haul, which Mme. Vanbillemont will use to make soup for the family's own dinner. M. Vanbillemont boils the shrimp *(above right)*, then strains them and pours them into baskets, ready for market. During the resort season, visitors in town sometimes come to buy shrimp on the spot. On most days, though, Mme. Vanbillemont goes out to sell the shrimp door to door to her neighbors *(opposite)*. The tender, succulent shellfish will be used in such Belgian dishes as creamed oysters and shrimp or shrimp-and-cheese fritters *(Recipe Index)*.

icant insight into Belgian cooking. We had moved with the crowd, following the dancing *Gilles*—young men of families fortunate enough to have inherited heirloom costumes designed centuries ago for entertainers of a visiting Spanish grandee. The *Gilles'* costumes were lavish and primitive, with bold patterns in red and black, bells on the belts, large fringed epaulettes, and feather headdresses that towered nearly five feet in the air. The moment for which everyone waited came when the *Gilles* pelted the crowd with a barrage of Seville oranges. As the oranges flew through the air, the spectacle clarified for me the meaning of Belgium's puzzling cuisine: it reflects the country's complex history and is a composite of the culinary preferences of its many earlier rulers. Ravished by memories of the dishes I had tasted, and carried away by the gaiety surrounding us in Binche, so close to France, I found myself repeating a cliché I had often heard and had just as often disputed: "French cooking is indeed superb, but Belgian cooking is divine."

Large Appetites in Little Luxembourg

The grand duchy of Luxembourg extends 55 miles from north to south and 35 miles from east to west (Frances and I have been on American Western ranches almost as large), and is bordered by Belgium, Germany and France. The grand duchy shares with Belgium the Forest of Ardennes, teeming with the best game in Europe, and with Germany the Moselle River and the exquisite vineyards lining its banks. I feel Luxembourg shares the provincial cuisine of France, although it allows Germany's cooking to underpin, or perhaps undermine, it.

The Luxembourgers' capacity for work, food and pleasure is legendary, and their energy is formidable indeed. Men and women work from morning till night, tending vines, ploughing fields, and running machines, but afterward everyone seems to be intent on roistering. From what we have seen in the outdoor cafés, a Luxembourger appears to enjoy nothing more than eating as much food as he can hold, while listening to a blaring brass band (there are at least 200 of these cacophonous ensembles in the grand duchy) and washing the food down with gargantuan draughts of frothy, heavy beer or the local Riesling wines.

Typical Luxembourg food is especially attractive when it consists of seasonal river specialties: trout, crawfish and pike, simply fried or grilled. And seasonal tarts called *tartes des quetsches (Recipe Index),* made from local plums, are among the best pastries made in the Low Countries. But the grand duchy's more substantial dishes are, for the most part, not to everyone's taste: *geheck,* a soup of entrails (it is considerably better than it sounds), pickled pig's trotters, jellied cow's udders, heavy meat-and-suet dumplings the Luxembourgers call *liewerknuddelen.* All these dishes, when we ate them in rural restaurants, were served with massive portions of boiled or fried potatoes. If these ponderous creations had little culinary attraction for me, they do have great appeal for German visitors as well as for the Luxembourgers.

But what Frances and I did adore were Luxembourg's refreshing, pale-gold wines. Because they were young and tart, they had an exhilarating effect upon me. And even Frances drank more wine there than anywhere

Opposite: The Belgians' great fondness for shellfish is reflected in this rich harvest of the Flanders coastline. At top right, in oyster shells, is *gratin d'huîtres d'Ostende,* oysters and shrimp bathed in cream sauce and sprinkled with cheese. Below it is *moules au gratin,* baked mussels topped with bread crumbs. Both dishes are bedded in rock salt, which holds the heat. At left are *moules à l'Anversoise,* mussels that are both steamed and served in a delicate wine and herb sauce.

else. Many of the Luxembourg wines are so young—some still fermenting in the bottle—that they have a *pétillant,* or faintly bubbly, character that older, more mature wines lack. The few Luxembourg Moselles that are exported to America—such as Rizaner, Auxerrois and Riesling—inevitably lose this sprightly quality when they travel, and although still drinkable and often delightful, cannot compare, for us at least, with those we drank on the spot.

In addition to the enticements of its wines, Luxembourg is a fascinating place to visit. The city of Luxembourg is the grand duchy's thousand-year-old capital—originally the greatest fortress in Europe and now the residence of the royal family, Grand Duke Jean and Princess Josephine-Charlotte. And south of the city in Esch-sur-Alzette, the duchy's steel-producing area, it was a delight to find elaborate flower gardens, neat parks, farms and vineyards flourishing right next to gigantic, smoke-spewing industrial plants.

Rich ore deposits and steel manufacture have made this little change purse of a country one of the most prosperous in Europe. There is no unemployment; wages and social security benefits are higher than in France, Belgium or Germany. And Luxembourg's Baroque castles, bucolic landscape and romantic Maeterlinckian forests never lose their luster for me even if my feeling about the grand duchy's food is something less than fervent. And as to that, I need have no qualms. After all, the Luxembourgers' national song is "Mir Wöllen Bleiben Was Mir Iss" ("We Want to Stay as We Are")—a clear indication that whatever I think of their food, they could hardly care less.

The Netherlands: Neither Staid nor Stolid

The first time Frances and I saw Holland was with our 16-year-old son as a guide, in 1966. Jonathan had been on holiday there and was about to return to New York; we were spending the summer in France, and on the spur of the moment decided to fly to Amsterdam and have an evening with him before he left Europe.

That one hectic night in the Netherlands' capital was enough to make us want to remain there forever. Our son, who knew the city well by then, authoritatively took us in hand. He had had his fill of Dutch boardinghouse cooking, and suggested that we go to what his friends had told him was the best—and, naturally, the most expensive—restaurant in town: the Indonesia.

Until then, we had thought of Amsterdam, as perhaps many Americans do, as a staid and stolid city. But with our energetic son as our guide, we were soon disabused of this notion. Amsterdam, as he put it so accurately, was "a swinging town." We were intrigued by the young men in ruffled shirts and tight trousers and the girls in the miniest of miniskirts. From all sides in these swarming streets—and Amsterdam is one of the most densely populated cities in Europe—the sounds of blaring jazz rose brazenly above the screeching of brakes and the honking of horns; at that moment, Times Square in New York City seemed a peaceful oasis by comparison.

But we discovered another aspect of Amsterdam, too. On our way to

Opposite: Though it is as distinctively Dutch as the carefully preserved town of Marken where it was photographed, *hutspot met klapstuk,* a robust meat-and-vegetable stew, also appears in nearly the same form in northern Belgium, where it is called *hochepot.* Its basic ingredients are boiled potatoes, carrots and onions cooked with boneless beef; but other vegetables are added freely to the dish as well, and because of this haphazard blending, the dish has entered the English language in the form of the word hodgepodge.

the restaurant we took a brief detour and drove along the banks of the Amstel River just outside of town. This broad, seemingly still river reflected the evening light of an icy blue sky. The farther bank extended flat as far as the eye could see to meet the sky at what seemed to be a right angle. Straight-edged geometrical Dutch houses—they made us think of the purity of Vermeer and Mondrian—old windmills and tall slender trees were silhouetted against the luminous background, with rays of light streaming through verdant foliage. In summer the Amstel is alive with boats, banners flying in the wind; and in winter, when frozen over, it is a sparkling arena for a frenzy of skating activity and color. Once away from the crowds and noise of Amsterdam, we felt, it was possible to see the Netherlands as the country's great landscape painters had. Frances said later that while driving she had felt as if she herself were a small figure in a brooding landscape by Jacob van Ruisdael.

The interior of the Indonesia restaurant was yet another world: spacious, serene and quietly elegant. The food of the faraway former colony is especially appealing to Hollanders—they call it *rijsttafel,* or rice table —and the restaurants that serve it are favorite dining-out places.

All the food for our dinner had been partially prepared in the kitchen, then completed and kept hot at our table on simple stoves set over can-

Forty percent of the Netherlands, like this lush pasture 10 miles south of Amsterdam, is below sea level. The Dutch have reclaimed such areas, called polders, by cutting the region off from the sea with dikes and pumping out the water. Canals and man-made rivers like the one seen here serve to drain the polder, act as fences for the cows, and provide navigable waterways.

dles. It was served by a chef assigned just to us. He was small, gentle and handsome, as Indonesians always seem to be. Wearing a batik jacket and black skullcap, he moved swiftly from the serving of one exquisite morsel to another, and, pleased by my curiosity, happily explained what they were and the contents of their accompanying sauces. It was a veritable banquet, a constant series of surprises contrived to delight the senses. With the virtuosity of a magician pulling rabbits out of a hat, he produced *saté,* beef bits on tiny skewers dipped in a fiery hot curry sauce, and then instantly served us glazed sweet potatoes to ease the sting. Goat's meat came with soya-bean sauce, followed by shrimp and carrots; the highly spiced pork slices were tempered by fried bananas. It went on and on, and even Jonathan, whose appetite can match any Dutchman's, finally called it quits.

Returning to our hotel later, we found the streets even more joyous than before. Unhappily, with an early plane to take, we had to bid Amsterdam and our son adieu, vowing to return at the earliest possible moment. The moment came three years later. We were visiting in London and found we had a few days free, and on impulse we caught a flight to Amsterdam. Frances, steeped in the history of the indomitable Dutch people and the reclamation of their land, told me as we landed that the

Schiphol Airport was diked in and lay 13 feet below sea level. It does give one pause to realize that without the remarkable feats of engineering that produced their dikes, dams, sluices and pumps, most of the Dutch wouldn't be there at all—they would be under water. But the ever-encroaching sea had other and less sinister meanings for me; I looked forward more to tasting its fruits than to learning about the hydraulic achievements responsible for its control.

The herring of Holland have always especially interested me. I had eaten brined Dutch herring in America where they are imported in great quantities, but my first taste of a salted herring in Amsterdam I can only describe as perplexing. New, or so-called green, herring are sold in early May from carts on the city's streets much as ice cream and popsicles are sold in New York City in summer. Dutchmen eat them on the run, buying them already cut up and served with minced onion, or consuming them whole in two or three enthusiastic bites. My puzzlement came from the fact that the fish are so lightly brined that at first taste they seemed to me almost raw. With each successive mouthful, however, I found myself savoring their silky sealike flavor more and more, and began to understand the love the Dutch have for these salty silvery fish.

But there were no first and second thoughts about lunch eaten in a *broodjeswinkel*—a sandwich shop somewhat like our delicatessens—where we feasted on the freshest of steak tartare, made, as it always should be, without a speck of fat; *half-om,* a curious combination of liver and corned beef; a glazed loin of veal cut in the thinnest of slices; a battery of sausages and cheeses—Gouda, Edam and the spiced Leyden and Friesian cheeses—all accompanied by hot rolls, the creamiest of creamery butter and heavy Holland beer.

Although a number of cultivated Hollanders complained to me of the monotony and simplicity of most home cooking—the lack of sauces, no wine, only beer—I realized that their food (and I have had the same thought about American food) does not have to be monotonous or simple at all. One dinner in Amsterdam illustrated this most graphically. Hugh Jans, the noted Dutch cartoonist and food columnist, cooked it for us in his own spacious, well-equipped kitchen. We started with a pea soup *(Recipe Index)* that is ordinarily a meal in itself—a winter one at that—which Hugh, because he meant us only to taste it, served in bouillon cups instead of the usual large bowls. The soup was quite different from any other pea soup I had ever tasted before. Instead of the smooth, simple purée of peas I expected, the soup in addition to split peas contained cubes of pig's feet, salt pork and slices of sausage, the whole flavored with crushed summer savory.

The plaice (we would call it flounder) that followed was even more elaborate. It had been topped with bacon, coated with bread crumbs, grated almonds and Holland's famous Gouda cheese, then baked in the oven only long enough for the fish to cook through and the topping to brown *(Recipe Index).* As simple as this technique may sound, it was in reality a culinary feat. Even French cooks would think twice before attempting it; they call the process a "complete gratin," which involves the perilous process of cooking both the raw fish and its topping at the same time in-

Opposite: Dutch green pea soup is at its best on a gray wintry day, but there is no reason it cannot be enjoyed year round. Its rich color is intensified by the fresh green vegetables that are combined with the green split peas, and rounds of spicy sausage and strips of pork give the soup its rugged character.

61

A carefree Amsterdam student demonstrates an approved way to eat herring in Holland: hold it by the tail and consume it bravely in several large bites. The salted fish are sold from pushcarts throughout the Netherlands and often are eaten on the spot as a snack. Although a purist might insist on eating the herring plain, many Hollanders prefer to garnish it with chopped onions as this girl has done.

stead of poaching the fish first and then topping and browning it later.

The main course was *lamstongen met rozijnensaus,* or lamb's tongues with raisin sauce *(Recipe Index).* And complaints about Dutch cooks to the contrary, Hugh produced a sauce that was superb, composed of garlic, brown sugar, marjoram, cumin, raisins and white wine. It was quite a dish. Then, as if to make up for the lavishly sauced tongue that an average Dutchman might consider extravagant and unorthodox cooking, Hugh served a dessert that looked like crisp fried doughnuts—"simple country apple fritters," he explained. When he told me the batter had been made solely of flour mixed with beer *(Recipe Index),* I expected the dessert to taste as deadly as it sounded. But I can state unequivocally that never before had I tasted a fritter to equal it. Simplicity indeed!

Holland's restaurants don't pretend to simplicity at all, and perhaps for this reason eating out is a special event for the Dutch. The grander restaurants generally seem to leave native cooking to Dutch housewives, but even in these establishments, where frankly French dishes and wines predominate, there are a number of Dutch specialties that retain a secure place on the menu.

We discovered this at De Beukenhof in Oegstgeest, a short drive from Amsterdam. Here a 16th Century farmhouse had been transformed into a sumptuous restaurant surrounded by immaculate gardens. Despite the anachronistic furnishings—upholstered sofas, modern lighting and an up-to-the-minute bar—the interior still had the unmistakable look of a Holland interior as painted by a Dutch master. This impression was underlined when the restaurant's manager proudly showed us an upstairs room in which Rembrandt, he said, had painted, and then led us to an enormous built-in chest of drawers, explaining that in Rembrandt's time the drawers had been used as beds. We then went down to dinner and, affected by the authentic atmosphere of the restaurant, we chose only dishes that were decidedly Dutch.

We bypassed the French hors d'oeuvre for dishes that were new to us, and began with a traditional glass of *jenever,* the Netherlands' national apéritif. Although *jenever* is what our word gin derives from, it is not really gin as we know it, but a clear, slightly thick spirit with just the faintest aftertaste of juniper; it is usually served cold. With it came slices of smoked Dutch eel unlike any smoked eel I have ever encountered before. Perhaps because eels, like herring, are so plentiful in Holland, they tasted fresher, and were as lightly smoked as the lightly brined herring I had had a few days earlier.

Eels and herring are taken for granted in the Netherlands, but the Dutch are justly proud of their Texel lamb, a breed that feeds in the salt marshes of the low-lying Frisian Islands that guard Holland's coastline. Texel lamb is as famous in Holland as salt-marsh-bred *pré-salé* lamb is in France. The rack of lamb served to us had a fine, characteristically salty flavor, but I must admit it was slightly overdone for my taste. (The Dutch insist on having their meats well done, even if they prefer their fish almost raw.) Despite an impressive array of pastries offered at De Beukenhof, we had promised ourselves a dessert of Dutch pancakes and headed for the Pannekoekenhuisje (literally, "pancake house") in the nearby ancient little town of Leyden. Though many sites in Leyden commemorate the stay of our Pilgrim forefathers in that city, there was certainly no reminder of Puritanism in the consumption of pancakes we witnessed there.

Lured by the technique diners at the next table were using to eat their pancakes, though not sure we could manage them as dexterously, we courageously ordered some. While waiting for them to arrive, we agreed that we felt as we had as children, watching Italians twirling slippery strands of spaghetti securely around a fork. Our neighbors, obviously trained from childhood to handle the complex maneuver, first poured spirals of a golden syrup much like treacle over the entire surface of the pancake (it must have been at least eight inches in diameter), then secured it with a fork and used another fork to roll it into a thick cylinder. Finally, each diner sliced his pancake into jelly-roll-like rounds and consumed it without further ado. When our dessert arrived, I managed the technique fairly smoothly, having cooked and rolled crêpes for many years, but Frances didn't fare so well—her pancake looked more like a misshapen muff. But she ate it anyway, saying defensively, "It may look messy to you"—and it surely did—"but it tastes delicious to me."

We discovered afterward that these pancakes, composed merely of flour, eggs, milk and butter, are sometimes as large as pizzas, and are eaten all over the Netherlands, not only spread with syrup, but just as often with jam or fruit. At their most elaborate, the pancakes are made into a cake called *flensjes (Recipe Index)*, constructed by piling at least seven pancakes in a stack. Spread between the pancakes as one is placed upon another are layers of applesauce, jam or rhubarb purée. The entire cake is then served like a pie and cut into wedges at the table. Most Americans would be satisfied with a wedge or perhaps two; we were astonished to see a Dutch diner enthusiastically tackling a stack at least four inches high all on his own.

Like all the inhabitants of the other Low Countries, the Dutch are hearty eaters, to put it mildly; but they have Western Europe's longest life expectancy and one of the lowest death rates in the world. Frances and I have hazarded all kinds of guesses as to why but have not by any means come up with verifiable conclusions. The one thing we are sure of is that everywhere we went in the Netherlands the people ate enormously, and it is obvious that their food agreed with them. Sturdy and honest, unpretentious but highlighted with sophisticated surprises, it seemed to us to reflect the essential character of the Dutch people themselves.

Overleaf: For three centuries the cheese market has been a local institution at Alkmaar, a town in northwest Holland. Once a week, from April to September, tradition is served by costumed cheese porters who load their sledlike barrows with golden wheels of Gouda and grapefruit-sized balls of Edam cheese that have been brought to town by barge. Gouda and Edam, native to the Netherlands, are both mild, semisoft cheeses, and they taste very much alike. The scarlet color that identifies Edam for Americans is affixed only to those balls that are to be exported.

To serve 6 to 8

4 tablespoons butter
6 medium-sized Belgian endives (about 1 pound), trimmed, washed and finely chopped
2 medium-sized leeks, including 2 inches of the green tops, trimmed, thoroughly washed to rid them of all sand, then finely chopped
1 medium-sized baking potato (about ½ pound), peeled and finely chopped
1 tablespoon salt
¼ teaspoon white pepper
6 cups milk
4 tablespoons butter, softened

To serve 6 as a first course

4 tablespoons unsalted butter, softened, plus 4 tablespoons unsalted butter
6 large firm endives, with tightly closed unblemished leaves
Salt
White pepper
¼ cup strained fresh lemon juice
A 6- to 8-ounce chicken breast, skinned and boned
¼ cup flour
1 cup chicken stock, fresh or canned
1 cup heavy cream
⅛ teaspoon ground nutmeg, preferably freshly grated
1 egg yolk
½ cup freshly grated imported Gruyère cheese
6 slices boiled ham, each ⅛ inch thick and about 6 inches wide and 8 inches long

Soupe à l'Ardennaise *(Belgium)*
CREAM OF ENDIVE SOUP

In a heavy 3- to 4-quart casserole, melt 4 tablespoons of butter over moderate heat. When the foam begins to subside, add the endives and leeks, and stir until they are evenly coated with the butter. Reduce the heat to low, cover tightly, and cook for about 10 minutes, or until the vegetables are soft and translucent but not brown. Stir in the potato, salt and pepper, pour in the milk, and bring to a simmer over moderate heat, stirring from time to time. Reduce the heat to low again and simmer uncovered for about 45 minutes. When the soup is finished the potatoes will have dissolved almost completely to create a light purée.

Taste for seasoning, swirl the softened butter into the soup, and serve at once from a heated tureen or in individual soup plates.

Chicorée et Volaille Bruxelloise *(Belgium)*
BRAISED ENDIVES STUFFED WITH CHICKEN

Preheat the oven to 325°. With a pastry brush, spread 2 tablespoons of the softened butter evenly over the bottom and sides of a baking-serving dish large enough to hold the endives in one layer.

With a small, sharp knife trim off the bases of the endives (making sure not to cut so deep that the leaves separate) and wash the endives under cold running water. Pat them completely dry with paper towels, then arrange them side by side in the buttered dish and with a pastry brush spread them with the remaining 2 tablespoons of softened butter. Sprinkle the endives with ½ teaspoon salt and ¼ teaspoon of white pepper, and pour the lemon juice over them.

Cover the endives with a sheet of wax paper cut to fit flush with the inside rim of the dish. Then bake in the middle of the oven for about 1½ hours, or until the bases of the endives are tender and show no resistance when pierced deeply with the point of a skewer. With tongs or a slotted spatula carefully transfer the endives to a plate. Pour off any liquid remaining in the dish and set the dish aside.

Raise the oven temperature to 375°. In a small flameproof baking pan, melt 1 tablespoon of the butter over moderate heat. When the foam begins to subside, add the chicken breast and turn it about with a spoon until it glistens on all sides. Remove the pan from the heat, sprinkle the chicken with ¼ teaspoon salt and ⅛ teaspoon white pepper, and cover it with wax paper cut to fit inside the pan. Poach the chicken in the middle of the oven for 8 to 10 minutes, or until the flesh feels firm to the touch. Transfer the chicken to a plate and, with a sharp knife, cut it into ¼-inch dice. Place the diced chicken in a small bowl and set aside.

In a heavy 1½- to 2-quart saucepan, melt the remaining 3 tablespoons of butter over moderate heat, stir in the flour, and mix thoroughly. Pour in the chicken stock and, stirring constantly with a wire whisk, cook over high heat until the sauce thickens heavily and comes to a boil. Reduce the heat to low and simmer for about 5 minutes to remove any taste of

Belgian endives, compact clusters of pale yellow and white leaves familiar to Americans as a salad ingredient, are cooked in Belgium in many artful ways. At top, a delicate cream of endive soup adjoins a meaty lamb stew with endives. In the foreground is an elegant composition of braised endives stuffed with chicken, wrapped in ham and smothered in a velvety sauce.

raw flour, then stir in the cream, nutmeg, ¼ teaspoon of salt and a pinch of white pepper. Taste for seasoning and add more salt or pepper if necessary. Pour about ¼ cup of the sauce over the reserved chicken dice and mix well. Then beat the egg yolk into the remaining sauce and when it is completely absorbed stir in the cheese.

Increase the oven heat to 400°. With a sharp knife, slit each endive in half lengthwise, cutting to within about 1 inch of the base. One at a time, spread the endives open butterfly fashion and flatten one half gently with the side of a cleaver or large knife. Divide the chicken mixture into 6 equal portions. Spread one portion of the chicken mixture on the flattened sides of each endive, then fold the other half of the endive over the filling and wrap each stuffed endive securely in a slice of ham.

Arrange the wrapped endives side by side (seamed side down) in the baking-serving dish and spoon the reserved sauce evenly over the top. Bake in the middle of the oven for about 10 minutes, or until the sauce begins to bubble. Then place the baking dish under a preheated broiler (about 3 inches from the heat) for a minute or so to brown the sauce further. Serve at once, directly from the baking dish.

Lapin à la Flamande *(Belgium)*
RABBIT IN PRUNE SAUCE

Combine the raisins, prunes and cognac in a small bowl and set them aside to marinate at room temperature for at least 3 hours. If the cognac does not cover the fruit completely, stir gently from time to time to keep all the fruit well moistened.

Pat the pieces of rabbit completely dry with paper towels and sprinkle them on all sides with the salt and a few grindings of pepper. In a heavy 4- to 4½-quart casserole, fry the diced bacon over moderate heat, stirring occasionally. When the dice are crisp and have rendered all their fat transfer them to paper towels with a slotted spoon.

Pour off and discard all but about 3 tablespoons of the bacon fat and add 2 tablespoons of butter to the casserole. Melt the butter over high heat and brown the rabbit in the hot fat, a few pieces at a time, turning them frequently with tongs or a slotted spoon and regulating the heat so that they color richly and evenly without burning. As they brown, transfer the rabbit pieces to a plate.

Pour off all but about 2 tablespoons of the fat remaining in the casserole and drop in the small white onions. Sliding the casserole back and forth frequently to roll the onions around, fry for about 8 minutes, or until they are golden brown. With a slotted spoon, transfer the onions to a separate plate.

Stir 1 tablespoon of flour into the fat remaining in the casserole. Then pour in 1½ cups of the water and bring to a boil over high heat, stirring constantly with a rubber spatula and scraping in the brown particles that cling to the bottom and sides of the pan.

Add the thyme and the reserved bacon dice. Return the pieces of rabbit and any liquid that has accumulated around them to the casserole. Turn the pieces about until they are thoroughly moistened. Reduce the heat to low and cover the casserole with both a sheet of foil and the casserole lid to seal it as tightly as possible.

Simmer the rabbit for 1 hour. Then add the reserved onions and stir in the raisins, prunes and cognac. Simmer tightly covered for about 1 hour longer, or until the rabbit is tender and shows no resistance when pierced with the point of a small, sharp knife.

With a slotted spoon, transfer the pieces of rabbit to a heated deep platter and arrange the onions, raisins and prunes attractively around it. Drape the platter loosely with aluminum foil to help keep the rabbit warm while you prepare the sauce.

In a small enameled saucepan or skillet, bring the sugar and the remaining ¼ cup of water to a boil over high heat. Stirring constantly with a metal spoon, cook briskly, uncovered, until the syrup begins to caramelize and turns a golden tealike brown. Still stirring, pour in the red wine vinegar and gradually stir in about ½ cup of the liquid remaining in the casserole.

Pour the entire contents of the saucepan or skillet back into the casserole and, still stirring constantly, simmer the sauce over low heat for one or two minutes. Taste the sauce for seasoning, then pour it over the rabbit and serve at once.

¾ cup (about 4 ounces) seedless raisins
12 pitted dried prunes
⅓ cup cognac
A 4- to 4½-pound rabbit, cut into small serving pieces
1 tablespoon salt
Freshly ground black pepper
¼ pound slab bacon, cut in ¼-inch dice
2 tablespoons butter
12 small white onions, each about 1 inch in diameter, peeled
1 tablespoon flour
1¾ cups water
¼ teaspoon thyme
1 tablespoon sugar
1 tablespoon red wine vinegar

The mainstay of this richly sauced Flemish stew is rabbit, a practical alternative to hare, one of the favorite game foods of rural Belgium.

To serve 6 to 8

3 pounds lean boneless lamb
    shoulder, trimmed of excess fat
    and cut into 1½-inch cubes
2 teaspoons salt
Freshly ground black pepper
4 tablespoons butter
3 tablespoons vegetable oil
1½ cups finely chopped onions
1½ teaspoons finely chopped
    garlic
3 cups beef stock, fresh or canned
1 cup water
1 small bay leaf
4 whole cloves
2 tablespoons finely chopped fresh
    parsley
½ teaspoon crumbled dried thyme
2 pounds small new potatoes (12 to
    16), each about 2 inches in
    diameter, peeled and cut in half
6 small Belgian endives
1 tablespoon cornstarch dissolved in
    2 tablespoons cold water

To serve 4

Rock salt or coarse salt (optional)
2 dozen large mussels (about 3
    pounds), shucked, with the
    deeper half shell of each reserved
2 tablespoons finely chopped
    shallots
2 tablespoons finely chopped fresh
    parsley
1 teaspoon crumbled dried tarragon
½ teaspoon finely chopped garlic
½ teaspoon freshly ground black
    pepper
1½ cups soft fresh crumbs made
    from homemade-type white
    bread, pulverized in a blender or
    finely shredded with a fork
2 tablespoons butter, cut into small
    bits
1 lemon, cut lengthwise into
    quarters

Ragoût de Mouton aux Chicons *(Belgium)*
LAMB STEW WITH ENDIVES

Pat the pieces of lamb completely dry with paper towels, place them in a bowl, and sprinkle with the salt and a few grindings of pepper. Toss the meat about gently with a wooden spoon to distribute the seasonings evenly. In a heavy 5- to 6-quart casserole, melt the butter with the oil over high heat. When the foam begins to subside, add 5 or 6 pieces of lamb and turn them frequently with tongs or a slotted spoon, regulating the heat so that the pieces color richly and evenly without burning. As they brown, transfer them to a plate and brown another 5 or 6 pieces.

When all the lamb is browned, pour off and discard all but about 2 tablespoons of the fat from the pot. Add the onions and garlic and, stirring frequently and scraping in the brown particles that cling to the bottom and sides of the casserole, cook over moderate heat for about 5 minutes, or until the onions are soft.

Return the lamb and any liquid that may have accumulated around it to the casserole. Add the beef stock, water, bay leaf, cloves, parsley and thyme and, stirring constantly, bring to a boil over high heat. Reduce the heat to low, cover partially, and simmer for 30 minutes. Add the potatoes and simmer partially covered for 30 minutes longer.

Meanwhile, with a small, sharp knife trim the bases of the endives and wash them under cold running water. (In Belgium, part of the bitter center core at the base is sometimes cut out when the endive is trimmed. You may remove about ¼ inch of the core with a small knife or apple corer, but be careful not to cut so deeply that the leaves spearate.)

Add the endives to the stew and continue to simmer for 15 to 20 minutes more, or until the lamb and vegetables are tender but not falling apart. Stirring constantly, pour in the cornstarch mixture in a thin stream and simmer only long enough for the sauce to thicken lightly. Taste for seasoning and serve the ragout at once, directly from the casserole or arranged attractively on a heated deep platter.

Moules "Le Zoute" *(Belgium)*
BAKED MUSSELS WITH HERBS

Preheat the oven to 350°. Line a large shallow roasting pan or jelly-roll pan with rock salt (or coarse salt) to a depth of ½ inch. Scrub the reserved mussel shells thoroughly under cold running water, then pat them dry. Arrange them in a single layer in the salt-lined pan and place a mussel in each one. Combine the shallots, parsley, tarragon, garlic and pepper in a bowl and mix well. Then add the bread crumbs and toss thoroughly together. Sprinkle the top of the mussels evenly with the crumb-and-herb mixture, masking the mussels completely. Then dot each mussel with a few of the butter bits and bake in the middle of the oven for 10 minutes. Place the pan under a preheated broiler (about 3 inches from the heat) for a minute to brown the crumbs lightly. Transfer the mussels from the pan to a large heated platter, garnish with lemon and serve at once.

NOTE: The bed of salt is not indispensable to the success of this dish. You may, if you like, bake the mussels in any shallow baking dish large enough to hold the shells snugly in one layer.

Gratin d'Huîtres d'Ostende *(Belgium)*
CREAMED OYSTERS AND SHRIMP IN SHELLS

Preheat the oven to 450°. Shell the shrimp. Devein them by making a shallow incision down their backs with a small, sharp knife and lifting out the black or white intestinal vein with the point of the knife. Wash the shrimp under cold running water and pat them dry with paper towels, then chop them coarsely. Melt 2 tablespoons of the butter in a small skillet. When the foam begins to subside, drop in the shrimp and, stirring constantly, cook over moderate heat for 2 or 3 minutes, until they begin to turn pink. Set aside off the heat.

Pour the oyster liquor into a large measuring cup and add enough milk to make 1¾ cups. Stir in the wine. In a heavy 8- to 10-inch skillet, melt the 4 remaining tablespoons of butter over moderate heat, but do not let it brown. Then stir in the flour and mix together thoroughly. Pour in the milk, oyster liquor and wine mixture and, stirring constantly with a whisk, cook over high heat until the sauce boils and thickens lightly. Reduce the heat to low and simmer for about 3 minutes. Then beat the egg yolk lightly in a bowl, add about ¼ cup of the sauce, and whisk the egg-yolk mixture into the sauce in the pan. Add the pepper and salt and taste for seasoning. Remove the pan from the heat and stir in the reserved shrimp.

Fill a large shallow baking dish to a depth of about ¼ inch with rock salt or coarse salt. (The salt will not only act as a bed for the oysters but also help keep them hot after they are cooked.) Spoon about 1 tablespoon of the shrimp sauce into each oyster shell, top with an oyster, and blanket the oyster with a second tablespoon of the shrimp sauce. Arrange the filled shells side by side in the salt-lined baking dish. Bake in the top third of the oven for about 8 minutes, or until the sauce has barely begun to bubble. Sprinkle the oysters evenly with the bread crumbs and the cheese. Return them to the oven for another 3 or 4 minutes, or until the cheese melts and the crumbs brown lightly. You may then, if you like, slide them under the broiler (about 3 inches from the heat) for a minute or two to brown the tops further. Serve at once.

Erwtensoep *(Netherlands)*
GREEN PEA SOUP

In a heavy 6- to 8-quart casserole combine the split peas, pig's feet, salt pork and water. Bring to a boil over high heat, skimming off the foam and scum as they rise to the surface. Reduce the heat to low, partially cover the pan, and simmer for 3 hours. Then add the potatoes, leeks, celery root and celery leaves, and simmer, partially covered, for 30 minutes.

With tongs or a slotted spoon, transfer the pig's feet and salt pork to a cutting board. Remove and discard the skin, gristle and bones from the pig's feet, then cut the meat and the salt pork into ½-inch dice.

Return the diced meats to the soup and add the sliced sausage, crumbled summer savory and a few grindings of black pepper. Stirring constantly, bring the soup to a simmer over moderate heat and cook for a few minutes to heat the sausage through.

Taste for seasoning and serve at once from a heated tureen or in individual soup plates.

To serve 4

½ pound medium-sized raw shrimp (16 to 20 per pound)
6 tablespoons butter
2 dozen fresh oysters, shucked, with the deeper half shell of each oyster and all the oyster liquor reserved
½ to 1 cup milk
2 tablespoons dry white wine
3 tablespoons all-purpose flour
1 egg yolk
¼ teaspoon white pepper
1 teaspoon salt
Rock salt or coarse salt (optional; *see note opposite*)
¼ cup soft fresh crumbs made from homemade-type white bread, pulverized in a blender or finely shredded with a fork
½ cup freshly grated imported Gruyère or Emmentaler cheese

To serve 8 to 10

2 cups dried green split peas (1 pound), thoroughly washed
2 large fresh meaty pig's feet
½ pound mildly cured salt pork in 1 piece with rind removed
4 quarts water
4 medium-sized boiling potatoes (about 1½ pounds), peeled and cut into ¼-inch dice
4 medium-sized leeks, including 2 inches of the green tops, trimmed, washed to remove any sand, and finely chopped
1 medium-sized celery root (celeriac), peeled and cut into ¼-inch dice
¼ cup finely chopped fresh celery leaves
½ pound precooked smoked sausage, such as *kielbasa,* sliced into ¼-inch-thick rounds
¼ teaspoon crumbled dried summer savory
Freshly ground black pepper

The fish soup at right and the chicken soup beyond it have more in common than they appear to. Both Flemish, they are called *waterzooi* ("water on the boil"), and are prepared on a vegetable base (although the vegetables may differ) and with a broth that is thickened somewhat before serving. Furthermore, they are splendidly practical, in that they comprise both soup and main course.

Waterzooi de Poissons (Belgium)
FISH STEW

Combine the 3 pounds of fish trimmings, sliced onions, parsley sprigs, bay leaf and whole black peppercorns in a 6- to 8-quart enameled or stainless-steel pot. Pour in the white wine and water and, stirring occasionally, bring to a boil over high heat.

Reduce the heat to low and simmer, partially covered, for 30 minutes. Then strain the stock through a fine sieve set over a deep bowl or saucepan, pressing down hard on the fish trimmings and vegetables with the back of a spoon before discarding them.

In a heavy 4- to 5-quart enameled or stainless-steel casserole, melt the 2 tablespoons of butter over moderate heat. When the foam begins to subside, stir in the celery. Cover tightly and reduce the heat to low. Simmer for about 5 minutes.

When the celery is soft but not brown, spread the pieces of eel, perch, pike and carp evenly on top, and dot the fish with the bits of butter. Pour in 6 cups of the strained fish stock and add the crumbled thyme. Bring to a simmer over high heat, then reduce the heat to low and cover the casserole tightly. Simmer for 6 to 8 minutes, or until the flesh flakes easily when a piece of the fish is prodded gently with a fork. Be careful not to overcook the fish.

With a slotted spoon or spatula transfer the pieces of fish to a heated tureen. Bring the stock remaining in the casserole to a boil over high heat and cook briskly, uncovered, for 6 to 8 minutes, or until it reaches the intensity of flavor you like. Taste the stock for seasoning, pour it over the fish in the tureen and serve at once.

To serve 6

3 pounds fish trimmings: heads, tails and bones from any white-fleshed fish
1 large onion, peeled and thinly sliced
8 sprigs fresh parsley
1 large bay leaf
½ teaspoon whole black peppercorns
2 cups dry white wine
3 quarts cold water
2 tablespoons butter
1 cup finely chopped celery
1 pound eel, cleaned, skinned and cut crosswise into 2-inch lengths
1 pound perch, cleaned, trimmed and cut into ½-inch-thick pieces
1 pound pike, cleaned, trimmed and cut into ½-inch-thick pieces
1 pound carp, cleaned, trimmed and cut into ½-inch-thick pieces
6 tablespoons butter, cut into ¼-inch bits
¼ teaspoon crumbled dried thyme
Salt

Waterzooi à la Gantoise (Belgium)
FLEMISH CHICKEN IN LEMON CREAM SOUP

Combine the fowl, giblets, beef, veal shank and water in a heavy 8- to 10-quart pot. Bring to a boil over high heat, skimming off the scum and foam as they rise to the surface. Add the onions, celery, leeks, carrots and salt, then reduce the heat to low and simmer partially covered for about 2½ hours. When the bird is tender, lift the pieces out of the stock with tongs and place them on a plate. Discard the veal bones and giblets and set the beef aside for another use. With a small knife, remove and discard the skin and bones from the fowl and cut the meat into strips about 2 inches long and 1 inch wide.

Strain the entire contents of the pot through a fine sieve set over a heavy 5- to 6-quart casserole, pressing down hard on the vegetables with the back of a spoon before discarding them. Let the liquid rest for a few minutes, then with a large spoon skim off and discard as much fat as possible from the surface.

Boil briskly, uncovered, over high heat until the soup has cooked down to about 10 cups, then reduce the heat to low. When the soup is barely simmering, beat the egg yolks and cream together with a whisk or fork and pour it into the soup in a thin stream, stirring all the while. Add the strips of chicken and continue to stir until the *waterzooi* thickens slightly and the chicken is heated through. Do not allow the soup to come anywhere near a boil or it will curdle. Add 1 tablespoon of the lemon juice and the white pepper, taste for seasoning, and add the remaining lemon juice if you prefer the soup somewhat tart. Serve at once from a heated tureen or in deep individual soup plates.

To serve 8 to 10

A 5-pound stewing fowl, cut into 8 pieces
The fowl giblets
1 pound lean beef chuck or shin
1 veal shank, sawed into 1-inch pieces
4 quarts water
3 cups coarsely chopped onions
3 medium-sized celery stalks, trimmed and coarsely chopped
2 medium-sized leeks, white part only, trimmed, thoroughly washed to remove any sand, and coarsely chopped
2 medium-sized carrots, scraped and coarsely chopped
2 teaspoons salt
4 egg yolks
1 cup heavy cream
1 to 2 tablespoons strained fresh lemon juice
⅛ teaspoon white pepper

To make about 24 fritters

BATTER
2 cups sifted all-purpose flour
1 pint (2 cups) beer, at room
    temperature

APPLES
5 medium-sized tart cooking apples
1 cup sugar
1 tablespoon ground cinnamon
Vegetable oil for deep frying
Confectioners' sugar

Appelbeignets (Netherlands)
APPLE FRITTERS

Sift the flour into a deep mixing bowl and make a well in the center. Slowly pour in the beer and, stirring gently, gradually incorporate the flour. Continue to stir until the mixture is smooth, but do not beat or overmix. Set the batter aside to rest at room temperature for 3 hours before using.

Fifteen minutes or so before you plan to make the fritters, peel and core the apples and cut them crosswise into ⅓-inch-thick rounds. Lay the rounds side by side on a strip of wax paper. Then combine the sugar and cinnamon in a small bowl and sprinkle the mixture evenly over both sides of each apple round.

Preheat the oven to its lowest setting. Line a large shallow baking dish or jelly-roll pan with a double thickness of paper towels and set it in the middle of the oven. Pour vegetable oil into a deep fryer or large heavy saucepan to a depth of about 3 inches and heat the oil until it reaches a temperature of 375° on a deep-frying thermometer.

One at a time, pick up an apple slice with tongs or a slotted spoon, immerse it in the batter and, when it is well coated on all sides, drop it into the hot oil. Deep-fry 3 or 4 fritters at a time for about 4 minutes, turning them occasionally, until they are delicately and evenly browned. As they brown, transfer the fritters to the paper-lined pan and keep them warm in the oven while you coat and deep-fry the remaining apples.

Arrange the fritters on a heated platter and sprinkle them lightly with confectioners' sugar just before serving.

To serve 4

3 pounds mussels in their shells
    (about 2 dozen)
10 tablespoons unsalted butter
½ cup finely chopped onions
½ cup finely chopped shallots
¼ cup plus 2 tablespoons finely
    chopped fresh parsley
2 tablespoons fresh chervil or 1
    tablespoon crumbled, dried
    chervil
2 cups dry white wine
Freshly ground black pepper

Moules à l'Anversoise (Belgium)
MUSSELS IN HERB SAUCE

Mussels—like clams or oysters—must be purchased with tightly closed shells. If the shells of an open mussel do not close when run quickly under cold water, the mussel must not be used. If the shells do not open when cooked, they must be discarded.

Scrub the mussels thoroughly under cold running water with a stiff brush or soapless steel-mesh scouring pad. With a small, sharp knife scrape or pull the black ropelike tufts from the shells and discard them.

In a heavy 8-quart casserole, melt the butter over moderate heat. When the foam begins to subside, add the onions, shallots, ¼ cup of the parsley and the chervil. Stirring frequently, cook for about 5 minutes, or until the onions and shallots are soft and translucent but not brown. Watch carefully for any sign of burning and regulate the heat accordingly.

Stir in the wine and a few grindings of pepper, then add the mussels, placing them hinge side down. Cover the casserole tightly and bring to a boil over high heat. Reduce the heat to low and simmer for 5 to 7 minutes, until the mussels open, discarding those that remain closed. With a slotted spoon, transfer the mussels to a heated tureen or to individual serving bowls. Strain the stock through a fine sieve lined with a double thickness of dampened cheesecloth directly over the mussels. Sprinkle them with the remaining 2 tablespoons of parsley and serve at once.

Homely ingredients—apples, flour and beer—are transformed into crisp, delicate confections in these Dutch fritters, dusted with sugar.

III Poland

A Steadfastly Preserved Cuisine

During a Polish folk art festival in Cracow, an artisan from the nearby village of Zalipie touches up a clay pot emblazoned with gay flower designs. Zalipie is famous as a place where everything gets decorated: houses, barns, chicken coops and even pigsties are painted with the same cheerful motifs that embellish the glass and pottery seen here.

Surely there are few literate Americans, young or old, who have not heard of these famous figures: Copernicus, the founder of modern astronomy; General Pulaski, a hero of the American Revolution; Madame Curie, the discoverer of radium; Frédéric Chopin, the composer; Wanda Landowska, the harpsichordist; the pianists Ignace Jan Paderewski and Artur Rubinstein. But how many of us know them as Poles? And, except for the hundreds of thousands of Poles who have emigrated to our shores, who in the United States knows anything at all about Polish cooking? Flatly, very few Americans do; even among culinary experts Polish dishes are often confused with Russian, German, Austrian and Hungarian dishes bearing similar, unpronounceable names. But vagueness about Polish identity and confusion about the nomenclature of Polish dishes are understandable in the murky light of this Slavic country's chaotic history.

Since its beginnings a thousand years ago, Poland has been rent apart, patched together, expanded and contracted like an accordion played by a madman. At one point, the country's borders stretched from the banks of the Oder in Germany to the Dnieper in Russia, and from the Baltic to the Black Sea; then, after 1772, Poland was, bit by bit, divided among—or more accurately, devoured by—Russia, Prussia and Austria, until by 1795 the country had been literally erased from the map. Then, after World War I, it was cartographically reborn, only to be brought 20 years later to the edge of oblivion once more by the Nazis. Decimating Poland's population and destroying many of its major cities, they sought to incorporate this almost empty shell of a country into the Greater Reich. But miraculously, Poland survived. It was reconstituted by the victorious Allied powers of World War II into almost 121,000 square miles of pastoral lands, forests and lakes wedged between East Germany on the west and the U.S.S.R. on the east, with its northern border the Baltic Sea, and its southern border shared with Czechoslovakia. This is the Poland we know today—the Polish People's Republic.

That Poland could have held on to its customs, traditions and cuisine through these repeated and often violent transmutations can be attributed only to the indomitable Polish spirit—a fiery, nationalistic spirit nourished by the Roman Catholic Church. Poland, despite its Communist orientation, remains, as it has been for over 900 years, a predominantly Catholic country, and at least 90 per cent of the Poles are still extremely devout. I find it an interesting paradox that it has been the religious spirit of the Poles—their soul, if you will—that has kept the Polish cuisine and its character alive.

The elaborate ceremonials of the Church (as well as the pagan rites on which some of them are based) still play a prominent role in the lives of the Poles and in what they eat. The dishes served at christenings, weddings, harvest and other festivals, and most important, at Easter and Christmas, glow in the frame of traditional menus and holiday rituals. Before the Easter feast begins—a monumental array of dishes arranged buffet style—the food is blessed at home by a priest, or a portion of each dish is taken to the church in baskets and blessed by the priest on Holy Saturday. A suckling pig roasted whole is likely to be prominent on an Easter feast table, bolstered perhaps by hams, coils of sausages, and roast veal, and always hard-boiled eggs and grated horseradish. But whatever the food presented, the place of honor on the table will be given the paschal lamb, either sculptured of butter and festooned with small Polish flags, or fashioned of white sugar with eyes a heavenly blue.

The Christmas Eve dinner differs from that of Easter because while it is a feast, it is also a fast—that is, no meat is served. But the meal is plentiful and varied nonetheless, consisting of soups, fish, noodle dishes and pastries. There is an interplay of pagan and Catholic rites: sheaves of grain are set in the corners of the dining room to assure good crops, and hay is laid beneath the white tablecloth in commemoration of the holy manger. Among the innumerable dishes eaten on Christmas Eve (and Poles are hearty eaters, to say the least) may be a special *barszcz Wigilijny (Recipe Index),* a cousin to the borscht familiar to many Americans, but much more refined—a clear soup made of the essence of beets and mushrooms, usually with *uszka,* "little ears" of dough stuffed with mushrooms *(Recipe Index).* Or there may be carp or pike, with which Poland's lakes abound, prepared in a number of elaborate and original ways; one, *szczupak à la polonaise,* consists of a whole fish, often three feet long, poached and served with a fish-stock-based horseradish and sour-cream sauce *(Recipe Index).* Typical, too, not only for the Christmas Eve dinner but other meals as well, is a dish of Jewish origin, *karp po żydowsku (Recipe Index),* slices of carp in a sweet-and-sour sauce with raisins and almonds; the fish is chilled until the sauce has jellied to an aspic.

Perhaps the most popular fish in Poland is herring, which is served traditionally on Ash Wednesday, the first day of Lent. On such an occasion the herring may be baked in cream, but they are popular year round, and are often simply fried in butter or eaten in their brined pristine state right out of the barrel. The food limitations imposed on Catholics by Lent have challenged the imagination of Polish cooks for centuries, and their attempts to circumvent the restriction against meat resulted in a number of curious dishes. One I find paricularly amusing (and the Poles laugh about it themselves) is cooked beaver's tail. The ingenious rationale is that the beaver, although a warm-blooded animal, keeps its tail in water much of the time, thus endowing this appendage with the characteristics of fish and removing it from the proscribed category of meat.

The crowning glory of any festive Polish meal is the pastry, a national specialty that is sometimes spectacular enough to rival the pastry of France, Russia, Austria and Hungary—from which many of the Polish pastries doubtless arose. An Easter cake called *babka wielkanocna (Recipe Index)* is distinctly Polish and to my mind the most delectable of all yeast cakes of its type. It is made of a rich yeast dough containing innumerable egg yolks and vast quantities of butter and flavored with white raisins, grated lemon and orange rind. Once the ingredients are combined, the dough is kneaded by hand for at least 40 minutes before it is put aside to rise. *Babka* in Polish means grandmother, but knowing how it is made, I would be more inclined to think *babka* meant baby—so cuddled, coddled and cooed over is it before it is baked and after it is removed from the oven. A housewife's reputation as a cook has been known to rest on the successful rising or catastrophic falling of her *babka*. On farms where the yeast may still be homemade and often unpredictable, the dough for the *babka* is placed gently on a feather pillow, sometimes on an eiderdown, for the rising; everyone is expected to walk about on tiptoe and is forbidden to speak above a whisper or, horror of horrors, slam a door, lest the dough react perversely and fail to rise. When the *babka* is done it is once again placed on a pillow and then, like a baby being put to sleep, rocked gently from side to side until it cools.

An American housewife would no doubt find this performance enchanting and poetic, but she is not likely to be persuaded to emulate it. Fortunately, however, when she decides to make *babka* she will use an envelope of active dry yeast guaranteed to behave as it should whether a door is slammed or not; an electric mixer to knead the dough if she isn't athletic enough to knead it herself; a thermostatically controlled oven in which to bake the cake; and a recipe that will give her predictable results. There are innumerable recipes—and good ones, too—for making *babka,* but Polish families guard them like jewels, passing them on as heirlooms from one generation to the next. The best *babka* recipe I know I received in barter, as it were, from a Polish friend who exchanged it for a treasured soufflé recipe of mine.

Only the most affluent citizens of Poland today own modern stoves and electric mixers. Those who do are mostly city dwellers, and they, for the most part, buy their *babki,* breads and pastries in cooperative markets or privately owned bakeries. The bakery that is most renowned in Warsaw is Blikle's, which still stands where it did one hundred years ago, on

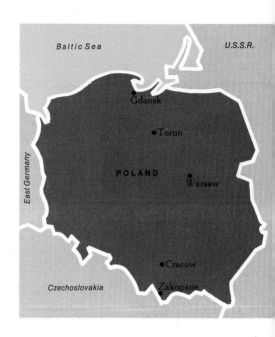

Several times in the past few centuries Poland has been erased from the map as a nation, but its people and language, customs and cuisine have endured. From Zakopane in the Tatra Mountains to Gdańsk (once called Danzig) on the Baltic Sea, the country's cooking reflects its people's ancient peasant ties to field and forest and their continued observance of the culinary traditions of religious feasts and other ceremonies.

Poland's pig production is exceeded by only five countries, and canned hams are one of the best-known Polish exports. This 390-pound sow and her chubby piglets lead a pampered existence on a farm near Cracow, growing sleek on a carefully balanced diet that includes milk and potatoes and vitamins.

Nowy Swiat Street. Although Blikle's makes excellent *babki*, its *pączki (Recipe Index)*—like our jelly doughnuts—are so sought after, especially for Shrove Tuesday and New Year's Eve, that people queue up by the dozens to buy them fresh. Blikle's makes other marvels as well. Among them are *tort orzechowy (Recipe Index)*, a rich walnut torte with coffee butter cream, and *makowiec (Recipe Index),* a Christmas cake shaped like a jelly roll and filled with black poppy seeds, honey, raisins and almonds. Then there is the *mazurek (Recipe Index),* a fragile pastry topped with almonds or chocolate meringue.

Frances and I recently tasted one of Blikle's world-famous honey cakes sent to us by a Polish friend, who told us it would keep for at least two months and be all the better for it. Unfortunately, we never gave it a chance—the cake was so moist and delicious that we consumed it in one sitting down to the last crumb. In this spicy cake, the Poles have used their baking skill to take full advantage of one of their favorite natural resources. Even in other countries where honey is produced it is freely admitted that the quality of Polish honey is unexcelled. The Polish honey-producing season is comparatively short, but the amount gathered is extraordinary. Whether or not proletarian Polish bees are more industrious than other bees, I have heard that they somehow manage to fill

Not all of Poland's pigs end up as exported hams. This sampling of traditional country pork products suggests the almost limitless variety of ham, bacon and sausages enjoyed by the Poles at home. Hanging at left is *wiejska szynka,* a mountaineers' ham that has been pickled and smoked; next to it is a slab of *wędzony bekon,* smoked bacon. The long thin sausages are *kabanosy* and those hanging to the right of them are *zulawska.* In the lower right corner are two smoked hams, and the thick, wrinkled sausages are *kiełbasa tatrzańska,* named after the Tatra Mountains in the extreme south of Poland.

their hives twice a season as compared with more indolent bees elsewhere, which seem content to fill their hives only once.

This abundance makes understandable, too, the Polish fondness for mead, a drink that is all but unknown in America. Honey is the base of this centuries-old potion—a drink that is, I must say, much too sweet for my taste. We tend to associate mead with the ancient Greeks, who called it the nectar of the gods, but the Poles stubbornly maintain that the pagan Slavs who settled in Poland invented their own mead. This was prepared, and mead still is, by diluting honey with water and mixing it with hops—the longer the fermentation the better and more potent the drink. There are meads in Poland a hundred or more years old, aged, like fine cognac, in casks; but old mead is extremely rare, and when you can get it at all, its price is formidable. Polish mead is now mass-produced, comparatively inexpensive, and widely exported. There is an old saying in Poland about mead—*idzie w nogi*—that means "goes to the legs." I had found this curious because exported mead is never more than 14 per cent alcohol. But when I first drank it, I discovered to my surprise that not only did it raise my spirits but *idzie w nogi,* it decidedly went to my legs.

The traditional food at religious and other holiday feasts in Poland might be described as elaborations on dishes that are similar but much

simpler everyday fare. Serving them at celebrations, refined and in profusion, has glorified them but has not in any sense impaired their essentially Polish characteristics. These qualities reflect both the northern climate of the land and its agriculture, but as in all cuisines it is the country's imaginative and resourceful cooks who have lifted the preparation of their food to gastronomic importance.

Because Polish winters can be quite severe, the Poles developed ingenious ways of preserving their foods to tide them over the barren months. Even today, despite modern canning and freezing techniques, ancient preserving methods are still used in the countryside. Cucumbers, herrings, tomatoes, beets, cabbages and turnips are brined in salt, and it would be a singular Polish farm that didn't have barrels of these sharply flavored vegetables and salty fish stored in its kitchen and cellars the whole year round. Fruits are preserved in a variety of ways—dried, made into jams and jellies, and even pickled. Of all the preserved fruits, plums, pickled in vinegar and water and flavored with sugar, cinnamon and cloves *(Recipe Index)*, are especially enticing. On ordinary occasions these preserved plums are exquisite accompaniments to a simple roast loin of pork, but on festive days the roast is elevated to greater heights by being encrusted with a golden glaze of applesauce *(Recipe Index)*.

Polish stick-to-the-ribs winter soups are another example of the Poles' way of building a crescendo from simplicity to complexity with a dish, depending upon whether it is meant for everyday consumption or for celebrations. The simpler soups are made with a rich, fatty meat-stock base to which grains such as barley or buckwheat groats are added. They increase in complexity when white or red shredded cabbage or any other stored or fresh vegetables the cook may have at hand go into the pot. A substantial vegetable-barley soup called *krupnik (Recipe Index)* is always accompanied by marvelous gray or dark Polish bread—the very bulk of the soup and bread makes it a perfect one-dish meal. And these hearty soups are very often stamped, as are countless other national dishes, by a taste that is characteristically Polish—the smoothly herbal flavor of sour cream and dill.

We know that many of the dishes of Poland were influenced by the Germans, Hungarians, Austrians and Russians, but it comes as a surprise to learn how much of the food in Poland has Italianate names. Certain pasta products in Poland are known as *makaron*. The tomato is called *pomidor* in Polish and *pomodoro* in Italian; cauliflower is *kalafior* in Polish and *cavolfiore* in Italian; green vegetables in general bear the name *wloszczyzna* which, entertainingly, means "Italian commodities." These Italianate words, now indissolubly part of the Polish language, are directly traceable back to Queen Bona Sforza, the daughter of the Sforza family of Milan. In the same way as the Medici family introduced Italian cooking into France when Catherine de Médicis married King Henry II in 1533, so did Queen Bona affect the cooking of Poland when she married King Sigismund I in 1518.

Earlier, in the 14th Century (also through romance, if not marriage) Jewish dishes had already become an important part of Polish food. Historical fact is hazy on the subject, but it seems that Poland's Casimir the

Opposite: A loin of pork, glazed with applesauce, dominates this festive Polish table. Embellishing the roast are tiny purple plums that have been pickled and flavored with cinnamon and cloves. Behind it is an unusual sauerkraut salad, tossed with diced apples and grated carrots and seasoned with caraway.

Continued on page 86

Bees and Bishops and Honey by the Ton

Beekeeping in Poland, an efficient industry that now produces more than 4,000 tons of honey a year, goes back to pagan days when honey was believed to be a gift of the forest gods. As the basis of mead and a source of sugar, honey was precious indeed, and the bees that produced it were objects of awe. Even today, killing one is regarded as an evil act. But anything is fair to induce the bees to work harder. Modern apiarists often truck their beehives to places where the bees can find more pollen and nectar for their honey-making. But in olden days more mystical means were used. On the hollow trunks that formed their hives, the Poles affixed magical designs to please the bees. And for bees unmoved by art, apiarists had another tactic: they stuffed the hives with tempting herbs.

Roofed with pine boards, a clutch of old-fashioned Polish beehives made from tree trunks rises out of a small yard in the open-air Ethnographic Museum in Cracow. They are five or six feet high and can hold a vast quantity of honey. At right, above, are a hive with a bee carved on it and one with the likeness of a bishop, typical of the figures thought in earlier days to exercise a magic influence on the yield of honey. The tempting array at bottom right, spread out on an inlaid 18th Century table, shows some of the honey-based delicacies in the Polish larder: honey cake coated with chocolate, ginger cookies flavored with honey, and Krupnik, a spiced honey liqueur. Strawberries and other fruits were sometimes used to flavor mead.

The most renowned bakery in a country that loves its pastries is Blikle's, which celebrated its centennial in Warsaw in 1969. Blikle's *pączki*—preserve-filled doughnuts—are admired by the great and near great of Poland and also, as it happens, made a notable friend in France. From 1919 to 1921 a young lieutenant in the French military mission to Poland lived upstairs above Blikle's. Forty-six years later he returned on a state visit and publicly recalled his fondness for Blikle's *pączki*. His name: Charles de Gaulle.

Great fell in love with a Jewish beauty, Esterka. Her influence upon him was so great that he made Poland a haven for the oppressed Jews of almost every country in Europe. Soon thereafter, Jewish dishes appeared on Polish tables: noodles with goose fat, stuffed goose necks, baked potato puddings and *karp po żydowsku,* the cold carp in jelly that has become a Christmas Eve tradition.

There is no telling what dishes the Jews of Poland might have invented had they not abided by their dietary law against the eating of pork, because the pork of Poland is considered superior to that of most other countries. Polish pigs are raised with loving care, fed on grain, milk and potatoes; all chemical or synthetic additives are, thus far at least, taboo. This purist approach to hog raising produces a flesh of the palest delicate pink—almost white—with the firmest yet tenderest of textures. So admirable is this pork that it has become perhaps the country's best-known product. Canned hams account for a major part of Poland's total export sales, and these boneless, fat-free hams are prized all over the world. In Poland itself, however, the pork product most extensively used is sausage. More than 70 kinds of sausage, or *kiełbasa,* are made in Poland and are prepared in numerous ways: cut up and served cold with horseradish sauce or mustard, boiled in beer, baked or cooked in stews.

The distinctive flavor of many of the sausages is the result of smoking them over the juniper wood that grows in the forests of Poland—forests that cover almost a quarter of the land. They provide other contributions to the Polish cuisine, too. More important than juniper wood are the vast quantities of mushrooms—golden chanterelles, brown-capped boletus, honeycombed morels—that grow on the shady forest floor and are picked by the hundreds of thousands during a long season that extends into the late autumn. The Poles use them fresh, dried, marinated, pickled or salted. In parts of Poland during the mushroom season it is a rare meal indeed that does not include them—as hors d'oeuvre, in soups, sauces or stuffing, as a vegetable or simply as a seasoning.

Nor are the pleasures of Polish mushrooms relished only in the homeland. Fresh Polish mushrooms are in demand all over Europe and are often available in the markets within 48 hours after they are picked. Dried mushrooms are exported around the world and can be bought more and more easily in the United States—although admittedly at a shockingly steep price. The Poles string these delicacies on cords and hang them as utilitarian decorations, much as Latin people do with their clusters of garlic, red onions and chilies.

Polish forests are the source not only of juniper and mushrooms but game, an important ingredient in Poland's most famous dish, *bigos,* or hunters' stew *(Recipe Index).* Bigos is almost as ancient as Poland itself and has become, in effect, its national dish. Culinary historians, agreeing for once, hold that *bigos* originally was made of cabbage, onions, mushrooms and a variety of other vegetables as well as apples or prunes, but that its basic ingredient was always leftover game. Game has never been in short supply in Poland, and in the past it accounted for much of the opulence of the aristocracy's cuisine.

In the 18th Century, at an Easter feast given in the palace of Prince

Paweł Sapieha in Dereczyn, and presented on what must have been the largest of tables, were four whole boars (representing the four seasons of the year) stuffed with hams, sausages and piglets; 12 stags (for the number of months in the year) stuffed with whole wild fowl and rabbits; 52 *mazurki* cakes (for the number of weeks in the year); 365 *babki* (for the number of days in the year), each decorated with poetic quotations written in sugar glaze.

From a meal such as that one (and hundreds of just as incredibly sumptuous ones are reported to have occurred, each nobleman seeking to outdo the other in lavishness and originality of presentation) there were sure to be leftovers. And what more logical way to use them, any sensible cook would ask, than to make a *bigos* by combining the leftover game with cabbage, root vegetables and spices that enhance the flavor of game.

The nobility's passion for the hunt called for long stays in the forest, and *bigos* became a staple food of the huntsman, partly because it could be reheated so successfully over outdoor fires (in fact, Poles, even today, think *bigos* not fit to eat unless it is reheated at home six or seven times). That the dish has endured these hundreds of years is testimony to its basic goodness. So important did *bigos* become that one of Poland's great poets, Adam Mickiewicz, was all but carried away when he described a *bigos* being cooked in the woods during the hunt: *"bigos* is no ordinary dish . . . based on good cabbage sliced and sour, which, as is said, by its own zest melts in one's mouth, it rests in a pot while in its moist bosom the choicest meats are enfolded; scullions boil it then, and the heat draws out the delicious juices until, overflowing the pot's rim, the *bigos* scents the air with fragrance."

Bigos as it is made today is a somewhat different dish from its earlier versions—there are many ways to prepare it now—but its basic character remains the same. Some cooks use fresh cabbage, some prefer sauerkraut and others combine them. To hear two Polish cooks arguing about this crucial point gives one an idea of how seriously the matter is taken. But however individual cooks may feel about the cabbage, they agree that the sky is the limit as far as the cooked meats that go into the *bigos* are concerned: cooked ham, sausages, roast fresh ham, roast poultry (preferably duck or goose), always a piece of boiled fatty pork, and other meat oddments, naturally including any cooked game—hare, venison, partridge and the like. They will even go so far—quite a concession in these socialist times—as to add a wineglass or two of old Madeira to the finished *bigos* as the high-living nobility used on occasion to do.

But modern Polish cooks have one traditional conviction about *bigos* that I disagree with strongly—they persist in making the *bigos* days before they plan to serve it. I know, of course, that *bigos* (or any similar stew such as an Alsatian *choucroute garni,* which *bigos* resembles to a remarkable degree) has a good chance of improving upon reheating if to begin with it was indifferently prepared. Cooking it again has the effect of intensifying its flavor by the culinary process known as reduction, in other words, by boiling down its excess liquid to produce a concentrated essence. But I firmly insist that reheating *bigos* is entirely unnecessary, although not disastrous, if it has been perfectly made at the start. After a

Overleaf: In the high Chochołowska Valley of Poland's Tatra Mountains, shepherds milk their flock. The milk will be used to make *oscypki,* a smoked cheese produced, with slight variations in name and procedure, in the mountainous regions of most Slavic countries. These men drive their sheep to the upland valley each May and stay on until it is time to return to lower pastures in September. Paint smudges on the animals' heads identify each man's sheep.

violent altercation about the question of reheating *bigos* with one of my Polish friends, I proceeded, as I usually do, to put the matter to a clinical test. I prepared a large pot of the best *bigos* I could make, and found to my delight that eaten directly when finished it tasted superb—and, more important, better than the remaining *bigos,* which I reheated day after day for a week. This experience proved to me again how often culinary myths explode when carefully and objectively examined. I can only assume that when this recooking myth about *bigos* arose, the stew had been poorly prepared; continual reheating gave it the richly flavored but muted acidity it could have had had it been properly made in the first place.

Bigos today is one of the main dishes of the New Year's Eve celebration, which in Poland is the most festive secular occasion of the year. And not the least contribution to the gaiety is the amount of vodka consumed. Of course, the consumption of vodka is not restricted to New Year's Eve; it is drunk by Poles on every possible occasion, including before, during and after a meal. When compared with the long history of *bigos* in Poland, that of vodka is short—a mere four or five hundred years. According to Polish historians, drinking vodka socially was considered bad form in the old days by the aristocracy. Serfs and peasants, unconcerned with niceties, drank their home-brewed vodka very much as our Kentucky mountaineers drank the corn liquor from their stills.

Originally vodka was crudely made from rye. When a commercial market for it was found in the 19th Century, however, the Poles and the Russians as well started making the spirit from potatoes, which were cheaper than rye and available in great quantity. Today, although potatoes are still used in some areas, the best vodka, now scientifically refined, comes as before from rye. Americans may not be aware of the many varieties of Polish vodka, because very little other than the clear, flavorless vodkas are consumed in the United States. One that Americans are coming to know more and more is the greenish-gold, aromatic vodka that takes its name from the grass called *żubrówka* (and there is a blade of it in every bottle) with which the vodka is flavored. Many kinds of vodka are produced in Russia and other Slavic countries, but *wódka* Żubrówka is uniquely Polish because the grass, upon which bison feed, grows only in the Białowieża virgin forest in eastern Poland.

The Poles maintain with some heat that they make the world's best vodka—an argument I would just as soon avoid. But a Polish acquaintance tells a story that I find most amusing, if not necessarily conclusive. He was standing one cold winter day in the Warsaw airport when a delegation of Russian officials bound from Moscow for a meeting in Paris came into the terminal. They had only a few minutes to spare, and without a moment's hesitation they marched as one man into the liquor store, bought all the Polish vodka in sight, and strode back to their plane.

Polish vodka is also made into many kinds of liqueurs. One of the most important, called *Goldwasser,* is produced in Gdańsk, or Danzig, as the city was known when it was part of Germany. *Goldwasser* is a sweet, colorless vodka-based liqueur flavored with herbs and spices, and in each bottle float tiny flakes of pure gold. Browsing through Escoffier's *Le Guide Culinaire,* I was fascinated to discover Escoffier's recipe for *soufflé*

Rothschild—a magnificent airy creation flavored with candied fruits—requires as one of its ingredients *l'eau de vie de Danzig,* or *Goldwasser,* its German name, still used by the Poles.

Escoffier also gives recipes for asparagus and cauliflower followed by the words *à la polonaise,* meaning in effect that the vegetables are to be served in the Polish style. Although the Poles do indeed serve these seasonal vegetables in the manner he describes—boiled, then sprinkled with bread crumbs fried in butter—there is another more noteworthy seasonal dish that Escoffier had apparently never tasted: *chłodnik,* a cold summer soup. If he had, there is not the slightest doubt in my mind that he would have included it in his masterwork, given the soup a French name and appended to it the words *à la polonaise.*

Unlike other Polish summer soups made of fresh fruits and berries, which I am inclined to think of as desserts rather than soups because they tend to be oversweet and are served with sweet or sour cream, chilled *chłodnik* could not be called anything but a soup in the proper sense of the word. And what a glorious soup it is! In Poland it is usually made when crayfish are in season, but shrimp can be used as successfully when crayfish are not available. Reading a recipe for *chłodnik* might very well put one off, so disparate and surprising do the ingredients appear at first glance. Grated beets, water, vinegar and a little sugar are used to make the stock which is then chilled, combined with cold crayfish (or shrimp), sliced scallions, radishes, cucumbers and the indispensable dill—the whole enriched with thick sour cream, and served garnished with slices of lemon and finely chopped hard-cooked eggs. *Chłodnik* bears no resemblance to any other cold soup I know; if Polish poets haven't yet sung about it as they have about *bigos,* were I poet, I would.

To acquaint myself further with Polish food as it is eaten in Poland today, I sought the assistance of the Polish Embassy in Washington. The response could not have been more gracious. Ambassador and Mme. Michałowski invited Frances and me to a formal dinner at which the dishes would be prepared in the authentic style, and which, I was delighted to learn, would be cooked by wives of the embassy's staff.

Everything I had felt about Polish food was confirmed for me that night. The hors d'oeuvre—Polish ham thinly sliced, a whole pike in glistening aspic, a salad of finely cut sauerkraut mixed with carrots, apples and caraway seeds *(Recipe Index)*—were delicious; the meat course—a braised beef stuffed with Polish mushrooms and accompanied by a sour-cream sauce *(Recipe Index)*—a tour de force; the pastries—tortes masked with butter cream or coated with nuts and fruits, and four different kinds of *mazurki*—superb beyond belief. Yet there was not the slightest hint of pretentiousness or ostentation that one might have expected at a dinner such as this. And during a lively and entertaining after-dinner discussion about food and cooking in different parts of Poland—the influences upon it, what was a true Polish dish and what was not—in which Ambassador Michałowski revealed himself as most knowledgeable, I found myself reflecting briefly on world affairs and couldn't help thinking rather wistfully: would that all debates in the world's embassies were limited to arguments about food.

In silence broken only by the clop of hooves, droshkies carry the groom and the wedding party to the bride's house.

A Podhale Wedding Takes Two Days of Feasting – and Then Some

Walled on three sides by the Tatra Mountains and by Czechoslovakia, the pocket of Poland known as Podhale clings lovingly to its past. Actually, that past was not always bright, and many Poles who emigrated to America around 1900 were escaping the poverty of Podhale. But now it is a favorite holiday region, and one of the attractions for tourists (Poles and Americans of Polish descent as well) is the pride with which the *górale,* or "mountaineers," of the area cherish their traditions. Among the most spectacular of these is the festivity of a wedding. No *górale* family would dare skimp on the preparations, nor did the families of Marysia Lukaszcyk and Jan Bryniarski from the village of Murzasichle near Zakopane. With relatives and friends they spent weeks preparing, then feasted, danced and sang for two full days. And on the following Sunday there was yet another party for those who had been too busy working to enjoy the first one.

After the wedding,
Marysia Bryniarski
emerges happily from the
church *(left)* escorted by
two "wedding hosts." The
groom is escorted out by
"wedding hostesses," then
stands at his bride's left
(below) looking slightly
abashed as the wedding
party poses for a portrait.
The bride (wearing a
laurel wreath) and the
groom are decked in white
ribbons, and their
attendants have red ones.

Overleaf: As the party goes back to
the bride's house for the feast, the
earlier silence is replaced by
singing, music and an amiable bit
of make-believe kidnaping by guests
dressed as *cyganie* (gypsies) and
mounted on horseback. They drop a
chain across the road, stopping the
procession, and demand ransom.
The custom recalls wilder days
when robbers preyed on caravans
and wedding cavalcades, demanding
money for safe passage. The chain
itself is an old symbol of good
fortune, in a region once so poor
that iron was a precious commodity.

The bride's aunt, Maria Lukaszczyk *(above, right)* and two friends prepare the breads and pastries for the grand wedding feast. Stacked on the table are layers for a cake that will be filled with chocolate and ground hazelnuts. The women in the background are folding the dough for *chrust,* a type of sugared biscuit, some of which are seen on the two plates in the foreground. Also on the table are cakes and several loaves of homemade bread. In the picture at left, the bride's mother prepares several veal roasts. Among the other specialties for the big meal are pickled herring, meat loaf and bouillon with noodles.

A rich torte is part of the
ceremonial with which the
newlyweds are welcomed back to
the bride's house. Bread and salt,
representing wealth, are customarily
offered to the bridal couple; here
the torte takes the place of bread.
Next comes the feast, and later,
nonstop dancing in the barn.

To serve 6 to 8

1 pound medium-sized firm young
  beets, peeled and coarsely grated
6½ cups cold water
3 tablespoons red wine vinegar
5 teaspoons salt
1½ teaspoons sugar
1 pound uncooked shrimp
1 cup sour cream
2 medium-sized cucumbers, peeled,
  sliced lengthwise in half, seeded
  and cut into ¼-inch dice
4 medium-sized scallions, including
  2 inches of the green tops,
  trimmed, washed and cut
  crosswise into ¼-inch-thick
  rounds
4 red radishes, thinly sliced
4 tablespoons finely cut fresh dill
  leaves
3 tablespoons strained fresh lemon
  juice
A pinch of white pepper
1 lemon, thinly sliced (optional)
3 hard-cooked eggs, chilled and
  finely chopped (optional)

Chłodnik
COLD BEET SOUP WTH SHRIMP AND VEGETABLES

In a 3- to 4-quart enameled or stainless-steel saucepan, bring the grated beets and cold water to a boil over high heat. Reduce the heat to moderate and cook uncovered for 10 minutes. Then reduce the heat to low, stir in 2 tablespoons of the vinegar, 2 teaspoons of the salt and 1 teaspoon of the sugar, and simmer partially covered for 30 minutes. Drain the beets in a fine sieve set over a large bowl. Set the beets and the cooking liquid aside separately to cool to room temperature.

Peel the shrimp. Devein them by making a shallow incision down their backs with a small, sharp knife and lifting out the black or white intestinal vein with the point of the knife. Wash the shrimp under cold running water. Then bring 1 quart of water to a boil in a small pan, drop in the shrimp and cook briskly, uncovered, for about 3 minutes, or until they turn pink and are firm to the touch. Drain and coarsely chop the shrimp. Set aside to cool.

When the beet cooking liquid is completely cooled, beat in the sour cream with a wire whisk. Then stir in the beets, shrimp, cucumbers, scallions, radishes, 2 tablespoons of the dill, the lemon juice, the remaining tablespoon of vinegar, 3 teaspoons of salt and ½ teaspoon of sugar, and a pinch of white pepper. Taste for seasoning, cover the bowl tightly with plastic wrap, and refrigerate for at least 2 hours, or until the *chłodnik* is thoroughly chilled.

To serve, ladle the soup into a large chilled tureen or individual soup plates. Sprinkle the remaining dill on top and, if you like, garnish the *chłodnik* with thin slices of lemon and chopped hard-cooked eggs.

To make 1 large cake

CAKE
1¼ cups lukewarm milk (110° to
  115°)
1 package active dry yeast
6 tablespoons sugar
2½ to 2¾ cups all-purpose flour
½ teaspoon salt
10 egg yolks
¾ pound plus 2 tablespoons
  unsalted butter, softened
1 cup white seedless raisins
2 tablespoons finely grated orange
  peel
1 tablespoon finely grated lemon
  peel

Babka Wielkanocna
EASTER CAKE WITH RAISINS

Pour the lukewarm milk into a small bowl and sprinkle it with the yeast and ½ teaspoon of the sugar. Let the mixture stand for 2 or 3 minutes, then stir to dissolve the yeast completely. Set the bowl aside in a warm, draft-free place (such as an unlighted oven) for about 10 minutes, or until the mixture almost doubles in volume.

Place 2½ cups of the flour, the remaining sugar and the salt in a deep mixing bowl and make a well in the center. Pour in the yeast mixture and the egg yolks and, with a large spoon, gradually stir the flour into the liquid ingredients. Continue to stir until well mixed, then beat in ¾ pound of butter a few tablespoonfuls at a time. The dough should be firm enough to be gathered into a medium-soft ball. If necessary, stir in up to ¼ cup more flour, adding it by the tablespoon.

Transfer the dough to an electric mixer equipped with a kneading hook and knead for about 20 minutes, or until the dough is very smooth, glossy and elastic. Or knead the dough by hand—pushing it down with the heels of your hands, pressing it forward and folding it back on itself —for about 40 minutes.

Garnishes of shrimp, cucumbers, radishes, scallions and fresh dill enhance Polish *chłodnik,* a cold beet-and-sour-cream soup.

Shape the dough into a ball, place it in a lightly buttered bowl and dust the top with flour. Drape a towel over the bowl and set it aside in the draft-free place for about 1 hour, or until the dough doubles in volume. With a pastry brush, spread the 2 tablespoons of softened butter over the bottom and sides of a Turk head mold or, less traditionally, a 2-quart *Gugelhupf* pan. Sprinkle the butter with the remaining ¼ cup of flour and tip the pan from side to side to spread it evenly. Invert the pan and rap it sharply to remove the excess flour.

Punch the dough down with a single blow of your fist and into it knead the raisins, orange peel and lemon peel. Pat the dough evenly over the bottom of the buttered and floured mold, drape with a towel, and set aside in the draft-free place again for 1 hour, or until the dough has doubled in volume and risen almost to the top of the mold.

Preheat the oven to 375°. Bake the cake in the middle of the oven for about 40 minutes, or until it is golden brown. Turn the cake out onto a cake rack and let it cool briefly at room temperature while you prepare the icing.

In a small bowl, combine the confectioners' sugar, water and lemon juice, and beat vigorously together with a spoon until they are smooth. Pour the icing slowly over the top of the warm cake, allowing it to run down the sides. Let the *babka* cool to room temperature before serving.

WHITE ICING
2 cups confectioners' sugar
¼ cup cold water
2 teaspoons strained fresh lemon
   juice

99

To serve 4

MUSHROOM STOCK
3 ounces imported European dried
    mushrooms, preferably dried
    Polish mushrooms
4 cups boiling water

BEET STOCK
2½ pounds medium-sized firm
    young beets, peeled and coarsely
    grated
5 cups cold water
2 tablespoons red wine vinegar
2 teaspoons salt

½ teaspoon salt
¼ teaspoon sugar
1 tablespoon strained fresh lemon
    juice

To make about 5 dozen dumplings

STUFFING
6 tablespoons butter
½ cup finely chopped onions
1 tablespoon soft fresh crumbs
    made from homemade-type white
    bread, trimmed of crusts and
    pulverized in a blender or finely
    shredded with a fork
3 ounces dried mushrooms, cooked
    and cooled (see barszcz
    Wigilijny, above)
1 egg white
1 teaspoon salt

DOUGH
1 whole egg plus 1 egg white
1 tablespoon cold water
2¼ teaspoons salt
1 cup all-purpose flour

Barszcz Wigilijny
CHRISTMAS EVE BEET SOUP

Place the mushrooms in a 2- to 3-quart enameled or stainless-steel sauce-pan and pour the boiling water over them. Let them soak at room temperature for at least 2 hours. Then place the pan over high heat and bring the soaking water to a boil. Lower the heat and simmer uncovered for about 2 hours, or until the liquid is reduced to ½ cup. Drain the stock through a fine sieve set over a bowl and set the mushrooms aside to be used, if you like, for *uszka,* the tiny dumplings usually served with this soup. Reserve the stock.

Meanwhile, in a 3- to 4-quart enameled or stainless-steel saucepan, bring the grated beets and 5 cups of cold water to a boil over high heat. Reduce the heat to moderate and cook uncovered for 10 minutes. Then reduce the heat to low, stir in the vinegar and 2 teaspoons of salt, and simmer partially covered for 30 minutes. Strain the beet stock through a fine sieve into a bowl, pressing down hard on the beets with the back of a spoon to extract all their juice before discarding them.

Return the beet stock to the saucepan in which it cooked, add the reserved mushroom stock, ½ teaspoon of salt, the sugar and lemon juice, and bring to a boil over high heat. Taste for seasoning and serve at once, accompanied, if you like, by *uszka (below)*.

Uszka
TINY DUMPLINGS FILLED WITH MUSHROOMS ("LITTLE EARS")

In a heavy 6- to 8-inch skillet, melt 2 tablespoons of the butter over moderate heat. When the foam begins to subside, add the onions and, stirring frequently, cook for about 5 minutes, or until they are soft and translucent but not brown. Stir in the bread crumbs and, when they glisten with butter, remove the pan from the heat and mix in the mushrooms. Then put the mixture twice through the finest blade of a food grinder.

Melt the remaining 4 tablespoons of butter in the same skillet. Add the ground mushroom mixture and, stirring from time to time, cook over low heat until most of the liquid in the pan has evaporated. Remove the skillet from the heat and stir the egg white and 1 teaspoon of salt into the mushroom stuffing. Taste for seasoning and cool to room temperature.

Meanwhile, prepare the dough in the following fashion: In a deep bowl, beat the egg, egg white, water and ¼ teaspoon of the salt together with a spoon until they are smooth. Beating constantly, sift in the flour a few tablespoons at a time. Continue to beat, or knead with your hands, until the dough can be gathered into a compact ball.

On a lightly floured surface, roll the dough into a paper-thin rectangle about 15 inches long and 9 inches wide. Turn the dough at right angles after each rolling and sprinkle flour over and under it to prevent it from sticking to the board. Then with a pastry wheel or sharp knife cut the dough into sixty 1½-inch squares. Cover them with a dampened kitchen towel to keep them moist while you fill and shape the dumplings.

To make each *uszka,* place about ¼ teaspoon of the mushroom filling in the center of a square of dough. With a finger dipped in cold water, moisten the edges. Fold the square in half diagonally to create a triangle and press the edges securely together. Then lift up the two points of the base and pinch them together. As the dumplings are shaped, cover them with a dampened towel and set aside.

In a heavy 3- to 4-quart casserole, bring 2 quarts of water and 2 teaspoons of salt to a boil over high heat. Stirring gently with a wooden spoon, drop in the dumplings, a large handful at a time. Reduce the heat to low and simmer each batch for 5 minutes, or until the dumplings are tender to the bite. With a slotted spoon, transfer them to a bowl and drape foil over them to keep them warm.

As soon as all of the dumplings are cooked, arrange them in individual soup plates and ladle a hot clear soup such as *barszcz Wigilijny* *(above)* over them. Although the Poles often serve as many as 12 *uszka* per bowl, you may prefer to serve somewhat fewer and reserve the rest (covered with plastic wrap and refrigerated) for future use. They will keep in this fashion for up to a week. Or you may freeze some of the uncooked dumplings; in that case, defrost them thoroughly before cooking.

Bigos
HUNTER'S STEW

Place the dried mushrooms in a small bowl, pour in enough boiling water to cover, and soak for at least 2 hours, or until the mushrooms are soft and flexible. Drain the mushrooms, reserving the soaking liquid, and cut them crosswise into paper-thin slices. Set aside.

Drain the sauerkraut, wash it thoroughly under cold running water and then let it soak in a bowl of cold water for 10 to 20 minutes, depending on its acidity. A handful at a time, squeeze the sauerkraut until it is completely dry. Then pull the strands apart with your fingers.

Drop the tomatoes into boiling water for 15 seconds, then peel off the skin. Cut out the stems and cut the tomatoes in half crosswise. Squeeze the halves to remove the juice and seeds, then coarsely chop the pulp.

In a heavy 4- to 5-quart casserole, melt 4 tablespoons of the butter over moderate heat. When the foam subsides, add the onions and apple. Stirring frequently, cook for about 5 minutes, or until the onions are soft and translucent but not brown. Remove from the heat and stir in the mushrooms, their soaking liquid, the sauerkraut, cabbage and tomatoes.

Preheat the oven to 350°. In a heavy 10- to 12-inch skillet, melt the remaining 3 tablespoons of butter in the vegetable oil over high heat. Brown the beef, venison (or lamb) and pork in the hot fat in separate batches, turning the cubes of meat frequently with tongs or a slotted spoon. As they brown, transfer them to the casserole.

Pour the chicken stock and Madeira into the fat remaining in the skillet and bring to a boil over high heat, stirring constantly and scraping in the brown particles that cling to the pan. With a rubber spatula, scrape the contents of the skillet into the casserole. Add the *kiełbasa*, allspice, salt and a liberal grinding of pepper to the vegetable-and-meat mixture. Cover the casserole tightly and bake in the middle of the oven for 1½ hours. Uncover and continue to bake for 30 minutes longer, or until the meats and vegetables are tender. Taste for seasoning and serve at once, directly from the casserole or from a large heated bowl.

To serve 4 to 6

4 large imported European dried
 mushrooms, preferably dried
 Polish mushrooms
½ to 1 cup boiling water
1 pound fresh sauerkraut
7 tablespoons butter
1 cup finely chopped onions
1 medium-sized tart cooking apple,
 peeled, cored and coarsely
 chopped
½ pound white cabbage, trimmed,
 cored, washed and finely
 shredded
2 medium-sized firm ripe tomatoes
2 tablespoons vegetable oil
1 pound lean beef chuck, trimmed
 of excess fat and cut into 1-inch
 cubes
½ pound lean boneless venison,
 trimmed of excess fat and cut into
 1-inch cubes, or substitute ½
 pound lean boneless lamb,
 trimmed of excess fat and cut into
 1-inch cubes
½ pound lean boneless pork,
 trimmed of excess fat and cut into
 1-inch cubes
½ cup chicken stock, fresh or
 canned
½ cup dry Madeira
½ pound fresh *kiełbasa (page
 105),* cut into rounds 1 inch
 thick, or substitute fresh or
 smoked commercial *kiełbasa,* cut
 into 1-inch rounds
4 whole allspice
1½ teaspoons salt
Freshly ground black pepper

Bigos—a superb Polish stew—is surrounded here by its diverse ingredients: chunks of beef and pork, a string of dried Polish mushrooms and a bowl of cabbage, onions, tomatoes, sausage and apples. Although *bigos* is now commonly served in Poland as a substantial dinner course, it was originally a breakfast dish prepared in the forest for aristocratic hunting parties.

To serve 6 to 8

A 5- to 5½-pound pork loin in one piece, with the backbone sawed through lengthwise but left attached and tied to the loin in 4 or 5 places with kitchen cord
1 teaspoon salt
Freshly ground black pepper
8 whole cloves
1 cup thick applesauce

Pieczony Schab
ROAST LOIN OF PORK WITH APPLESAUCE GLAZE

Preheat the oven to 350°. Rub the pork loin on all sides with the salt and a liberal grinding of pepper. Stud the loin with the cloves, spacing them along its length as evenly as possible.

Place the pork loin fat side up in a shallow roasting pan just large enough to hold it comfortably. For the most predictable roasting results, insert the tip of a meat thermometer horizontally at least 2 inches into one side of the loin. Be sure the tip of the meat thermometer does not touch any fat or bone.

Roast the loin undisturbed in the middle of the oven for 1 hour. Remove the pan from the oven and, with a spatula, spread the applesauce evenly over the top of the loin. Roast for about 30 minutes longer, or until the applesauce has become a golden brown glaze and the meat thermometer indicates a temperature of 160° to 165°.

Transfer the roast pork to a heated platter and let it rest for about 10 minutes for easier carving. Traditionally, the roast pork is accompanied by pickled plums and sauerkraut-and-apple salad *(Recipe Index)*.

To make about 6 dozen cookies

PASTRY
2 cups plus 2 tablespoons all-purpose flour
2 cups confectioners' sugar
4 hard-cooked egg yolks
1 teaspoon vanilla extract
½ pound plus 1 tablespoon unsalted butter, softened

ALMOND TOPPING
1 egg, lightly beaten
4 ounces (1 cup) sliced blanched almonds

Mazurek Wielkanocny
FLAKY FINGER COOKIES TOPPED WITH ALMONDS

Sift 2 cups of flour and the confectioners' sugar into a deep mixing bowl. With the back of a spoon, rub the egg yolks through a fine sieve directly into the flour-and-sugar mixture. Stir until well combined, then add the vanilla and beat in ½ pound of butter a few tablespoons at a time. Continue to beat vigorously with the spoon, or knead with your hands, until the dough is smooth and can be gathered into a compact ball. Wrap in wax paper and refrigerate the dough for at least 1 hour.

Preheat the oven to 375°. With a pastry brush, spread a large baking sheet with the remaining tablespoon of softened butter. Sprinkle the 2 tablespoons of flour over the butter and tip the sheet from side to side to spread it evenly. Invert the sheet and rap the bottom sharply to remove the excess flour.

On a lightly floured surface, roll out the dough into a 12-inch square that is less than ¼ inch thick. Trim the edges to make a perfect square. Cut the dough into quarters and, with a long, wide metal spatula, carefully transfer the quarters to the baking sheet, placing them side by side in their original positions. Cover the dough with a sheet of lightly floured wax paper and gently roll the dough again to join the seams. Peel off the wax paper and brush the entire surface of the dough with the beaten egg.

Sprinkle the top of the dough evenly with the cup of sliced almonds, pressing them gently into the surface. Bake in the middle of the oven for 20 to 25 minutes, or until the pastry is golden brown. Remove the pan from the oven and, with a lightly buttered knife or pastry wheel, cut the pastry into strips about 2 inches long and 1 inch wide. With a metal spatula carefully transfer the *mazurek* to a wire cake rack and let them cool to room temperature.

In a tightly covered container, the cookies may safely be kept for as long as 2 to 3 weeks.

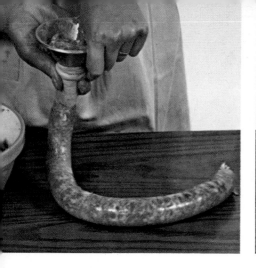 

To make sausage by hand, tie a knot about 3 inches from one end of a cleaned sausage casing and fit the open end over the spout of a wide-based funnel, easing most of the casing up onto the spout. Then spoon the meat mixture into the funnel and push it through into the casing with your fingers *(far left)*. Knot the open end *(left)* and roll the sausage gently on a firm surface to distribute the filling evenly.

Kiełbasa
GARLIC-FLAVORED PORK SAUSAGE

Place the pork in one bowl and the beef shin in another and sprinkle each with 1 tablespoon of salt. Toss to distribute the salt evenly and set aside in a cool, not cold, place for 24 hours.

Place the sausage casing in a bowl, pour in enough warm water to cover it by 1 inch, and soak 2 or 3 hours, until it is soft and pliable.

Put the pieces of pork once through the coarsest blade of a meat grinder, then put the beef through the finest blade 4 times. In a deep bowl, combine the ground meats with the remaining ½ teaspoon of salt, the pepper, garlic and saltpeter. Knead the mixture vigorously with both hands, then beat with a wooden spoon until smooth and fluffy.

Wash the sausage casing thoroughly but gently under cold, slowly running water to remove all traces of the salt in which it was preserved. Hold one end securely around the faucet and let the cold water run through to rinse the inside of the casing. To make each sausage, tie a knot about 3 inches from the end of one length of casing. Fit the open end snugly over the funnel (or "horn") on the sausage-making attachment of a meat grinder. Then ease the rest of the casing up onto the funnel, squeezing it together like the folds of an accordion. Spoon the meat mixture into the mouth of the funnel and with a wooden pestle push it through into the casing. As you fill it, the casing will expand and gradually ease away from the funnel in a coil. Fill the casing to within an inch or so of the open end; do not stuff it too tight or it may burst. Slip the casing off the funnel and knot the open end. You may cook the sausages immediately or refrigerate them safely for 5 or 6 days.

Before cooking, prick the casing in 5 or 6 places with the point of a skewer or a small knife. Coil the sausages in concentric circles in a heavy 10- to 12-inch skillet and pour in enough water to cover them completely. Bring to a simmer over moderate heat, then simmer uncovered for about 40 minutes. *Kiełbasa* is traditionally sliced into rounds ½ inch thick, fried in a little vegetable oil until no trace of pink shows in the meat, and served with sauerkraut and boiled potatoes. It may also be served cold, or used in *bigos* and *erwtensoep (Recipe Index)*.

If you do not have a meat grinder, ask the butcher to grind the pork coarsely and the beef very fine. Following the recipe, combine the meats with the seasonings, and fill the sausages as illustrated above.

To make 3 sausages, each about 30 inches long

4 pounds boneless pork shoulder, cut into 1-inch pieces
1 pound beef shin, cut into 1-inch pieces
2 tablespoons plus ½ teaspoon salt
3 three-foot lengths of hog sausage casing
½ teaspoon freshly ground black pepper
4 cloves garlic, finely chopped
¼ teaspoon curing saltpeter *(see Glossary)*

IV Romania and Bulgaria

Pastoral Themes, Turkish Touches

An earthen bowl of *ciorba*, a versatile sour soup that ornaments the Romanian cuisine, rests on a table at the Village Museum in Bucharest. Made with beef and an assortment of vegetables—there are countless other versions *(page 116)*—this *ciorba* is accompanied, inevitably, by a chunk of fresh bread.

No two peoples so closely related politically and geographically could be so dissimilar in personality as the Romanians and the Bulgarians —at least as viewed from our own brief but intense encounters with them. The Romanians we met were pleasure-loving, romantic and given to the delights of eating and drinking. The Bulgarians were far more direct. Not that they disdained the pleasures of the table, or fun and games, so to speak, but they struck us as essentially sober, serious, dedicated to their ideals, and doggedly devoted to hard work.

When it comes to cooking, however, the two Communist countries are more closely related. Both are intent on using their considerable technical knowledge to feed their people more nutritiously than ever before, and both are developing methods of food production that have tended to standardize their cuisines. But at the same time they are determined to recapture and conserve the dishes of their past—in "folkloristic" restaurants and in their homes as well.

Historically, perhaps the most important link between Romania and Bulgaria is one they share with other Balkan countries—the humiliation and deprivation they suffered under Turkish rule, which began in 1393 and ended, finally, in 1878. This 500-year vassalage is still in their memories; it is bitterly referred to in their literature and daily speech as the *jug,* the yoke, in Romania, and as *pod igoto,* under the yoke, in Bulgaria.

Whatever the hardships imposed upon them by their despotic rulers, the Romanians and Bulgarians did at least inherit an important culinary legacy from the Turks; it is perhaps the most pervasive element in their

In the great Halele Obor market in Bucharest, a farm woman offers a pickled cabbage for sale. Chances are it will be bought for making *sarmale,* the meat-stuffed cabbage rolls that are practically a Romanian national dish. The Halele Obor, literally, "cattle market," dates back five centuries to the earliest days of Bucharest and is now the site of a large cooperative selling all manner of fresh and canned food.

cooking. Of some importance, too, are the influences brought to bear upon Romania by the old Austro-Hungarian Empire, of which it was a part, and upon Bulgaria by the Greeks and the Armenians. One could assume, in the light of these interwoven culinary strands, that neither Romania nor Bulgaria could possibly have a cuisine unmistakably its own —and, from my point of view, neither of them really does. Yet because of the Turkish influence underlying the most important dishes of both countries and because, after all, they share a border of nearly 400 miles, there exists what might be termed a Romanian-Bulgarian cuisine.

Romania: A Lively and Wholesome Blend

Brillat-Savarin's oft-quoted and by now banal aphorism, "Tell me what you eat: I will tell you what you are," would, if one believed it at all, apply least to a Romanian. What a Romanian eats hardly reflects what he is or appears to be. He speaks a language akin to Italian, claims descent from ancient Roman conquerors, and, in fact, even looks and often acts like an Italian. Yet the indigenous Romanian food he eats has a pastoral simplicity that in no way can be compared with the multifaceted variety and brilliance of Italian cooking.

There is, however, one basic dish common to both Italians and Romanians—ground cornmeal boiled in water and made into a porridge, called *polenta* in Italian and *mamaliga* in Romanian *(Recipe Index).* This culinary kinship may go all the way back to the days when imperial Roman legions occupied Romania and indeed gave it its name. Yet it is significant that while the Italian word for the porridge is derived from the Roman word *pulmentum,* the Romanian word, *mamaliga,* is apparently Turkish in origin—*mamà* being Turkish for food.

The first time Frances and I saw *mamaliga* made was in the kitchen of a rustic restaurant, La Doi Cocoşi, The Two Cocks, a few miles outside of Bucharest, Romania's capital. I remember vividly the sight of a brawny, ruddy-faced woman pouring cornmeal into a *ceaun*—a vast black iron pot —filled with boiling water, all the while stirring it with a long-handled wooden spoon. Within about 10 minutes, the cornmeal had thickened into a farina-like mass, dense enough for the spoon to stand upright in it unsupported. In village homes *mamaliga* is turned out on a platter like a pudding, cooled, then cut into portions with a taut string; but here, at La Doi Cocoşi, the porridge was unceremoniously dumped into a huge basin that was kept warm in a pan of hot water. I found this *mamaliga* as decidedly bland as *polenta;* but like *polenta* when served with tomato sauce in Italy, *mamaliga* takes on another dimension when moistened with melted butter or fatty meat juices and served with *pastramă.*

Romanian *pastramă* sounds like, but has little to do with, the meat known in the United States as pastrami, which is made of highly spiced beef studded with black peppercorns, and is in fact an invention of the Slavic Jews. The Romanian word *pastramă,* like *mamaliga,* derives from the Turkish; *păstra* in Turkish means "to keep" or, as we would say, to preserve, cure or brine. Of all the types of commercial or homemade *pastramă* Frances and I tasted in Romania—lamb, beef, goose breast, or pork —it was the pork *pastramă,* surprisingly, that came closest in flavor to our Jewish pastrami, because it was so highly seasoned with crushed peppercorns, garlic and other spices. But except for lamb, any meat used for *pastramă* is first heavily salted and then smoked. Americans usually steam pastrami to cook it, but *pastramă* is simply grilled, as are many other meats in Romania, and as a general rule it is accompanied simply by cold *mamaliga* when the *pastramă* is hot, and by hot *mamaliga* when the *pastramă* is cold.

Because we stayed at the Athenée Palace Hotel in Bucharest, we were fortunate enough to meet Alexandru Gheorghiu, the foremost expert on *pastramă* in Romania. For 10 years he had been head of the Athenée's smoking room (or *carmangerie,* as it is called), and had spent 30 years before that perfecting his art. To compare Mr. Georghiu's version of *pastramă,* especially the one made of pork, to ordinary *pastramă* we had eaten elsewhere in Romania would be like comparing our superb country-cured hams to our mummified, chemically cured supermarket hams.

After tasting this densely textured and richly spiced grilled pork *pastramă* in the sumptuous dining room of the hotel, I avoided the international dishes on the menu taken from the classic French, Italian, Austrian and Hungarian cuisines (and it was a most impressive list indeed) and chose instead a native dish, *ciorba de peste (Recipe Index),* which Frances and I had first tasted on the Danube delta in the easternmost part of Romania. The people there, called Lipovans, came to the area from the north in the 18th Century, and are blue-eyed and blond in contrast to the dark, Latinate-looking people we had seen elsewhere in the country. The Lipovans are primarily fishermen, and so prodigious is their energy and so rich the Danube's harvest that they provide at least half of the fresh-water fish eaten throughout Romania.

We were guests at a small party in the fishing village of Matita where a local version of *ciorba* was being prepared. It was an exceedingly simple soup-and-fish dish made with a large Danube fish called *stuica,* resembling our pike, and a savory collection of onions, red and green peppers, tomatoes and vinegar that flavored the broth. The *ciorba* took only minutes to cook, and it was served as two separate courses—first the cut-up fish and vegetables with a sauce made from a cupful of broth heavily seasoned with garlic, and then bowls of the broth straight from the pot. The Athenée's version of *ciorba de peste,* however, was something else again. The base of this soup was not merely water flavored with vegetables and vinegar as it had been on the delta, but a classic *fumet,* or fish stock, that had been strained and then thickened with a purée of fish to give it more flavor and body. Even more impressive to my professional eye were the neatly trimmed fish steaks that had been poached to perfection in the broth, and the acidulated broth itself, garnished with diced crisp cucumbers. Here was a meaningful example of a country dish that had been transformed from simple origins and elevated, as it were, to another level of culinary importance.

I rarely think of food except in its own terms, but I couldn't help seeing in the difference between country and city *ciorba* an analogy with the remarkable change in Romania's economic fortunes. Since the country began an ambitious 15-year development program in 1960, it has un-

For 500 years the Balkan peoples lived under the Turkish yoke, and though the Romanians and Bulgarians have strong national differences, many similarities in their traditional cooking reflect this shared historical bondage. Now both countries are modernizing and improving their agricultural production, but at the same time fostering their native cuisines.

Continued on page 112

In a Romanian Country Kitchen, Cornmeal Mush Comes Out "Mamaliga"

What could be more Romanian than *mamaliga,* the staple food of the country people who make up over 60 per cent of the nation's population? *Mamaliga de aur* they call it, bread of gold, because of its rich yellow color. Yet an American might readily recognize it as cornmeal mush, solidified to slicing firmness. The pictures on these pages, taken in the kitchen of La Doi Cocoşi, a rustic restaurant in a Bucharest suburb, show the beginning and the end of the classic *mamaliga*-making process. Above, Maria Christa sifts the cornmeal prior to stirring it with boiling water in a cast-iron pot, called a *ceaun,* until it has the consistency of porridge. Ordinarily in the restaurant the *mamaliga* is then turned into a heated pan to keep warm, but here Mrs. Christa demonstrates the home-kitchen way: having let the *mamaliga* cool and become firm, she turns it out onto a round board and slices it with a string.

110

dergone an astonishing growth in industrial strength and a parallel increase in agricultural output. We did not inspect any factories, but at the marketplace in Bucharest we did see at firsthand the results of the agricultural boom—that disastrous floods later were to interrupt.

Because the Romanian People's Republic permits a measure of private enterprise, the produce of individual farmers—radishes, lettuce, leeks, carrots, tomatoes, cabbages, eggs, fruits, nuts and fowl—were presented for sale on long wooden tables on one side of the marketplace. The food was beautifully fresh and wholesome but, like the country *ciorba,* limited. Directly across the street was a mammoth enclosed government-run cooperative market burgeoning with food of far greater variety and sophistication (although I suspect not necessarily of higher quality). Here were carcasses of beef, lamb, pork, and cages of live chickens and ducks; basins of pure tomato paste with such a distinctive flavor as not to be matched anywhere, even in Italy; barrel after barrel of pickled cucumbers and tomatoes; sauerkraut in brine; whole cabbages and separate cabbage leaves in large tubs of brine. In one section was the most varied and dazzling array of peppers—red and green, large and small, sweet and hot —that I have ever seen anywhere. (Romanians and, we were to discover, Bulgarians as well use peppers in their cooking in an astonishingly imaginative number of ways.)

Elsewhere there were stalls with row upon row of jellies made from every kind of berry and fruit; jars of honey; cans of imported delicacies; mounds of walnuts and hazelnuts; and cheeses of all sorts. I saw Romanian cheeses that looked like Roquefort and Brie, and discovered upon tasting them that the Romanians had been no more successful in duplicating these classic French cheeses than Americans have in their imitations. Much more interesting were Romania's native cheeses, such as the simple soft white *brynza* or the firmer yellow and mild Kashkaval —both made of sheep's milk. This overflowing cornucopia was an impressive display in a once-impoverished country—and it was also impressive to see that, whether or not it was the result of government price control, everything was remarkably inexpensive.

The sight of all those beautifully fresh vegetables in the marketplace made me think of the Romanian *ghiveciu (Recipe Index),* a combination of vegetables and meat resembling a stew, made in a Turkish *güveç,* or earthenware pot, from which the dish takes its name. Having attempted many versions of *ghiveciu* in my own kitchen, and, I must admit, with disappointing results, I determined then and there to see a *ghiveciu* actually made in a Romanian household so that I could evaluate once and for all the quality of this dish. Frances and I immediately visited the Romanian Government Tourist Agency where the officials were most helpful. So efficient were they, in fact, that in what seemed only moments we found ourselves ensconced in splendor in a chauffeured car driving through the countryside, headed we knew not where.

The only traffic on the roads consisted of teams of horses harnessed to creaking canvas-covered wagons reminiscent of those of America's pioneering days. Along a good stretch of the trip the houses were huddled together, tipped toward each other as if for support, with dirt paths lead-

Opposite: The main attraction at a Romanian picnic is likely to be the spicy sausages called *mititei (on the grill)* and their traditional accompaniment of peppers in oil *(center).* Other elements of a simple country meal often include rye bread and white goat cheese *(bottom),* sharp black olives and sour cream with dill *(top),* which is usually eaten with the cheese.

Romanian pork *pastramă* is an example of that logical impossibility, an object greater than the sum of its parts. Above is some smoked *pastramă*, which started out as plain slices of pork, shown with the herbs and spices that transformed it. At left is black pepper, and clockwise from it are nutmeg, sweet red pepper, saltpeter, salt, sugar, allspice berries and garlic. Romanians are also very partial to mutton and goat *pastramă*, but these versions are merely salted. Romanian *pastramă* is only very distantly related to the highly spiced American pastrami made of beef.

ing up to them where children and adults walked about barefoot. Patches of green showed here and there in backyards where chickens, ducks and geese wandered freely. Yet poor as many of the houses appeared, the villagers looked strong and vigorous, even the old men and women, some walking with canes. One scene was particularly striking, an echo of Romania's Turkish past, perhaps, when women were treated as chattels. Four sturdy men, arms crossed and muscles bulging, walked abreast, chatting and joking while a few feet behind them a young red-cheeked woman cheerfully hauled a small, newly uprooted tree on her back.

Our driver finally pulled up at a small farmhouse where Mr. and Mrs. Varabiov, the owners, shyly welcomed us. I had no idea then, nor do I care now, how this rapid communication had been effected (there was no telephone in sight), but to my delight Mrs. Varabiov immediately offered us a glass of *tuica,* a brandy distilled from her own home-grown plums, and then silently and smilingly set about preparing a *ghiveciu.* With Frances taking notes, I watched everything Mrs. Varabiov did, keeping track of the amounts of the ingredients she was cutting up so skillfully. As I had hopefully expected, the dish in the making in that tiny but scrupulously clean kitchen was considerably different from the one so authoritatively described in misguided cookbooks as Romanian *ghiveciu.*

Arranged on the table were almost as many different types of vegetables as I had seen in the market, and a cut-up breast of veal. *Ghiveciu* as I had made it was a comparatively simple affair (many recipes for the dish do not include meat), but when I saw what this Romanian housewife was doing I realized that it was a complicated production indeed. After browning the chunks of veal in pork fat and removing them to a platter, Mrs. Varabiov patiently browned one vegetable after another in separate batches—and there were at least eight kinds, among them celery root and acorn squash. But the moment of excitement came for me after our hostess returned the meat and vegetables to the pot. She moistened the colorful mélange with stock and the marvelous tomato paste I had tasted at the market, poured in a cup of red wine—and then unexpectedly tossed in a large handful of luscious green grapes. For me, this preparation of *ghiveciu* (often referred to by Romanians as *"ghiveciu national"*) was a re-enactment of the country's tangled culinary history: the wine and pork fat represented a defiance of 500 years of Muslim dietary prohibitions; the grapes were a borrowing from the Hungarians, who are much given to cooking meat with fruits, and the casserole in which the whole was baked was, of course, a *güveç,* the Turkish pot.

Many other, more intricate dishes in Romania reflect not only Turkish and Hungarian but other influences too: *sarmale (Recipe Index),* brined cabbage leaves filled with a pork mixture and cooked on a bed of bacon and sauerkraut (the sauerkraut and cabbage are clearly Austrian); *musaca (Recipe Index),* made of potatoes, veal and wine, with a browned topping of eggs and cream (certainly Greek); an airy soufflé called *torta romaneasca* (definitely French; *Recipe Index);* and *satou (Recipe Index),* a zabaione-like custard flavored with sweet wine (obviously derived from the Italian). But here too, as with *ghiveciu,* no matter what the origins of these unusual creations—and I could list many more—the way Romanians cook them today makes each dish distinctly their own.

If the evolving Romanian cuisine was impressive, the quantity and quality of the wines the average Romanian drinks impressed me even more. Had Brillat-Savarin known those warmhearted people he might have said more accurately: "Tell me what you *drink;* I will tell you what you are." The Romanian wines, like so many Romanians we met, are mercurial, flowery and gay. Many of these wines, white or red, sweet or dry —from the celebrated vineyards at Cotnari, Murfatlar, Segarcea and Tîrnave, among others—have such distinguished qualities that they have earned prizes and medals in many European wine competitions. It can scarcely be wondered then that Romania during the past century has become one of Europe's largest producers of wine.

In fact, the Romanians' love of wine is such that they drink it even before it becomes wine. In autumn after the grape harvest—a festive time —small outdoor restaurants called *mustării* blossom all over Romania for the purpose of dispensing must, unfermented grape juice, and *turberel,* a must that has just begun to ferment. In every *mustării,* must and *turberel* are always accompanied by *mititei* ("smaller than small"), sausages made of ground beef, mixed with staggering amounts of chopped garlic, shaped into cylinders and impaled on skewers *(Recipe Index).* They are then grilled over charcoal and, inevitably, served with *mamaliga* and, usually, with wine.

Mititei have so universal an appeal in Romania that one can find them not only in the smallest village taverns and roadside stands but even in as elegant an establishment as the Athenée Palace. Although Frances and I had eaten *mititei* and drunk wine all over Romania, we associated this particular combination of food and drink with perhaps the most enchanting night—and sadly the last one—that we spent in Romania.

It began at 10 p.m. at the Athenée Palace and ended at 8 a.m.—10 hours of eating and drinking we shall never forget. We learned from our convivial companions, the tourist officials who had helped us in our quest for *ghiveciu,* that such a night is called a *noapte alba,* or a "white night," a spontaneous celebration that occurs only once in a great while—"at the right moments in life." The platters of *mezelicuri* or hors d'oeuvre—*mititei,* sliced fresh vegetables, cheese, nuts and olives—were refilled again and again through the night, and the wine flowed continually. Two bottles of wine and we were all on a first-name basis. Four, six or eight bottles later Frances and I sang, to the hilarity of the others, in what we pretended was Romanian, then joined their circle to dance a Romanian *perinita,* a folk dance as wild and gay as an Italian *tarantella.* As the sun came up and the birds twittered in the trees we ended the revelry and bade our Romanian friends farewell, kissing and hugging as if we had known one another all our lives.

We had arrived in Bucharest from the airport in a clanking taxi with a broken-down seat, and we left in a similar one, but now we were armed with flowers, two bottles of wine and a last minute request to sign the Athenée Palace's "Golden Book." On an earlier page of the guest book was a warm note of appreciation inscribed by another recent American visitor, Richard M. Nixon.

Continued on page 119

A Savory Romanian Melange from the Danube Delta

After coursing through half of Europe, the Danube flows into the Black Sea at Romania's eastern border in a maze of meandering streams. This delta region is enormously rich in wildlife—birds, including huge flights of ducks; frogs (the Romanians call them *pui de baltă,* or "marsh chicken"); and above all fish. Ten thousand tons of fish come from the delta waters each year, about half the quantity harvested in all Romania. Inevitably a good many of them end up in fish *ciorba.* In these pictures Petru Ustinescu, a delta fisherman, prepares a *ciorba* for a gathering of friends. He begins with two pike and a large *somn,* a type of catfish. Above, he cleans the fish and slices them crosswise part way through so they will cook more evenly. At left, he washes the fish, which are then placed in two pots, and boiled with vegetables and seasoning. At right, with the cooking done, Ustinescu removes the fish and vegetables. They will be eaten separately and the broth drunk by itself. Nothing else is needed—except bread and, perhaps, a little wine.

Bulgaria: Its Own Mix of Past and Present

Having said that Romania and Bulgaria have much in common—borders, controlled economies, and as far as their food is concerned, a Turkish heritage and many similar dishes under different names—I should point out, too, that their overall differences are more profound than one might suppose. Though both were part of the Ottoman Empire for almost five centuries, Romania, while paying exorbitant taxes to the Turkish sultan, was more or less ruled by the local nobility. Bulgaria, however, was not only one of the empire's provinces but was occupied, if not in fact inundated, by the Turks. For the Bulgarians, *pod igato* had and still has deeper and more poignant meaning than has the *jug* for the Romanians.

During the period of occupation, Muslim dietary restrictions were even more in evidence in Bulgaria than in Romania. On the whole, the Bulgarian people managed to hold on, courageously if covertly, to their pre-Turkish culinary traditions and customs. But it would be singular indeed for any nation dominated for so long not to have absorbed, despite itself, the culinary traditions of its conquerors. Inevitably, then, Bulgarian cooking has at its base, even more than Romanian, the major elements of the exotic Turkish cuisine. Even the Greek and Armenian influences on the cooking were largely Turkish-oriented, since Greece and Armenia were also part of the Ottoman Empire for centuries.

Nevertheless, present-day Bulgarian cooking, especially in restaurants, has achieved a contemporary profile while still reflecting this Turkish, Greek and Armenian past. In fact, Frances and I were very much aware of the intensely nationalistic character of the cooking, and impressed by the care taken by Bulgarian cooks at home as well as in restaurants to make the most of the quality of the food itself rather than attempting to elaborate it in fanciful ways.

One factor contributing to this culinary stability is that Bulgaria has no restaurant tradition; travelers in the old days ate in monasteries or were invited into private homes. Consequently, restaurant standards have been set by the state with an emphasis on cleanliness and efficiency. But these establishments, small or large, are not the mechanized monsters one might assume them to be. They do reflect a preoccupation with hygiene and nutrition, yet at the same time manage to serve their dishes most attractively.

We first observed this in a mountaintop restaurant outside Sofia. The service was neither institutional nor crudely rustic, but displayed an innate orderliness and taste that we came to expect from the Bulgarians. The sienna-colored plates we ate from were classically designed with black linear patterns or bright blue peacock's eyes set in feathery fan-shaped tails. And the food was distinguished by an elegant simplicity. The Bulgarians place great emphasis upon fresh vegetables, cheeses and nuts of all varieties, and they are, to put it mildly, addicted to yoghurt. This bacterially fermented milk, deliciously sour and powerfully nutritious, is consumed on every possible occasion, not because all Bulgarians really believe it accounts for their legendary longevity, but simply because they love it.

What we ate in the restaurant that night might have been conceived by an efficient American home economist, but it could only have been em-

Opposite: On a fertile, well-cropped pasture in Bulgaria's Sredna Gora, or "central mountains," cows and water buffalo are about to be cooled by a summer shower. The cows are raised mainly for their milk; the buffalo also provide milk and serve as draft animals as well. The Bulgarians produce and consume a spectacular quantity of dairy foods, including the famous yoghurt for which their appetite is apparently insatiable.

At the open market in Gabrova, a thriving agricultural and industrial city in central Bulgaria, a customer ponders his selection of hot red peppers, an indispensable ingredient of many Bulgarian dishes. The buyer is a priest of the Orthodox Eastern Church, the country's predominant religion.

bellished by the hand of a Bulgarian artist. So plain a dish as a traditional country salad, for example, called *shopska salata,* composed only of tomatoes, cucumbers and cheese, had not been tossed together carelessly; instead, the small bright tomatoes and unpeeled cucumbers had been thinly sliced and esthetically arranged in overlapping concentric circles. As for the cheese, it was the ubiquitous brined goat cheese called *sirene,* similar to Greek *feta* and Romanian *brynza,* grated in delicate white strands and scattered in spirals over the vegetables. There was no dressing on the *shopska salata*—although other more elaborate Bulgarian salads often have complicated dressings of chopped walnuts, garlic, vinegar and oil —but the vegetables were so fresh and the cheese so salty, moist and fresh that none was needed. The *shopska salata* (named after the villagers, called Shopi, living in the environs of Sofia) was accompanied, as it was every time we had it thereafter, by a small, round, heated bread so fragrant that I knew it had come to our table directly from the oven. To add to my enchantment with the salad and the bread was a dish of mixed powdered spices called *ciubritsa,* named for its most important herb, *ciubritsa,* which is similar to tarragon. Bulgarians use the blend as a dip for bread, and the combination of the two was so delectable that if I were able to reproduce the *ciubritsa* at home (I have tried but with no success) I would give up ever buttering bread again.

In this restaurant we were also intrigued to discover that many of the dishes suggested by our interpreter turned out, although their names were unfamiliar, to be similar to dishes we had eaten in Romania. The first surprise was small, skinless grilled sausages called *kebabcha,* which, at first glance, I could have sworn were Romanian *mititei.* But when I tasted them, the difference was clear: although the basic construction of the sausages was the same—that is, ground meat mixed with spices, strung on a skewer and grilled—the Bulgarian version, *kebabcha,* was made of veal and pork rather than beef, and was subtly rather than intensely seasoned with garlic. The *kebabcha* seemed to reflect the understatement, restraint and refinement of the Bulgarians, just as the lustier *mititei* reflected the ebullience of the Romanians. And instead of being served with *mamaliga,* the Bulgarian sausages were surrounded by small, decorative mounds of scallions, chopped parsley and bright crisp radishes whose freshness dazzled our eyes.

The *ciorba* was similar too, except that the Bulgarian versions of this soup were flavored in the Turkish manner with lemon juice rather than vinegar. And on occasion, our interpreter told us, many Bulgarian *ciorba* are not acidulated at all. There was very little difference, however, between the grilled Romanian *pastramă* and the same grilled meat called *pastermá* here. We liked the *pastermá* well enough but were disappointed by the chunks of grilled lamb called *kebabs;* the Bulgarians never use a marinade to tenderize and flavor their meats. I can only assume that sooner or later either the quality of the meats may improve or modern Bulgarian cooks will learn the ancient, magic art of marination.

The generally inferior quality of meat in Bulgaria as compared to the superior meat in Romania was striking, but in a sense understandable. The Bulgarian government has placed great stress on the nutritional value of dairy foods, the byproducts of the grazing animals that are raised in huge herds on fertile upland pastures.

Thus the Bulgarians de-emphasize the production of meat, and milk their cows, sheep and goats literally dry. In the huge marketplace in Sofia, for example, the least impressive area, except that allotted to live fowl, was the display of butchered meat. But we came upon the byproducts in the dairy section with a shock of delight. Here were elaborate and colorful displays of Kashkaval cheese and creamy white *sirene* cheese, butter in tubs, and endless jars and crocks of yoghurt made from cow's, sheep's or water buffalo's milk. And the variety of breads—many of them made with butter, cheese and yoghurt—was unbelievable; simple round breads, breads in figure 8s, braided breads, long, narrow breads of the French type, and a rotund extravanganza called "bird of paradise" *(Recipe Index),* its surface artfully decorated with triangles of cheese, oval black olives, strips of red pepper and cubes of ham.

It occurred to me that Bulgarian meat not destined to be grilled or salted for *pastermá* is used mainly for sausages and other *charcuterie* in which the toughness of the meat is never apparent because it is always finely or coarsely ground. Younger and more tender meat such as veal is, of course, used in making *ghivetch,* the Bulgarian counterpart of Romania's *ghiveciu.* But often as not, the Bulgarians are perfectly content to make

this dish without any meat at all, relying upon their superb vegetables and spices for flavor. With or without meat, the *ghivetch* is considerably different from the *ghiveciu*. The Bulgarian version is spicier, and its outstanding feature is its crusty topping composed of yoghurt and eggs, an idea obviously taken from the Greeks, who use a similar topping for their eggplant-and-lamb *moussaka*.

The Bulgarians appear to have greater culinary respect for their game than for domestic meat or fowl. Their preparation of quail is a notable example. The birds are browned in butter with garlic and onions, then steamed with a combination of rice, currants and raisins in the Turkish fashion *(Recipe Index)*. Bulgarians make other game dishes with equal skill, as well they might—for rabbit, deer, pheasant, partridge and wild boar abound in the innumerable mountain fastnesses of the country.

We heard a vivid description of one way to serve game from a charming, cultivated woman, Mrs. Vasov, whom we met through the tourist office. She told us of a traditional holiday dish prepared in the mountain town of Bansko in southwestern Bulgaria; the best way to convey her enthusiasm for the subject is to quote Frances' notes on the conversation:

"A Saint Nicholas festival dish in Bansko. To listen to this intense description is to be there preparing it and finally eating it. 'This is how they do it,' she says, and tells it step by step: 'First a layer of fermented cabbage leaves is laid on the bottom of a huge pot, then a layer of pieces of pork. This they cover with another layer of cabbage leaves, then chunks of rabbit and chicken. On top, a layer of cabbage leaves, then all kinds of game in chunks and slices. Rice is added, then bacon strips, and on top of it all a final layer of cabbage leaves.'

" 'Like Polish *bigos,*' Michael exclaims (his eyes are alight).

" 'Much better,' Mrs. Vasov says. 'Wait, let me tell you.' And with her hands, she fashions in the air the final addition to this festive dish large enough to serve dozens of revelers. 'Like this,' she says, fingers curled, 'they take cabbage leaves; they fill them with rice and raisins, then fold them; pinch the edges together; roll them into little balls. *These* they hide among the cabbage leaves and the meats. Will these not be delicious surprises? Think of it. What a dish! What flavor! What a marvel! Can you imagine it? Such a selection of meats, something for everyone's taste—and the little cabbage ball surprises.'

"Michael wants to know if they bake this dish or cook it on top of the stove. 'That's the remarkable part of it,' Mrs. Vasov says. 'What do these women do? They seal the pot with dough to keep in all the flavors and they carry it to the town baker, who puts it in his oven where it cooks for the whole night. Believe me, when the next day the women pour this food from the pot onto big platters, Saint Nicholas day is celebrated for hours and hours—such eating, drinking, dancing and singing!' "

We never got to taste this marvelous dish—though we felt we almost had, from Mrs. Vasov's expressive words—but I did remark to Frances that it clearly had a family resemblance to a much less elaborate duck dish we had eaten in Romania, called *ratza ala Romania (Recipe Index),* which combines layers of cabbage with layers of duck and bacon.

The Stara Planina, or Balkan Massif *(balkàn* is Turkish for moun-

Opposite: In her kitchen in the Bulgarian hamlet of Schumata, Mrs. Iakim Tihov shows off a freshly made *ghivetch,* a vegetable-and-meat stew ample enough to feed her family for several days. Taking its name from *güveç,* Turkish for the earthenware vessel in which it is cooked, the dish is common to Bulgaria and Romania. This version differs from the Romanian in its spiciness—it contains small green hot peppers—and in the topping of beaten eggs that is added just before the dish comes out of the oven.

Continued on page 126

In Go the Ripened Plums; Out Comes the Slivova

In late summer each year, when the nights begin to
turn cool in the Bulgarian village of Schumata, the
time for making *slivova* arrives. By then the local
plums are ripe and all but ready to fall from the
branches *(right),* and families from miles around
bring basketloads to the shed shown above to start
making plum brandy. The fruit ferments in huge vats
for about a month, and then the mash is boiled and
distilled. The occasion calls for conviviality, music
making and, of course, the drinking of *slivova.* It is a
very special time, because in Schumata, they say, "the
slivova knows how to talk, how to sing, how to cry."

Inside the shed *(left)* a worker checks the still. Fermented plums and water are boiled in a vat enclosed in the stone oven in the foreground. Rising vapors pass in the pipe through a cooling vat, in the background, filled with cold water. The condensed vapor trickles from a small faucet at the bottom as *slivova.* Meanwhile, a self-appointed tasting board, in a festive mood, samples the newly distilled brandy *(above),* and Iakim Tihov, who is chairman of the *slivova*-making committee of Schumata and a bagpiper of local renown, greets the occasion with a cheerful Bulgarian air.

Surrounded by her wares, an herb merchant at a market in Plovdiv fills an order for *ciubritsa,* one of the most popular Bulgarian seasonings. Related to tarragon, it is used to flavor the stew called *ghivetch* and, mixed with salt and ground red pepper, makes a dip for bread. Many of this vendor's herbs are sold for use as medicines, and include such remedies as nettle seeds to combat diabetes, camomile for sore throats and anise for colicky babies.

tains), cuts across Bulgaria's center from east to west, its northern slope falling gradually to the fertile Danubian plateau; to the south is the rich soil of the Thracian Plain. Between the massif and the plain is the Tundzha Valley and the town of Kazanluk, with its famed Valley of Roses and equally famed walnut groves. Some of the roses are used by Bulgarians in their jellies, perfumes and soaps, but most are exported to Turkey and North Africa, where rose water and syrup are extensively used in cooking. The walnuts, however, are put to abundant use at home.

We Americans are perfectly content to eat walnuts out of their shells and use them in cakes and desserts, but otherwise we seldom cook with them. The Bulgarians, on the other hand, cultivate great groves of walnut trees, because walnuts—green or ripe—are essential to many of their dishes. In their marketplaces and restaurant kitchens we saw enormous mounds of shelled walnuts and beside them women immaculately dressed in white whose sole job, it seemed, was to shell them.

Of all the dishes in which Bulgarians use walnuts—soups, salads, stuffings, desserts—the one Frances and I loved most was, of all things, an ice-cold soup. Our introduction to this soup was most delightful because of an enthusiastic restaurant hostess who not only told us what this nectar was but precisely how to prepare it. What made the encounter so amusing was that our helpful hostess spoke four languages but knew only two words in English, as she said laughingly: "O.K." and "I-love-you." After much groping about in French, Italian and German, we finally settled on French, and it was in this language that we learned the recipe for the soup called *tarator (Recipe Index)*.

Our hostess described how to peel and cut up the cucumbers, sprinkle them with salt, let them sit for 15 minutes to rid them of their moisture, then combine them with yoghurt, chopped walnuts and garlic, stir in some sunflower oil and finally garnish the soup with dill. My respectful attention to her description and appreciative response to the tart, herbal flavor of the soup seemed to inspire her to tell us everything she knew about her beloved Bulgaria and the secrets of its cooking. She seduced us into tasting dish after dish, enumerating the ingredients that had gone into them and how they were made. After the soup, for example, we had peppers stuffed with *sirene* cheese; the fascinating aspect of this simple combination was that it had been coated with bread crumbs and deep-fried in fat *(Recipe Index)*. Upon my comment that I found *sirene* superior to the *feta* cheese I had often eaten in Greece, she insisted that we must have a *banitsa* made with *sirene (Recipe Index)*. *Banitsa,* she told us, was one of Bulgaria's famous dishes, and when it appeared I could easily understand why.

On the plate before me was a spiraling, figure-8 pastry with a texture so fragile that I instantly realized it had been made of the same strudel-type dough that the Middle Easterners use to make their celebrated pastry, *baklava.* Our hostess explained that *banitsa* was made in many other forms, especially as large and small pies (sometimes filled with spinach, even pumpkin), but that she had had the cook bake it for us in this shape because it was unusual.

We would have eaten our way through the entire menu had our hostess had her way, but fortunately for our digestion—after all, we had come only for a light lunch—she was obliged to greet some 30 or so young Russian student tourists who were on a holiday. She seated them, then rushed back to say goodbye to us. Frances and I had fallen in love with this outgoing, passionate-natured Slavic woman. In my ardor, I impulsively grabbed the carnations from the vase on our table, handed them to her, bowed, kissed her hand, and said, "O.K. I-love-you too."

She escorted us to the elevator, making us promise to stop before retiring that night at a *mekene,* as taverns are called, for *loukanka*—a hard, salami-type Bulgarian sausage—accompanied by a Bulgarian red wine. And she added that under no circumstances should we miss visiting the remarkable diet restaurant across the street from the Balkan Hotel where we were staying.

We had heard that in Bulgaria and Romania people requiring special diets were provided for in special government-run establishments. In Romania, we had avoided what we felt would be depressing, hospitallike food—hardly representative of the country's national dishes. But now, still under the influence of our hostess and the delicious food she had served us, even I (who dislike the restriction that the word diet puts upon me) was impelled to visit the diet restaurant immediately. Not only did I not regret this visit but I still cannot get over what we found there;

Overleaf: At a cooperative farm in Bulgaria's Valley of Roses, workers husk corn to be used both for animal fodder and for roasting on outdoor grills for human consumption. A population movement from farms to cities has caused concern in Bulgaria about maintaining agricultural output. But the government requires all students to give two months of rural labor a year, and many go into the countryside to work on cooperative farms such as the one shown.

my only regret now is that we didn't take the time to go to similar places I had heard about in Romania.

As we entered the spacious room that had the air of a fine restaurant, we were greeted by a young woman dressed in white who recognized us as foreigners and with unerring Bulgarian courtesy took us in hand. Since she spoke English—and exceedingly well—I was able to explain my interest in Bulgarian cooking, whereupon she told me she was similarly interested, but as a dietitian. During the half hour or so we spent there we learned as much about the Bulgarians as people as we had in their homes and in their finest restaurants.

While such restaurants are always charged with the festive atmosphere that eating out usually inspires—and in Bulgaria, as in Romania, there is often so much music and dancing one can hardly think, much less talk —in this diet restaurant, warmth and cheerfulness seemed to emanate from the diners alone. The patrons were mostly elderly, but to look at them one would never suspect that they were anything but healthy. Seated at round tables, they were involved in animated conversation, and seemed not at all reluctant when asked by the dietitian to discuss what they were eating and why.

The first discovery I made was that there were blackboards listing menus for specific ailments, but with several choices written in chalk on each one. And that wasn't all; there was a change of menus daily, and for all three meals. The food on the tables before each of the diners looked so tempting that I asked the dietitian if I could taste one dish that looked like a *ciorba*. I expected that at the very least it would be bland as most diet foods usually are. It was as good as, if a little different from, those I had enjoyed elsewhere in Bulgaria. And beginning to distrust my judgment, I asked to taste another dish—this time, a golden-brown pancake-like croquette. I discerned that it had been made of scallions, dill, parsley and eggs—a dish I would be happy to eat in my own house or serve to friends *(Recipe Index)*.

On the way to the kitchen, Frances remarked to the dietitian that the mood in the dining room was unusually pleasant considering that the diners could not all be in the best of health. The dietitian smiled gently, and explained that people dining there met often and made friendships; and that the older people, especially, looked forward to eating together rather than alone. Another psychological factor had been taken into account as well; those who had families with whom they preferred to eat could come to the restaurant three times a day, show their diet papers to the doctor in charge (whom we were about to meet), and choose their meals, have them boxed, then carry them off to dine at home. No meal, we learned, costs more than the equivalent of about 25 cents. When chatting with the doctor I asked if he prescribed any just plain reducing diets, of the type so popular in America. His answer was most revealing. "We are not yet at the point," he said, "where our men prefer thin women to heavy ones. We do not have cosmetic diets. If a serious physical condition produces obesity we know how to treat it."

Returning to our hotel, we ambled through the luxurious park in the center of beautiful Sofia where the flowers, enjoyed so much by Bulgarians, seemed as carefully and lovingly tended as the people we had just seen in the diet restaurant. It was getting late, but the suggestions offered to us by our hostess at luncheon had been so fruitful so far that we decided to go to a *mekene* for *loukanka* and a red Mavroud wine. In the lobby of our hotel there was a sign in Cyrillic—the script used by the Bulgarians and by the Russians as well—which we had learned said *mekene;* under the sign was a large piece of cardboard with a huge arrow drawn on it pointing the way. We had noticed the sign several times, but had never followed its suggestion. Now we set forth with a sense of excitement and curiosity.

Like Theseus with Ariadne's thread we followed arrow after arrow directing us down stairs, along hallways, through doorways and out into the street behind the hotel, where we were confronted by yet another arrow pointing to a steep stairway that we dutifully climbed. Having reached the top, we asked whomever we met along the way, *"mekene?"* Each one smiled, indicating another arrow pointing to *mekene*. We finally came to a pair of elegantly designed doors—but they were locked. Was this our long-sought tavern? Once more we tried, asking a passerby for the *mekene. "Slivova!"* he exclaimed, laughing, taking for granted that we wanted Bulgaria's plum brandy, and generously walked with us the full length of the block (which is quite a walk in Sofia), and at the end of it turned to the left and walked up the steps where, pointing to an arrow, he bowed good night. To our dismay, there before us was the lobby of our hotel and the wretched arrow under *mekene*. We turned to the right, stepped into the elevator, and went to bed.

Commiserating with each other because it was our last night in Bulgaria, Frances and I decided we could afford to have missed the *loukanka* and the wine after all, because Bulgaria had more than fulfilled for us so many of its other culinary promises. But maybe next time. . . .

Roast Lamb and Ritual Food at a Mountain Picnic

Bulgaria is a paradise for picnickers, both because two thirds of its land is forest and mountain terrain, and because its traditional solid fare is highly appropriate for eating outdoors. In these pictures, students from the Technical University of Sofia enjoy a feast on the stony banks of a stream high in the Rila Mountains. Their main dish is a whole spit-roasted lamb, so well done that it can be pulled apart *(above)*. Side dishes include grapes and stuffing of rice and giblets, and to drink there is *slivova* and Gamza, a red wine. But their meal also includes a particularly Bulgarian feature: *kurban,* a meat-stock soup with peppers and tomatoes *(right).* A survival from the ancient religious practice of animal sacrifice, *kurban* even today is as much a matter of ritual as of cuisine.

To make about 2 cups

A 1½-pound eggplant
2 medium-sized green peppers, roasted, peeled and deribbed *(see peppers in oil, page 143)*
1 medium-sized firm ripe tomato, peeled, seeded and finely chopped *(see bigos, page 101)*
¼ cup olive oil
3 tablespoons red wine vinegar
3 tablespoons finely chopped fresh parsley
2 teaspoons finely chopped garlic
1 tablespoon salt
Freshly ground black pepper

Kiopoolu (*Bulgaria*)
EGGPLANT AND PEPPER SPREAD

Roast the eggplant in the following fashion: Prick it in 3 or 4 places, then impale it on a long-handled fork and turn it over a flame until the skin chars and cracks. Or, pierce the eggplant, place it on a baking sheet, and broil it 4 inches from the heat for about 20 minutes, turning it so that it chars on all sides. Wrap the eggplant in a damp towel for 5 minutes, then peel off and discard the skin. Cut the eggplant in half, chop it fine, and mash the pulp to a smooth purée. Similarly, mash the skinned and deribbed green peppers.

Combine the eggplant and pepper purée in a deep bowl. Stir in the oil and vinegar a tablespoon at a time, then beat vigorously with a wooden spoon until the mixture is smooth. Add the chopped tomato, parsley, garlic, salt and a liberal grinding of pepper, and continue to beat until all the ingredients are well mixed. Taste for seasoning and refrigerate until chilled. Serve mounded on a platter as a first course or spread on dark bread as an accompaniment to drinks.

To serve 4

A 1-pound white cabbage
¼ pound lean slab bacon, cut into ¼-inch dice
A 5-pound duck, cut into 8 serving pieces
¼ cup finely chopped fresh fennel, or substitute ½ teaspoon powdered fennel
2 tablespoons finely chopped shallots, or substitute 2 tablespoons finely chopped scallions, white parts only
½ teaspoon finely chopped garlic
½ teaspoon crumbled dried thyme
¼ teaspoon crumbled dried sage
¼ teaspoon crumbled dried marjoram
1½ cups sauerkraut juice

Ratza ala Romania
BRAISED DUCK WITH CABBAGE

Remove the tough outer leaves of the cabbage, wash the head under cold running water, and cut it into quarters. Shred the cabbage by cutting out the core, then slicing the quarters crosswise in ⅛-inch-wide strips.

In a heavy 4- to 6-quart casserole, fry the bacon over moderate heat, stirring frequently until the bits are brown and crisp and have rendered most of their fat. With a slotted spoon, transfer the bacon bits to paper towels to drain. Pour all but 2 tablespoons of the fat remaining in the casserole into a cup or bowl and set aside.

With paper towels pat the pieces of duck completely dry. Then brown them in the casserole, 3 or 4 at a time, turning them frequently with tongs. As they brown, transfer the pieces of duck to a plate.

Preheat the oven to 425°. Discard all the fat in the casserole and in its place add the reserved bacon fat. Drop in the shredded cabbage, fennel, shallots or scallions, garlic, thyme, sage and marjoram. Stirring frequently, cook uncovered over moderate heat until the cabbage is limp but not brown. Add the sauerkraut juice and stir until it comes to a boil.

Arrange the pieces of duck on top of the cabbage, pour in the liquid that has accumulated around them, and scatter the reserved bacon bits over the top. Cover the casserole tightly and braise in the lowest part of the oven for 15 minutes. Lower the heat to 325° and continue to braise for about 1 hour longer, or until the duck is tender.

With a long spoon skim off and discard all the surface fat and serve the duck and cabbage directly from the casserole. Or mound the cabbage on a deep heated platter and arrange the duck pieces over or around it.

Surrounding a Bulgarian bird-of-paradise bread are crisply fried cheese-filled finger peppers *(top left),* a sweet and hot-pepper salad *(top right)* and, at bottom, a combination of chopped eggplant and peppers.

To make 1 round loaf

1 package active dry yeast
½ teaspoon sugar
¼ cup lukewarm water (110° to 115°)
3 to 3½ cups all-purpose flour
2 teaspoons salt
½ cup unflavored yoghurt
4 eggs
2 ounces *brynza* or *feta* cheese *(see Glossary)*, rubbed through a sieve or food mill (½ cup)
1 tablespoon salted butter, softened
1 egg lightly beaten with 1 tablespoon milk
¼ pound Kashkaval *(see Glossary)*, or substitute sweet Münster cheese, sliced ¼ inch thick and trimmed into 4 triangles about 4 inches long
A ¼-inch-thick slice boiled ham, cut into four 1-inch squares
4 ripe black olives, preferably Mediterranean type
A 1-inch square of sweet red pepper or pimiento, cut into a star

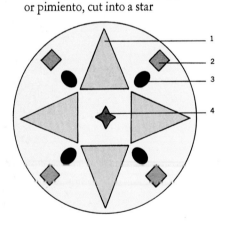

To serve 8

1 quart water
1 tablespoon salt
2⅔ cups finely ground yellow or white cornmeal
4 tablespoons butter, melted

Khliab Raiska Ptitsa *(Bulgaria)*
BIRD-OF-PARADISE BREAD

In a small, shallow bowl sprinkle the yeast and sugar over ¼ cup of lukewarm water. Let the mixture stand for 2 or 3 minutes, then stir well. Set the bowl in a warm, draft-free place (such as a turned-off oven) for about 5 minutes, or until the mixture almost doubles in volume.

Combine 3 cups of flour and the salt in a deep mixing bowl, make a well in the center, and pour in the yeast mixture, yoghurt, eggs and *brynza* or *feta* cheese. With a large spoon, gradually stir the flour into the other ingredients, continuing to stir until the mixture is smooth and the flour is completely absorbed. The dough should be just firm enough to be gathered into a ball. If it is too soft, add the remaining ½ cup of flour a tablespoon at a time, beating vigorously after each addition and using only enough of the flour to give the dough its proper consistency; it should not be too firm.

On a lightly floured surface, knead the dough by pushing it down with the heels of your hands, pressing it forward, and folding it back on itself. Continue the kneading for about 10 minutes, or until the dough is smooth and elastic. Sprinkle it from time to time with a little flour to prevent it from sticking to the board.

Shape the dough into a ball and place it in a lightly greased bowl. Drape with a kitchen towel and set aside in a warm, draft-free place for about 1 hour, or until the dough doubles in bulk.

With a pastry brush, spread a large baking sheet with the tablespoon of softened butter. Punch the dough down with a single blow of your fist, shape it into a round loaf about 8 inches in diameter, and set the round on the buttered sheet. Brush the entire surface of the dough evenly with the egg-and-milk mixture, then, following the diagram at left, arrange the cheese triangles (1), the ham cubes (2), olives (3) and red pepper or pimiento (4) attractively on top. Set the dough aside in a warm place for about 30 minutes to allow it to double in bulk.

Preheat the oven to 400°. Bake the bread in the middle of the oven for 15 minutes, then reduce the heat to 350° and bake for 30 to 40 minutes longer, or until the loaf is golden brown. Transfer the bread to a cake rack to cool. Serve at room temperature.

Mamaliga *(Romania)*
CORNMEAL PORRIDGE

In a heavy 2- to 3-quart saucepan, bring the water and salt to a boil over high heat. Pour the cornmeal very slowly into the boiling water, making sure that the boiling never stops and stirring constantly with a wooden spoon to keep the mixture smooth. Reduce the heat to low, cover tightly, and simmer for 10 to 12 minutes, or until the *mamaliga* is very thick and all the liquid in the pan has been absorbed.

Serve at once, mounded on a heated platter and moistened with the melted butter. *Mamaliga* may be served with meat and gravy as a substitute for bread or potatoes; or it may be served at room temperature as a separate course surrounded by black olives, hard-cooked eggs, dill and tarragon sprigs and accompanied by sour cream and *brynza* cheese.

Sarmale *(Romania)*
STUFFED CABBAGE LEAVES WITH SAUERKRAUT

To make about 12 cabbage rolls

Drain the sauerkraut, wash it under cold running water, and let it soak in cold water for 10 to 20 minutes, depending upon its acidity. A handful at a time, squeeze the sauerkraut until it is dry. Set aside in a bowl.

Remove the bruised and tough outer leaves of the cabbage and wash the head under cold running water. Drop it into a large pot of boiling water and cook briskly for about 10 minutes. Remove the cabbage with tongs, but let the water continue to boil. Carefully peel off as many of the outer leaves as you can without tearing them. Then return the cabbage to the boiling water and cook for a few minutes longer. Again peel off the softened outer leaves. Repeat the process until you have detached 12 perfect leaves. Pat them dry with paper towels and set them aside.

Bring 1 quart of water to a boil over high heat and stir in the rice. Boil briskly, uncovered, for 10 minutes, or until partially cooked. Drain the rice in a sieve or colander, run cold water over it and set aside.

Grind the pork together with ⅓ cup of the onions through the finest blade of a meat grinder into a deep bowl. Add the rice, thyme and salt, knead vigorously with both hands, then beat with a wooden spoon until the mixture is smooth and fluffy.

Lay the cabbage leaves side by side and, with a small knife, trim the base of each leaf of its tough rib end. Place about ½ cup of the pork filling in the center of each leaf (smaller leaves will take less), and roll up each leaf tightly, tucking in the ends to make a neat oblong package.

Preheat the oven to 350°. Melt the butter over moderate heat in a heavy 3- to 4-quart casserole. When the foam begins to subside, add the remaining 2½ cups of onions and, stirring frequently, cook for about 5 minutes, or until they are soft and translucent but not brown. Add the tomato-purée-and-water mixture and ground red pepper and bring to a boil. Then with a fork stir the contents of the pan into the sauerkraut.

Spread about one third of the mixture on the bottom of the casserole. Arrange 6 of the cabbage rolls side by side on top, then sprinkle them with ⅓ cup of the green pepper. Cover the rolls with half of the remaining sauerkraut mixture, arrange the rest of the cabbage rolls on top and again sprinkle them with another ⅓ cup of the green pepper. Add the rest of the sauerkraut mixture and pour in any liquid remaining in the bowl. Sprinkle with the final ⅓ cup of green pepper and arrange the bacon strips on top. Bring to a boil on top of the stove, cover the casserole tightly, and bake in the middle of the oven for 1 hour. Then arrange the tomato quarters in one layer across the top of the bacon, re-cover, and bake ½ hour longer.

Serve at once, directly from the casserole. Pork *sarmale* is traditionally accompanied by *mamaliga (opposite)*.

NOTE: *Sarmale* is characterized in Romania by the acidulated flavor of fermented cabbage leaves. To ferment a cabbage, place it in an 8- to 10-quart casserole and cover with 6 quarts of cold water. Add 1½ cups of salt and bring to a boil. Lower the heat and simmer, partially covered, for 10 minutes. Place a heatproof plate on top of the cabbage to keep it submerged and set it aside for 3 days. Separate the large leaves, drain, and use in place of the fresh cabbage leaves described above.

1 pound fresh sauerkraut
A 2½- to 3-pound white cabbage, raw or fermented *(see note)*
¼ cup long-grain unconverted white rice
1½ pounds lean ground pork
3 cups finely chopped onions
1 teaspoon crumbled dried thyme
1½ teaspoons salt
8 tablespoons unsalted butter (1 quarter-pound stick), cut into small bits
1 cup tomato purée, mixed with 1½ cups water
¼ teaspoon ground hot red pepper (cayenne)
1 cup finely chopped green pepper
6 lean bacon slices
4 tomatoes, cut lengthwise into quarters

To make 12 stuffed peppers

12 medium-sized Italian finger
   peppers (about 1½ pounds)
12 ounces *brynza* cheese, or
   substitute *feta* cheese *(see
   Glossary)*
6 ounces pot cheese
2 eggs, plus 2 eggs lightly beaten
Freshly ground black pepper
½ cup all-purpose flour
3 cups soft fresh crumbs, made
   from homemade-type white
   bread, pulverized in a blender or
   finely shredded with a fork
Vegetable oil for deep frying

To serve 4 to 6

STOCK
1 pound fish trimmings: the heads,
   tails and bones of any firm white-
   fleshed fish
1½ cups coarsely chopped onions
1 medium-sized bay leaf
1 teaspoon salt
6 cups cold water

FISH SOUP
½ pound boned skinless halibut or
   other firm white-fleshed fish,
   coarsely chopped
1 teaspoon salt
¼ teaspoon freshly ground black
   pepper
2 pounds halibut or other firm
   white-fleshed fish steaks, each cut
   1 inch thick
1 tablespoon finely chopped garlic
   mashed to a smooth paste with
   ½ teaspoon salt
1 medium-sized cucumber, peeled,
   seeded and cut into ¼-inch dice
2 tablespoons distilled white
   vinegar

Purzheni Chushki s Sirene *(Bulgaria)*
FRIED PEPPERS STUFFED WITH CHEESE

Following the directions for peppers in oil *(page 143)*, roast and peel the peppers. Cut out the stems and carefully scoop out the seeds, leaving the peppers intact.

Force the *brynza* or *feta* and the pot cheese through a food mill or rub them through a medium-meshed sieve into a bowl with the back of a spoon. Add 2 eggs and a few grindings of black pepper, and beat vigorously with a spoon until the mixture is smooth. Using a pastry bag fitted with a small plain tip, fill each of the roasted peppers with about 3 tablespoons of the cheese stuffing. One at a time, dip the peppers into the flour and shake gently to remove any excess. Turn the peppers about in the lightly beaten eggs and then roll them on all sides in the crumbs. If necessary, pat the crumbs into place with a small spatula to make them firmly adhere. Spread the peppers side by side on wax paper and refrigerate for about 30 minutes.

Pour the vegetable oil into a deep fryer or large heavy saucepan to a depth of at least 3 inches and heat the oil until it reaches a temperature of 375° on a deep-frying thermometer.

Fry the stuffed peppers in the hot oil, 3 or 4 at a time, turning them about with a slotted spoon for 2 to 3 minutes, or until they are richly and evenly browned. As they brown, transfer the peppers to paper towels to drain, then arrange them on a heated platter. Serve the peppers immediately, either whole as a first course or cut crosswise into 3 or 4 slices as a first course or an accompaniment to drinks.

Ciorba de Peste *(Romania)*
FISH SOUP WITH GARLIC SAUCE

Combine the fish trimmings, chopped onions, bay leaf, 1 teaspoon of salt and the 6 cups of water in a heavy 3- to 4-quart enameled or stainless-steel casserole. Bring to a boil over high heat, reduce the heat to low, and simmer partially covered for 30 minutes. Strain the entire contents of the casserole through a fine sieve into a deep bowl, pressing down hard on the fish trimmings and onions with the back of a spoon to extract all their juices before discarding them.

Pour the stock back into the casserole and add the chopped fish. Stirring occasionally, bring to a boil over high heat. Reduce the heat to its lowest point and simmer uncovered for about 15 minutes, or until the fish can be easily mashed with the back of a spoon. Purée the contents of the casserole in a food mill, or rub them through a coarse sieve, and return to the casserole. Stir in the 1 teaspoon of salt and ¼ teaspoon of pepper, and immerse the fish steaks in the soup. Bring to a simmer over moderate heat and poach partially covered for 5 to 8 minutes, or until the fish flakes easily when prodded gently with a fork. Do not overcook.

With a slotted spatula, transfer the steaks to a large heated tureen or individual soup plates. With a whisk, beat 1 cup of the soup into the garlic paste and pour the mixture into a sauceboat. Add the cucumber and vinegar to the remaining soup, taste for seasoning, and ladle over the fish steaks. Serve at once, accompanied by the garlic sauce.

Walnuts, a Bulgarian staple, and crushed ice lend interest to the cold yoghurt soup, with cucumbers and dill, called *tarator*.

Tarator (Bulgaria)
COLD CUCUMBER AND YOGHURT SOUP WITH WALNUTS

To serve 4

1 medium-sized or 2 small
  cucumbers
1½ teaspoons salt
2 cups unflavored yoghurt
⅓ cup walnuts, finely chopped
1 tablespoon finely cut fresh dill
½ teaspoon finely chopped garlic
2 tablespoons sunflower or olive oil
1 cup crushed ice cubes

With a small, sharp knife, peel the cucumber and slice it lengthwise into halves. Scoop out and discard the seeds by running the tip of a teaspoon gently down the center of each half. Cut the cucumber halves into ¼-inch dice, place in a small bowl, and sprinkle evenly with ½ teaspoon of salt. Set aside at room temperature for about 15 minutes. Then transfer the cucumber dice to a sieve, wash briefly under cold running water, and let them drain. Spread the cucumbers out on paper towels and pat them thoroughly dry.

Combine the diced cucumbers, unflavored yoghurt, chopped walnuts, dill, garlic and the remaining teaspoon of salt in a deep bowl, tossing them about with a spoon until they are thoroughly mixed. Stir in the sunflower or olive oil by the teaspoonful, making sure each addition is well absorbed before adding more.

Ladle the soup into 4 individual bowls or soup plates, dividing it evenly among them, and refrigerate the soup for at least 1 hour, or until thoroughly chilled. Drop about ¼ cup of crushed ice cubes into each bowl immediately before serving.

Ghiveciu National *(Romania)*
FRESH VEGETABLE STEW WITH VEAL AND GRAPES

Although the Romanians traditionally use a great variety of colorful vegetables in their national stew, you may, if you wish, eliminate some, increasing the quantity of others. For example, you may omit the acorn squash or cauliflower and double the amount of potatoes or eggplant.

Preheat the oven to 350°. In a heavy 12-inch skillet, fry the pork fat (if you are using it) over moderate heat, stirring frequently, until it is crisp, delicately browned, and has rendered all its fat. Remove the crisp bits with a slotted spoon and discard them. Pour the rendered fat into a measuring cup; there should be about ¾ cup. Pour 4 tablespoons of the fat back into the skillet and set aside off the heat.

Pat the chunks of veal completely dry. Season them on all sides with 1 teaspoon of the salt and a liberal grinding of pepper. Dip them in the flour and, when they are evenly coated, shake vigorously to remove the excess flour. Heat the pork fat in the skillet over high heat until a drop of water flicked into it splutters and evaporates instantly. Or, pour 4 tablespoons of the butter-and-oil mixture into a 12-inch skillet and place over high heat until the foam begins to subside. Brown the veal chunks in the hot fat, 7 or 8 at a time, turning them frequently with tongs or a spatula. Add more fat or butter and oil to the skillet as needed. As the veal browns, transfer the chunks to a heavy 6- to 8-quart casserole.

Add the onion slices and garlic to the fat remaining in the skillet and, stirring frequently, cook for about 5 minutes, until they are soft and translucent. With a slotted spoon transfer the onions and garlic to the casserole and spread them over the veal. Pour off all the fat from the skillet and in its place add 1 cup of the stock (or the stock-and-water mixture) and the tomato paste. Stirring constantly, bring to a boil over high heat. Pour the mixture into the casserole.

Cut the eggplant, potatoes, cabbage and squash into 1½-inch cubes, and cut the carrots, green pepper and celery root into strips about 2 inches long and ¼ inch wide. Separate the cauliflower into small flowerets.

Put 6 tablespoons of pork fat or butter and oil in the skillet and place it over moderate heat. Adding them to the skillet in separate batches and frying each batch just long enough to color the pieces lightly and evenly, fry the eggplant, potatoes, carrots, string beans, green pepper, celery root, squash, cauliflower and cabbage. As they brown, transfer the vegetables to the casserole with a slotted spoon, arranging each one in a separate layer. Add more fat to the skillet when necessary.

Pour off any fat remaining in the skillet, then add the remaining 3 cups of stock (or stock and water), the wine, parsley, marjoram, thyme and remaining salt. Bring to a boil over high heat, scraping in any browned particles clinging to the bottom and sides of the skillet. Pour the mixture down the sides of the casserole. Bring to a boil over high heat, then cover tightly and bake in the middle of the oven for 45 minutes. Add the tomatoes, grapes and peas, and bake covered for 15 minutes longer. Taste for seasoning, then serve directly from the casserole.

¾ pound fresh pork fat, cut into small dice, or 8 tablespoons melted butter combined with 4 tablespoons vegetable oil

3 pounds boneless breast of veal, cut into 1-inch chunks

2 tablespoons salt

Freshly ground black pepper

½ cup flour

3 medium-sized onions, peeled and cut into ¼-inch-thick slices

2 teaspoons coarsely chopped garlic

4 cups freshly made beef stock, or substitute 2 cups condensed canned beef stock combined with 2 cups cold water

2 tablespoons tomato paste

1 small eggplant (about ¾ to 1 pound), peeled

6 medium-sized boiling potatoes (about 2 pounds), peeled

½ small white cabbage (about ½ pound), trimmed and cored

1 pound acorn squash, peeled and seeded

3 medium-sized carrots (about ½ pound), peeled

1 large green bell pepper, stemmed, deribbed and seeded

1 medium-sized celery root (celeriac), about ½ pound, peeled

1 small cauliflower (about ¾ to 1 pound), trimmed and washed

¼ pound green string beans, trimmed, washed and cut in half lengthwise

1 cup dry red wine

2 teaspoons finely chopped parsley

½ teaspoon crumbled dried marjoram

½ teaspoon crumbled dried thyme

4 medium-sized firm ripe tomatoes, peeled, cut into quarters and seeded

¼ pound seedless green grapes, washed

¼ cup fresh green peas, shelled

Romanian *ghiveciu,* like its Bulgarian counterpart *(page 122),* is a vegetable stew with meat, but has no chilies or hot spices and emphasizes sweet young vegetables, accented by a sprinkling of green grapes.

Flaky, spiraled *banitsa,* often served with coffee, is a Bulgarian creation of paper-thin pastry wrapped around a cheese filling.

Banitsa (Bulgaria)
FLAKY CHEESE ROLLS

To make 16 rolls

½ pound unsalted butter, melted
   and cooled
1 pound *brynza* cheese, or substitute
   1 pound *feta* cheese
½ cup unflavored yoghurt
2 large eggs
16 sheets *filo* pastry *(see Glossary),*
   each about 16 to 18 inches long
   and 12 inches wide, thoroughly
   defrosted if frozen *(see note)*

Preheat the oven to 400°. With a pastry brush, spread 2 tablespoons of the melted butter on 2 large baking sheets.

Crumble the cheese between your fingers, then force it through a food mill set over a deep bowl or rub it through a fine sieve with the back of a spoon. Add the yoghurt and eggs, and beat vigorously with a spoon until the mixture is smooth. Transfer about half of the cheese mixture to a pastry bag fitted with a ⅓-inch-wide plain tip.

Assemble each *banitsa* in the following fashion: Place one sheet of *filo* on a kitchen towel and brush it evenly with a teaspoon of the butter. Carefully fold the fragile pastry in half crosswise to make a two-layered rectangle about 12 inches long and 8 or 9 inches wide. Brush the top with about ½ teaspoon of the butter. Pipe a strand of the cheese mixture from the pastry bag along one long side of the rectangle, starting and ending ½ inch from the ends. Then roll the pastry into a narrow cylinder, lifting the edge of the towel to help you, and brush it lightly but evenly with butter. Now gently curl one end around once or twice up to the middle of the cylinder, brushing it lightly with butter to keep it moist. Curl the other end around once or twice in the opposite direction, until you

142

have created an S-shaped spiral *(see photograph opposite)*. With the aid of a long spatula, transfer the filled cheese roll to a baking sheet. Then proceed to make the remaining *banitsa* similarly, lining them up side by side on the baking sheets. Bake the *banitsa* in the middle of the oven for 20 minutes, or until they are crisp and a delicate golden brown. Slide them carefully onto a large heated platter and serve at once as a first course or as an accompaniment to drinks.

NOTE: *Filo* tends to dry out and become brittle almost as soon as it is exposed to air. Once you have unrolled a packet of *filo,* remove the sheets one at a time and butter, fill and shape them at once, keeping the remaining sheets rolled up and loosely wrapped in a damp kitchen towel.

Mititei (Romania)
GRILLED BEEF SAUSAGES

To make about 18 small sausages

2 pounds lean ground beef, preferably neck, ground together with ¼ pound fresh beef kidney suet
2 teaspoons finely chopped garlic
½ teaspoon ground allspice
¼ teaspoon ground cloves
¼ teaspoon crumbled dried thyme
1½ teaspoons salt
⅛ teaspoon freshly ground black pepper
½ cup beef stock, fresh or canned
Vegetable oil

Combine the beef and suet with the garlic, allspice, cloves, thyme, salt and pepper in a deep bowl. Knead vigorously with both hands until the ingredients are well blended. Then pour in the stock and beat with a wooden spoon until the mixture is smooth and fluffy. Taste for seasoning.

Divide the mixture into 18 equal portions and roll each one into a cylinder about 3½ inches long and 1 inch thick, moistening your hands with cold water as you proceed.

Preheat the broiler to its highest setting. Brush the rack of a broiler pan lightly with oil and arrange the sausages side by side on the rack. Broil them about 3 inches from the heat for about 8 minutes, turning them with a spatula or tongs every few minutes until they are crisp and brown on all sides.

Serve the *mititei* at once from a heated platter. Traditionally, the sausages are accompanied by peppers in oil *(below)* and sour dill pickles.

Ardei cu Untdelemn (Romania)
PEPPERS IN OIL

To serve 4 to 6

6 medium-sized bell peppers, green or red
½ cup olive oil
½ cup white wine vinegar
½ cup cold water
2 teaspoons imported paprika
1 tablespoon salt
Freshly ground black pepper
12 ripe black olives, preferably Mediterranean type
Brynza cheese, or substitute *feta* cheese, cut into 1-inch cubes
8 to 12 scallions, trimmed and washed

Roast the peppers in the following fashion: Impale them, one at a time, on the tines of a long-handled fork and turn them over a gas flame until the skin blisters and darkens. Or place the peppers on a baking sheet and broil them 3 inches from the heat for about 15 minutes, turning them so that they color on all sides. As the peppers are roasted, wrap them in a damp towel and let them rest for 5 minutes. Rub them with the towel until the burned skins slip off, but leave the stems intact.

In a deep bowl combine the olive oil, vinegar, water, paprika, salt and a few grindings of pepper. Beat vigorously with a whisk or a fork until the ingredients are combined, then taste for seasoning. Add the peppers and turn them about with a spoon until they are coated on all sides.

Marinate at room temperature for 3 or 4 hours, turning the peppers over occasionally. Then cover the bowl tightly with foil or plastic wrap and refrigerate for at least 24 hours before serving. Peppers in oil are traditionally served on a platter, moistened with some of their marinade and garnished with black olives, cheese and scallions.

Serve as a salad course or as an accompaniment to *mititei (above)*.

V

Tunisia—Algeria—Morocco

An Exploration of the Exotic

A crabapple seller awaits customers in Sidi Bou Said, a suburb of Tunis famous for the sky blue of its doors, shutters and iron grillwork. The bittersweet crabapples, growing wild in the mountains, are smaller than most American varieties; the Tunisians, instead of making them into jellies and preserves, prefer them raw, right from the basket.

Frances and I looked forward to our first visit to North Africa with equal excitement but—as usual when we travel together—with different expectations. She had read a great deal about North Africa's history and the religion of its predominantly Muslim population; my eye was fixed firmly on North Africa's culinary compass, although I found its needle swinging disconcertingly in every direction. Would the cuisine be the classic one Tunisians, Algerians and Moroccans proudly claim it to be? Or would each country's cooking elude definition, mirroring the confusing culinary traditions of various rulers across the centuries?

During our flight to Tunisia, the first country on our North African itinerary, we studied the map. To our eager eyes, Tunisia had the shape of a flowering bush, with its back against Algeria on the west and its roots in the Sahara. On the north and east, it basked in Mediterranean sunlight. It was from the Mediterranean that Tunisia's first settlers had come —peaceful Phoenician traders who lifted their chief city, Carthage, to such heights of riches and culture that it was subsequently overrun by a succession of envious predators: Romans, Vandals, Byzantines, Arabs, Turks, Spaniards, Italians, and most recently, the French. The French had occupied Tunisia for 75 years, Algeria for 130 and Morocco for over 40. Now that they are no longer "protectors" of the Maghreb—as North Africa is called by its own inhabitants—I was all the more interested to see if the cuisine had withstood the blandishments of French cooking, surely the most pervasive in the Western world.

My ruminations ceased the moment we arrived at the Tunis airport, El

A Tunisian lad in Sidi Bou Said surveys a street vendor's selection of *kaaki*, bread sticks made simply with flour, salt and water. Small ones cost a penny or two, the large round ones about four cents. They are sold all over Tunis, but hawkers find business especially brisk near schools, since children are partial to *kaaki* as recess snacks.

Aouina. Although it is as modern as other airports throughout the world, its atmosphere made us wonder if we had not been wafted there on a magic carpet instead of a plane; we appeared to have landed in another world and in another age. Except for the blue-uniformed clerks, there were no other men in sight. But around us everywhere were ivory-skinned Muslim women draped in parchment-colored cloths—*safsari* that covered them from head to ankles. We were bewitched by their dark eyes rimmed with the smoky Arabic cosmetic, kohl, and by the effortless, graceful way in which they manipulated their draperies. Noting bundles, boxes and straw-covered bottles on the floor beside them, Frances surmised that the women were on a Muslim pilgrimage, and that the paraphernalia probably included the food they traditionally took with them on such trips. (Later we discovered that this was true indeed, and that their packages and bottles had undoubtedly contained, among other foods, *mhammes*—hand-rolled pasta made from semolina grain—sweet pastries; olive oil; orange and rose water for flavoring desserts, and a preserved meat called *quaddid*.) Absorbed by the clusters of murmuring, fluttering females, we were surprised by the sudden emergence of a definitely contemporary Western woman—blue-eyed, golden-haired, and chicly dressed—who was walking directly toward us. She could only have been Tanya Matthews, with whom we had corresponded through mutual friends; as had been prearranged, she had come to meet us.

Tanya, a well-known journalist, had been living for many years in Sidi Bou Said, a small suburb a few miles outside Tunis where we were to stay at the Hotel Sidi Bou Said, close to Tanya's house. We had expected to go directly there, but Tanya, knowing the purpose of my trip, suggested that we stop briefly for a snack at a typical Tunis café.

To our surprise and, I must confess, dismay, the city was teeming with cars and was as raucous and bustling as New York, Paris or London. But there the similarity ended. At the café there were only men—all wearing turbans or stiff maroon-colored hats called *chéchia* and the flowing woolen robes of North Africa, jellabas. Animatedly engaging in conversation, the men were sipping lemonade and eating an assortment of vegetables, each in its own little dish. I would have liked some wine, but knowing the Muslim prohibition against drinking it I was resigned to ordering lemonade when Tanya said, "Why not try a *boukha?*" This, she explained, was a native brandy distilled from figs, a centuries-old invention of the Jews of North Africa. A number of dietary laws, I knew, were shared by Muslims and Jews—a ritual animal slaughter and a stern proscription against the eating of pork—but, happily, a ban on the imbibing of alcohol was not one of them.

The *boukha* arrived at the table and was soon followed by the array of vegetables that customarily accompanies it: strips of carrots, celery, turnips and zucchini and tiny buds of cauliflower, all uncooked but sharply brined, and so artfully prepared as to keep their natural flavors intact. I could readily understand, as I alternately sipped my slightly sweet and very potent *boukha* and bit into each briny vegetable in turn, why this marriage of opposites was so successful.

I would have been perfectly content to sit for hours in the café, lulled

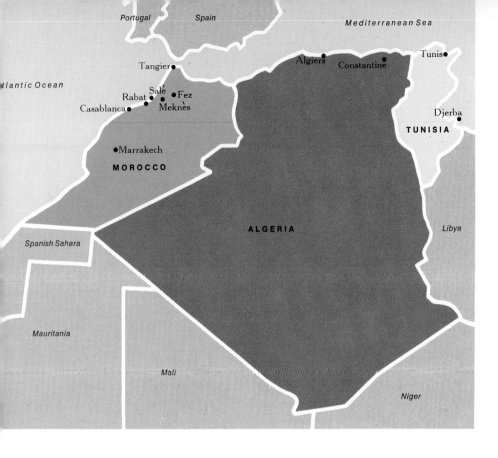

Morocco, Algeria and Tunisia occupy the northwest corner of the African continent, part of the region between Egypt and the Atlantic, the Sahara and the Mediterranean known in Arabic as Maghreb—the west. (The Maghreb also included Spain when that country was under Muslim sway.) The North African cuisine has qualities in common with the Arabic food of the Middle East, but it has its own sophisticated distinctions.

by the brandy and watching the passersby and the flower sellers offering their wares in packets of heavy green fig leaves. The leaves enclosed a single, open-petaled, fragrant jasmine—traditionally meant for women; for men the jasmine petals were tied together with fine red string, to be worn tucked over the ear, as our flower seller was doing. I bought flowers for Tanya and Frances, a long-stemmed one for myself, and bravely placing the flower behind my ear in true Tunisian fashion paid the bill with a flourish and escorted the ladies to the car.

If what we saw of Tunis had evoked fewer exotic notes than we had hoped for, Sidi Bou Said more than made up for it. While driving along the modern macadam road that leads to Carthage, now desolate, brown and barren, Tanya made a sharp turn onto a gray cobblestoned path worn glassy-smooth with age; we began a slow, steep ascent as if heading into the sky. At the very top we were blinded by a mass of gleaming white box-like houses overlooking the Gulf of Tunis, whose waters were tranquil, luminous and intensely blue.

Glistening mosaics, exquisite in design and color, lit our way up the sunny steps of the Hotel Sidi Bou Said to the cool, shadowed interior. As we followed the leather-slippered Arab boys carrying the luggage, our heels clacked anachronistically on the floor of a patio where four upright white beams formed a large frame through which we could see the burning sky. A pale-blue iron grille curved out from the window of our room; below it, orange trees and bushes of dazzling colors grew in profusion everywhere, and fountains trickled, delicately caressing the ear.

Tanya's house was even more entrancing. Faded blue doors opened onto a flower-filled patio surrounded by what seemed an endless series of rooms; I caught glimpses of a pink-flecked marble bathtub, a delicate Per-

Continued on page 152

147

Couscous: All Things to All North Africans

Infinitely varied, *couscous* is found everywhere in North Africa, from Suez to the Atlantic. The name is a confusing one because it applies both to a great many finished dishes and to the grains that are their basic common ingredient. The grains are pellets of wheat or semolina (though they may be corn, barley or groats) that are moistened with water and oil, dried and then steamed. Sometimes *couscous* is eaten alone, like pasta, or is sweetened and served as dessert, but generally it is served with a host of other ingredients—meats, fowl, vegetables, spices—which are piled on and around a foundation of grain. The result: *couscous*. That is the dish being prepared for dinner by the Tunisian woman shown here—and being prepared in countless other Tunisian homes at the same time.

In the patio of a Berber home in Sidi Bou Said, Madame Ben Ahmed assembles a *couscous* with her daughter's help. First she arranges the *couscous* grain in a serving dish, then places an array of vegetables and stewed chicken on top *(above)*. The grain was steamed over the pot in which the other ingredients were cooking, and has absorbed their flavor. The round bowl holds a peppery sauce to be poured over the completed *couscous*. At right, Madame Ben Ahmed shows the dish, a splendid collage of green peppers, potatoes, hard-boiled eggs, pumpkin, carrots, chick-peas, okra, chicken and, of course, *couscous*.

In Tunisian style, seated in a circle and using their fingers, the Ben Ahmed family eats the *couscous* on their tiled patio. In the past the head of the family would eat by himself first, often in a separate room; but this custom has been modified to the point where father now eats with everyone else—although he still starts first. The two jugs contain buttermilk; the bowl holds more of the hot sauce that was poured on the *couscous*. When the diners finish the sauce-soaked portion, the whole dish is refreshed with a new infusion *(above)*.

sian bedstead with finely wrought spindles, spots of red showing through aged gold leaf. But I came down to earth at the sight of the kitchen, where Tanya introduced me to Abdul, her smiling Arab cook; then she whisked Frances off and left me on my own to watch the preparation of what she said would be a simple lunch.

Looking about me, I thought it would indeed have to be a relatively simple meal. In a kitchen so small—roughly the size of a long wardrobe closet —it seemed inconceivable that dishes of any complexity could possibly be made, unless prepared by the most skillful of cooks. At a glance I took in the minuscule stove attached to a container of bottled gas, a tin-lined sink, a tiny refrigerator and a long, roughhewn table piled with an unplucked chicken, eggplants, bouquets of herbs, bottles of oil, vinegar and numerous spices, many of which looked unfamiliar. And equally unfamiliar was a variety of metal and ceramic pots.

Picking up a shallow, covered ceramic pot much like one of our casseroles, I asked Abdul in French what it was. *"Tajine,"* he answered, then attempted to explain something that made little sense to me. Frustrated, I lifted the chicken by its feet, and pointing to the vegetables and other ingredients, made a stirring motion with my forefinger in the empty *tajine.* My pantomime seemed ineffectual. Abdul merely smiled again and said, *"tajine,"* indicating the pot with one hand, the ingredients with the other. At last it dawned on me that *tajine* was the name of both the pot and the dish.

Suddenly there occurred the subliminal communication that takes place between cooks everywhere despite language and nationality. I quickly understood that *any* combination of ingredients, however disparate, was called a *tajine* if cooked in a *tajine.* Once we had established this much rapport, Abdul set to work, apparently confident that I would understand everything else he was going to do. Never have I seen a chicken plucked, eviscerated and cut up with such dexterity. And with equal dispatch, the chicken was browned in oil; a handful of spices, tomatoes, cut-up eggplant, chick-peas and crushed garlic were tossed into the *tajine,* and then covered with what seemed to me an inordinate amount of water. Abdul brought the mixture to a turbulent boil, and, to my consternation, let it continue to boil unabated instead of lowering the flame to allow the chicken to simmer as a practiced Western cook would have done. I controlled the impulse to express disapproval at what struck me as the crudest of techniques, and left the *tajine* to its fate. Abdul ignored it from this point on, and busily engaged himself with an entirely new dish. Certain that the *tajine* would be a disaster, I turned my attention to what I could only fear would be another.

Abdul placed a circular, tin-lined copper pan—it had no handles—bottom side up over a pot of boiling water (in a less modern kitchen the pan undoubtedly would have gone over a brazier), and then I watched him toss a couple of handfuls of fine semolina flour into a bowl, moisten it with water, and begin to stir it slowly with his hand. Little by little, the mixture began to thicken into a smooth batter, and the stirring hand movement, as if attuned to the changing texture of the batter, turned into a rapid clutching and releasing one. Almost before I knew it, the batter began to give off a snapping, rubber-band-like sound, and as the sound increased in intensity, my tension increased with it. Without stopping the clutching and releasing movement for a moment, Abdul carried the bowl to the stove. Then, using a small handful of the dough like a sponge, he lightly dotted it all over the very hot oiled surface of the upturned pan. In seconds, the pan was covered with what looked like the thinnest possible circular sheet of translucent mica, the copper beneath it showing through. Abdul then simply peeled the pastry off the pan and placed it gently on a plate. With the greatest of ease, he proceeded to make circle after circle of pastry, which I later learned was called *malsouqua (Recipe Index)*, precisely the same way as before. In my wildest culinary fantasies I had never imagined such a virtuosic performance.

At this crucial moment Tanya and Frances appeared with baskets bulging with purchases from the marketplace in Tunis. "Just in time for a *brik*," Tanya said. "A *what?*" I asked blankly, still under the spell of Abdul's culinary sleight of hand. "Abdul is making pastry for a *brik* with anchovies," she explained, "my favorite hors d'oeuvre." I took their baskets, my head still turned toward the kitchen, determined not to miss a thing. "We'll eat them out here before lunch," Tanya said to Frances as they walked through the patio. I asked Abdul in French, *"Brik aux anchois?"*

Baker and shopkeeper Bechir M'Gandef presides over his pastry store in Sidi Bou Said. The triangular pastry at right is *samsa (Recipe Index)*. In the center is *baklava,* an almond pastry soaked in honey. Behind it is a tray of Tunisian doughnuts called *yo-yo (Recipe Index)*, and a glass case filled with *twajin,* almond cookies dusted with powdered sugar. The bottles in the cabinets contain mint, rose, almond and peanut syrups that go into refreshing drinks.

to which he nodded, amused, and repeated in Arabic, *"Brik bil anchou-wa."* And then he graciously handed me the bowl of batter, as I in his place would have done, and indicated with a smile that I should try my hand. Every cook I know has had a great moment in his culinary life that surpasses description, so powerful is the sense of achievement. Mine was peeling a perfect, filmy circle of *brik* pastry from the pan and laying it on top of Abdul's.

Impressed as I was by the making of these extraordinary pastries, filling and frying them was even more dramatic. On each circle, Abdul dropped a mixture of chopped onions, parsley, capers and anchovies, and sprinkled it with Parmesan cheese. He heated some oil in a large frying pan, then broke an egg directly over the filling, folded the pastry into a half moon and placed it in the now spluttering oil. If anyone had told me that this could be done without sealing the pastry or without losing the egg, I would never have believed it. My startled eyes actually saw the ends of the pastry slowly coming together on their own as they fried in the oil. Abdul turned the *brik* over with a spatula as easily as I might have turned a pancake. In a few minutes, lying before me was a pale golden-brown crescent through which I could see the egg yolk—whole and neatly centered. What he had, in effect, done was to poach the egg while simultaneously cooking the filling and browning the *brik*. Technically, this dish alone *(Recipe Index)*—and I had not yet tasted it—convinced me that, whatever else I would discover about Maghreb cooking, Tunisia had a cuisine to be reckoned with.

Abdul served the *brik* to us in the patio, and Frances, always the most respectful of listeners, paid close attention to Tanya's instructions about how to eat this exclusively Tunisian specialty. "Be sure to start at the center, bite gently, then suck up the yolk," Tanya said, picking up a *brik* with both hands and holding it by the ends. But unlike Frances, I went blithely ahead, as usual, on my own. I made a thorough mess of it, ending up with the egg splattered all over me while Frances, sipping and swallowing, stopped only long enough to describe the *brik* as "divine." If my Tunisian table manners left much to be desired, I was still able to recognize that this dish was a masterpiece; the pastry was lacy edged and crisp, and the pungent, highly spiced filling made a perfect contrast to the blandness of the egg—or what I had managed to salvage of it.

Seated at the dining-room table, I recalled with a sinking feeling the chicken *tajine* to come. While we awaited its arrival, Frances described her visit with Tanya to the Tunis market. I had never known her to be so carried away. Although she told me all about the food she had seen, I knew that for her the experience had been a purely esthetic one. Eggplants were "royal purple," fresh almonds "lime-green velvet." She spoke of the crates of oranges, peaches and apricots as "still lifes" because they had been artfully displayed with their stems and leaves attached. Cages of lively, snow-white chickens were juxtaposed with a Soutine-like eviscerated lamb carcass, and there had even been a grisly Tunisian joke: a lamb's head, neatly skinned, set on a bed of green leaves, smiling, and sporting a smoking cigarette between its blackened teeth.

"Tunisians are artists," Frances said, and went on to describe the bunch-

Tea, liberally sweetened with sugar and flavored with mint, is North Africa's most popular drink. It is consumed at all times of day by all types of people, whether served simply, as in the humble Tunisian café above, or elaborately, as in Tunis' Le Malouf Restaurant *(opposite)*. There, the waiter's well-practiced showmanship not only impresses his customers but also helps cool the tea. A dash of rose water from the silver vial adds fragrance, but it is the sugar and mint leaves that convey the drink's peculiarly North African character.

es of carrots and other root vegetables that had been tied tightly so that they faced outward in the shape of open flowers—all arranged geometrically on shelves covered with bright blue paper matching the sky. Strips of canvas, each a different color, shaded the stalls and billowed like hammocks from one end of the market to the other. "Enough," she sighed, "to make a painter die of envy."

Throughout all this, Tanya was silent and smiling. She was clearly proud of her adopted Tunisia, and pleased that our visit was proving successful. And when Abdul appeared with the *tajine* her smile broadened with confidence. As soon as I tasted it, I realized that my unexpressed fears about its cooking had been premature. The rapid boiling had reduced the water, spices and vegetables to a thick aromatic sauce, and the chicken, instead of falling off the bones as I had expected it would, was remarkably moist yet intact. If I needed further convincing that Tunisians could be great cooks this did it.

The bread, called *pita,* was as fresh and fragrant as the butter Frances had seen churned an hour before in an ancient metal container. We ended this so-called simple lunch with plump, cool Muscat grapes. There would be further "gustatory glories" in Tunisia, Tanya promised as we bade each other goodbye.

On the way to our hotel, Frances recalled that at the market she had eaten a grilled sausage called a *merguez.* "Murderously hot," she said, "but I ate it for your benefit." It had been seasoned with a Tunisian spice, *hrisa (Recipe Index)*—a mixture of crushed dried hot red peppers, ground cumin and salt. Unlike Moroccans, the Tunisians prefer their food highly seasoned, and use *hrisa* in almost everything except desserts. In fact, Tanya had heard that *hrisa* thinned with olive oil and tomato purée was spread on bread and fed to babies. Frances was appalled at the idea but it did not surprise me: I know that highly spiced foods were and still are fed to babies in Mexico and southern India.

Tanya, indefatigable guide that she was, called for us one evening to drive down the coast to Hammamet to have dinner at a small restaurant in the ancient walled quarter of the city. It was quite dark when we arrived there, and the walled quarter as we approached it loomed like a vast, turreted castle, forbidding yet alluring. Inside the walls, tortuous alleys beckoned, but before we had taken more than a few steps, a group of noisy, gesticulating Arab children surrounded us, offering to be our guides. Tanya let them lead us, and strolled unconcernedly with them through dark passages where ancient doors were tightly closed, flush to faceless walls, the only light seeping eerily down from small naked electric bulbs scattered here and there.

We had heard of the legendary hospitality of the Muslims, but these doors, so firmly shut, seemed to make each home an impenetrable fortress. We walked a good way before Tanya told us where we were heading. As she explained later, the leader of the group, a black-eyed, ringleted urchin with an engaging smile, had been unwilling to give exact information without her subtle prodding. He was taking us to see his mother's embroidery in the hope that we might buy it. We soon discovered, as we were to rediscover time and again in North Africa, that however unfriendly and anonymous closed doors in the alleys of the old cities might seem, once they are opened to guest or stranger they reveal welcome, warmth and generosity.

The children led us through a dimly lit courtyard open to the sky. As in our hotel and at Tanya's house, there were numerous rooms surrounding it. Tanya explained that it was not uncommon for a North African family of several generations from infants to great-grandparents to live together in houses similar to this one. Although the atmosphere struck us as impoverished—sleeping children lay rolled up in thin blankets on the floor, and the communal kitchen was primitive—it was, in fact, luxurious compared to the lot of the many Tunisians who sleep in the streets and live solely on bread dipped in olive oil.

Curiously, we inspected the embroidery, which, unfortunately, was not to our taste. Nevertheless, the boy's mother invited us into another room where a group of older people were seated on the floor eating their dinner. It was steaming in a common bowl set on a low table; each diner dipped a chunk of bread into it and mopped up his share. When they asked us to join them, Tanya made elaborate and appropriate excuses but I, curious to taste the deep red, soupy concoction I had heard Tanya call *chakchouka,* accepted at once. I expected the *chakchouka* to be hot, but at

Rain or shine, shepherds and merchants meet every week to haggle over the price of sheep at the *souk,* or market, at El Harrach, 10 miles outside Algiers. In Muslim Algeria, where pork products are taboo, sheep are the main source of meat, and *mechoui,* a lamb roasted whole on a spit, is one of the cornerstones of the cuisine.

The *kouba,* or local Muslim shrine, of the farming hamlet of El Ganzra stands in dazzling contrast to the muted tones of northern Morocco's rolling hill country. Moroccans respect the sanctity of such shrines, which are common throughout the land, even though the names of the holy men buried in them may have been forgotten long ago.

the first bite it streaked across my tongue like a lash, and it took every effort of my will to keep from gasping.

By the time we arrived at the restaurant my numbed taste buds had recovered some of their sensibility, and I was ready to take on the dish I had been most particularly looking forward to—*couscous,* the pillar of North African cooking.

The restaurant had attained some eminence among visitors to Tunisia because of the fine quality of its cooking. Tanya knew the cook, and when she asked him if I could go into the kitchen he couldn't have been more gracious. "I would deem it an honor," he said in French, and led me into the small immaculate kitchen where the *couscous* was steaming in a pot in which it is traditionally made—a *couscoussier.* As in a double boiler, the top pot is inserted into the bottom one, but the top pot has small sievelike openings in its base. And the top pot is always left uncovered while the *couscous* is steaming, which ensures that the fine semolina of which *couscous* is made remains separated in small moist pellets instead of becoming a gummy mass.

I observed with interest the moistened band of cloth wedged between the top and bottom pots of the *couscoussier,* assuming—as it turned out, correctly—that the cloth was a primitive device to seal the two pots together. Thus the aromatic steam from the boiling *tajine* in the lower pot could rise in full force through the holes in the *couscoussier* above it and flavor the grains as they steamed. The *tajine* for our *couscous,* the cook said, removing the top pot so I could see it, was a special delicacy. Unlike the usual *tajine* of lamb or chicken, this was made of beef. I could identify the beef, of course, but was impressed at the number of varicolored vegetables swirling about it in the bubbling sauce: cabbage, carrots, turnips, zucchini, pumpkin, potatoes, chick-peas and tomatoes. Thinking of the *chakchouka* I had tasted en route to the restaurant, I asked the cook if the sauce was red because it contained *hrisa.* He delightedly informed me that it was, and added that the *couscous* when served would be moistened with some of the sauce, with the remaining sauce flavored with still more *hrisa,* served in a separate bowl.

Back at the table I warned Frances to tackle the *couscous* warily, reminding her of the *merguez* she had eaten at the Tunis marketplace and of my more recent confrontation with the *chakchouka.* When the *couscous* appeared on its large platter with the semolina in the middle surrounded by the vegetables and meat, it was not only accompanied by the bowl of *hrisa*-spiced sauce but by three small dishes of relishes as well: a simple combination of lime-flavored salted cucumbers and green peppers *(Recipe Index),* rounds of lime-flavored white turnips *(Recipe Index),* and a potato salad flavored with olive oil, lemon juice and caraway seeds *(Recipe Index).* And to compound my concern, each of these, except for the cucumber relish, was liberally spiked with *hrisa.*

I approached the Tunisian *couscous* like the conductor of a small orchestra, listening to each instrument in turn to make sure it was in tune: I first tasted the grains of *couscous,* and was gratified to find they had indeed absorbed the flavor of the *tajine;* then bit into a chunk of beef in which I could detect a faint note of *hrisa.* With each successive vegetable I sampled, the *hrisa* became more and more apparent. Having completed this cautious survey, I served myself a generous helping of *couscous,* meat and vegetables, and throwing caution to the winds, poured a large spoonful of the *hrisa*-flavored sauce over it. Despite the fiery *hrisa,* each flavor of this incomparable ensemble, called *kouski bil lahm (Recipe Index),* was clearly apparent. What with the relishes, which intrigued me further, I cannot remember for the life of me whether Frances and Tanya got their share of the *couscous,* although they assured me they had.

The meal ended with *tmar mihchi (Recipe Index),* heavily sugared date confections. What made them so remarkable was their stuffing, a paste of pistachio nuts flavored exotically with rose water. So dramatic a juxtaposition of the fiery *hrisa* to the luxuriously sweet dates underlined the imaginativeness with which Tunisians cook and serve their food.

I consumed the dates slowly, one by one, realizing with a feeling akin to nostalgia that we were to leave Tunisia the next day. But the nostalgia was not unmixed with excitement about what we had found in this enchanting country. Despite all my apprehensions that Tunisian cooking would be eclectic or at least French oriented, I had discovered the very reverse to be true. Every dish we had eaten during our brief stay had had a tone that was vibrantly and distinctively Tunisian.

Leaving Sidi Bou Said was painful, but we had a plane reservation for Algeria, where we were to spend a short time investigating the food be-

fore going on to Morocco. Tanya drove us out to the airport. We felt like old friends; she had accepted an invitation to stay with us in New York in a month, and we hoped to visit her in Tunis again not too long afterward. We made poignant farewells—and then discovered that we had not only missed the plane by hours but that there would not be another flight to Algeria for days. Tanya, used to coping with what seemed to foreigners in her care to be insurmountable problems, raised our spirits at once. We would return to Sidi Bou Said for the night, she said, fly directly to Morocco the next day, and in the interim she would tell us about Algeria, which she knew almost as well as she did Tunisia. By the time we got back to the hotel, we had begun to accumulate interesting facts simply from Tanya's running commentary.

Algeria's Nomads and Urbanites

Algeria is almost three and a half times the size of Texas—but less than a fifth of the land is agricultural. The most intensely cultivated part is in a fertile coastal strip called the Tell, which lies between the Mediterranean Sea and the Tellian Atlas mountain range. Here great quantities of grapes, citrus fruits and vegetables are grown. South of the Tell is the region called the High Plateau, which extends into Morocco on the west and rises to about 3,000 feet above sea level. Here animals graze and cereal grains are grown. The produce of the Tell and the Plateau is the basis of Algerian cooking: the cereals go into breads and *couscous,* the livestock ends up in lamb dishes, the fruits are used to flavor meats and desserts, and the grapes are pressed into wine for export or for drinking by non-Muslim Algerians. Virtually everywhere else, Algeria is desert, wasteland and mountains. These facts are important, I feel, for it is Algeria's topography that limits the country's cuisine when compared to the cuisines of its neighbors on either side.

In the vast Sahara (which covers most of Algeria), vegetation is scant, to say the least, yet the awesome, arid desert does contain some grazing land for goats, sheep and camels, as well as oases where dates are produced. It also harbors a sparse nomad population, approximately one person per square mile. It was to meet the needs of these intrepid people, the Bedouins, that the simple Algerian cooking evolved: on their long treks across the desert to feed and water their animals, they cook their lamb either by grilling it or by transforming it into the simple one-pot dishes called *tajine,* similar to their counterparts found all over North Africa.

Tanya gave us a poetic account of desert cooking, describing a feast she had attended. The high point of the meal was a *mechoui,* a whole spitted baby lamb that had been roasting for hours over a smoldering fire. As she spoke, we could almost see the weather-beaten faces of the tall, slender men seated cross-legged on patterned rugs, their turbans and woven woolen robes white under a starry sky, and the sand stretching away to infinity. Nearby were the camels, neatly hobbled. In a trench dug deep in the sand a fire glowed, and above it the lamb, richly anointed with butter, hung taut, its legs tied to a stick. A boy fanned the flames and basted the lamb with more spices and butter. The feast began when the meat had become tender enough to be picked off in strips with the fingers.

Opposite: Sheltered in the hollow of a mountain about 35 miles west of Fez, Moulay Idriss is Morocco's holiest city. It is named for the country's first Muslim ruler, who is buried in the sanctuary marked by green-tiled roofs. Each September tens of thousands of devout Moroccan Muslims pay homage to him by making a *moussem,* or pilgrimage, to the holy city.

After we had envisioned this desert *mechoui,* it came as a surprise to us to hear that *mechoui* is also made in Algeria's cities, although with some adaptations in the way it is prepared. City dwellers, Tanya explained, often cut their lamb into halves or quarters and roast them over charcoal-filled braziers just as we would barbecue our meats. So seriously do urbanites take their *mechoui* that before a Muslim feast it is not unusual to hear the bleating of lambs that are temporarily tethered on apartment balconies.

In the cities, of course, the influence of the French cuisine still persists strongly, an inevitable aftereffect of the long period of French occupation. For example, the French *baguette,* a long, thin, crusty loaf, seems to have superseded *kesra,* the round Arab bread made in clay ovens, which is still much in evidence in mountain villages. City dwellers buy their *baguettes* from the bakery in the morning—not in ones and twos, but more often in bundles that resemble armloads of kindling wood. As for desserts, one is as likely to see a school child eating an éclair as a *makroud el louse,* an indigenous Algerian cookie composed of finely ground almonds, grated lemon rind, sugar and eggs *(Recipe Index).*

The French influence is also clear in the Algerians' wine production. Coming from vineyards cultivated for generations by the French, the wines are surprisingly like the lesser ones of southern France and, in fact, were formerly exported to France in great quantities. Now that the French have left Algeria, it appears that the vineyards are receiving less attention, and I have heard that the once-pampered vines now have more the look of bushy trees. Of course, the Muslims do not drink wine anyway, and so production cannot be expected to remain at its former standards.

Although the influence of France persists, it is nevertheless not all-pervasive in the cuisine. Algerians prefer their food highly seasoned, and have always heightened the flavor of dishes borrowed from France with *hrisa,* cinnamon and other herbs and spices. And the Algerians naturally have retained many of their own dishes that they enjoyed for centuries before the French ever came. One example is *sferia,* a chicken *tajine* flavored with cinnamon and onions and accompanied by chick-peas and cheese-flavored croquettes *(Recipe Index).* I have since cooked this intriguing combination; while milder than most Algerian dishes, it is not French at all—and exceedingly good.

If the French have made an imprint on Algerian cooking, Algeria has, in a sense, returned the compliment. A number of restaurants in Paris and other cities serve Algerian food, and a few of these establishments are excellent. While many of the more exotic Algerian dishes are not regularly on the menus, an Algerian version of *couscous (Recipe Index)* is a great favorite among native Parisians as well as among exiled *pied-noirs,* as the Frenchmen who lived in Algeria were known when the land belonged to France.

An Eating Journey into Morocco

If on the map Frances and I had studied en route to North Africa, Tunisia looked like a flowering bush, Morocco resembled a pantalooned leg —its shin running along the Atlantic on the west, its calf touching Algeria on the east, and its foot flat on Spanish Sahara. We flew over the northern part of Morocco—with the narrow Strait of Gibraltar that separates it from Europe somewhere off to the right out our window—and landed in Casablanca, Morocco's chief Atlantic port. From the air, Casablanca, or "white house" in Spanish, struck us as aptly named. Under a blue dome-like sky, the city resembled a dazzling white pebble-strewn beach extending to the horizon. Once on the ground, however, we thought we must have seen a mirage from the air; for Casablanca's buildings, perhaps once white, were now a soft ivory color reminiscent of the Muslim women's *safsari* in Tunis.

Casablanca, planned by the French, is a cosmopolitan city with broad palm-lined avenues, air-conditioned office buildings, and department-store windows glittering with lavish displays—in short, we decided, a miniature Paris. To add to this impression, El Mansour, our hotel, rivaled in magnificence the Paris Ritz, one of the grandest hotels in the world. To our great fortune, Stephen Hughes, an English journalist and long-time Moroccan resident, was to act as our guide. He had already arranged introductions for us in Marrakech, Fez and Tangier to gentlemen as culinarily knowing as himself, and he saw to it, too, that our first dinner with him was an example of Moroccan cooking at its best.

Al Mounia, the Casablanca restaurant to which he took us, reawakened the awe I had felt when I first read *The Arabian Nights*. We were seated on low, luxuriously covered banquettes backed by embroidered pillows; I was tempted to recline against them in Oriental fashion so that I could admire the multicolored tiles that decorated every inch of the walls and ceiling, but I resisted the impulse and sat stiffly erect, as did the other diners, in front of our low table, an etched, highly burnished brass tray set on carved legs.

Waiters, the tassels of their tall fezzes whipping the air, moved swiftly and silently in backless pointed slippers called babouches. They smiled gently if inscrutably as we went through the Muslim predining ritual of hand washing. We held out our hands, palms cupped over a bowl, while the waiters poured warm rose-perfumed water into them from a long spout of a copper kettle, then gave us immaculate white linen towels. I felt like a pasha, but a nervous one, when Stephen told me that I was expected to eat with the thumb and two fingers of my right hand, using chunks of bread as an aid for scooping and dipping. Stephen showed us how to do it: he moved his thumb back and forth between his first and second fingers, forming, in effect, an activated, three-pronged fork. Remembering the carelessness with which I ate my first *brik* at Tanya's I now paid careful attention to Stephen, and decided that I would have no difficulty whatever.

I shouldn't have been quite so sanguine. When the first course appeared I could scarcely believe I was expected to eat it with my fingers; it was a whole bass, rose-tinted with paprika, its sauce seasoned with cumin, garlic and parsley *(Recipe Index)*. Frances was fearless. Following Stephen's lead she delicately plucked a piece of fish off the bones and quickly popped it into her mouth as if she had eaten this way all her life. In Moroccan fashion, she discreetly wiped her fingers on her bread, dipped it into the sauce, then ate it. I plunged in bravely, and instantly discovered why Frances had eaten the fish so quickly—it was simply too hot to hold. Except for that, though, I decided this finger eating wasn't difficult at all.

At the second or third helping of fish, I found that for the sheer sensual joy of tasting food in its pristine state, fingers are best, because a fork, even of the finest silver, intrudes with its own alien flavor and texture. This discovery prompted a stream of associations in my mind: ripe, sun-warmed tomatoes plucked from the vine and eaten on the spot; freshly baked bread eaten with the hands; a ripe banana; or even the lowly but delicious hamburger on a bun. For the first time I really understood why the Chinese and Japanese use chopsticks—as aids to direct the food *to* the mouth, but not to accompany it *into* the mouth. The lamb and honey *tajine (Recipe Index),* our second course, I savored in the same new way, and was enchanted besides by its sweetness, an unexpected nuance after the pungency of the fish.

Stephen suggested we have a rich dessert, a nut-filled pastry dripping with honey, but by now another sweet would have been too much of a good thing for me. We had, instead, what Moroccans consider a salad but seemed to me a perfect dessert: chilled orange sections arranged in a sunburst pattern in which the *suprêmes,* as the French would call them, overlapped one another in concentric circles on a beautifully designed ceramic platter. The *suprêmes* had been sprinkled with orange-blossom water, and finely powdered cinnamon and sugar radiated in alternating strands from the center outward in the pattern of a pinwheel *(Recipe Index).* It was almost too beautiful to eat but so enticing I could hardly wait to plunge in. The taste of the succulent orange was a tart, refreshing antidote to the honey-sweetened *tajine.*

I would have liked some Turkish coffee but Stephen, a stickler for tradition, explained that in a restaurant such as this one the only correct end to a Moroccan meal was freshly brewed green tea flavored with mint and a great deal of sugar—"loaf sugar," he added, "lovingly chopped into chunks with a special brass or silver-plated hammer." At the first sip it was apparent that this was not tea as I knew it but a lime-green liquid powerfully seasoned with mint, and almost unbearably sweet.

Even more unexpected was the spectacular manner in which it was served. Much as a sommelier in an elegant French restaurant is dressed so as to distinguish him from the waiters, the mint-tea server was as extravagantly costumed as a nobleman in an ancient Persian miniature painting. Holding a heavily embossed, long-spouted silver kettle several feet above the table, he poured the boiling-hot tea in a graceful arc into short narrow glasses—without spilling a drop.

After managing to down most of my tea, I learned to my distress that we were expected, according to Moroccan custom, to have two glasses more. But at each new serving, I somehow succeeded in switching my full glass with Frances' empty one, in a not-too-subtle effort to avoid offending Stephen and the hovering tea server. If they noticed my clumsy maneuver (I'm certain they did) they gave no sign.

Before leaving us that night, Stephen alerted us to the fact that a Madame Becheton would meet us early in the morning to introduce us to our French-speaking chauffeur, who was to drive us all over Morocco. Madame Becheton, he said, was a young, sophisticated Moroccan who ran a car rental service in Rabat, the capital, some 60 miles farther north on the coast. The next morning we found her waiting in the hotel lobby, smiling a cordial welcome. I asked her to tell the chauffeur that we wanted to avoid the usual tourist spots because the purpose of our trip was to sample as much Moroccan cooking as we could. Little did I expect that at the mention of food we would hit it off so well. She immediately asked if we would visit Rabat sometime in the next few days to have dinner with her and her husband. She would cook it herself, she said, and added with some pride that I would be able to see how a modern, liberated Moroccan working woman adapted the preparation of the traditional cuisine to the demands of contemporary living. We were delighted to accept, and meanwhile took off on our own explorations.

How very different were the outskirts of Casablanca from its modern center. As we whizzed through them on our way to Marrakech, we caught fleeting but vivid glimpses of crowds of Muslims: the men wore striped jellabas, babouches, and turbans as we had seen them in Tunis, but the women wore not *safsari,* but what in Morocco are also called jellabas —long-sleeved, hooded, straight sacks down to the ankles and seamed up the sides. In addition, most of the women were veiled; squares of dark, opaque cloth covered the lower half of their faces and their throats, leaving only their eyes exposed. The veil—yashmak—as well as the jellaba worn in the streets had an age-old purpose: protection for women from the advances of men. Once a girl reached puberty she had to wear the veil and jellaba until she married. Then she could reveal herself—but only to her husband, who might never have seen her face before.

The road outside the city was flanked by fields of grain as far as the eye could see. It was a lyrical landscape—gold, with only now and then a strip of green. Animating the scene were glossy, dark-brown horses; flocks of black-nosed sheep, their thick wool the color of *café au lait;* single-humped, thin-legged baby camels, little heads held high, ears perky and stiff. After we had driven for several hours, hamlets began to appear more frequently and closer to the road. We could see Berber women lined up with jugs, waiting their turn at ancient wells; the road, which until now had been almost free of traffic, was gradually becoming crowded with mules so overloaded with bales and baskets that we could see only their hooves. An old man in a snow-white turban, jellaba and babouches put-putted by, hunched over the handle bars of a motor bike of the latest design. Date palms appeared, then low squatting houses of red clay. Suddenly the landscape had become tropical. "Marrakech," our chauffeur said. And in minutes we were driving down a spacious avenue lined with jacaranda trees in full bloom, the purple flowers brilliant against the red houses.

Without even unpacking at our hotel, we telephoned Stephen Hughes' friend, Christopher Wanklyn, a Canadian writer who had lived for many years in the Marrakech *medina,* as the ancient Arab quarters of North African cities are known. Christopher had already made elaborate gastronomic plans. First we would tour the Marrakech market, and later have dinner at his home. We were enchanted, of course, especially since now we would see yet another aspect of North African living behind those ever-mysterious *medina* doors.

We had an unsettling sensation of *déjà vu* when we arrived at the unbelievably large market because every kind of fruit, vegetable and species of fowl that we had ever seen in an American or European market was here. Where we expected, perhaps, more exotic produce, there were young peas in their pods, watermelons, cauliflowers, cabbages, thick white and slender green asparagus, bright yellow lemons, dark red cherries, ripe and green almonds, tiny new potatoes, large white radishes, pale yellow grapefruit, baskets of strawberries and oranges.

The meat section was so immense as to make our largest American supermarkets seem meager by comparison; it looked like the world's warehouse of live turkeys, guinea hens, rabbits, ducks, chickens and squabs—each species housed in its own slatted cage. The creatures were sold live—stuffed squalling, quacking, squawking and clucking into shopping bags and baskets—and all the buying was done by men. Christopher explained that the animals were bought live to be slaughtered later in the Muslim ritual manner. And as for men doing the marketing, most Muslim women in Morocco are virtually cloistered as far as worldly affairs are concerned; moreover, all shops are run by men. Christopher pointed out that few Muslim women would even be capable of bargaining in true Arab style—a veritable tradition in itself, which we were observing at that very moment as buyer and seller haggled noisily over the price of a struggling chicken.

In another large area of the market were bins filled to the brim with dried legumes, spices and pasta of every kind, but an even larger area was allotted to countless sacks of semolina, ranging from coarse to fine, used for *couscous,* which the Moroccans, like the Tunisians and Algerians, consider their national dish. Out in the bright sunlight on high wooden tables were displayed blackened sheepsheads, obviously roasted over charcoal. In front of one of them stood a portly buyer in a white jellaba, his head swathed in a turban just as dazzlingly white, his eyes closed and his mouth expectantly open. Spearing a sliver of satiny pink mutton on the tip of a small dagger, the vendor placed it in his customer's mouth. As discreetly as we could, we observed the gentleman's pleasure at what was obviously considered by Moroccans a delicacy.

The last thing we saw—or, more accurately, smelled—before Christopher dragged us away was a small booth in which was sold a substance resembling butter, called *smen* in Arabic. *Smen,* Christopher said, is rancid or aged butter and is used extensively in Moroccan cooking. I had tasted imported bottled *smen* in New York and found it not quite to my liking, although not unpleasant in the least. In modern Morocco, Christopher told me, it is being slowly replaced by fresh butter and oil, both considerably less expensive and more easily available.

If anything could surpass what we had just seen, it was the transformation that had taken place at the vast square, the Place Jemaa el Fna, which we had crossed earlier on our way to the market and found virtually empty. Now the crowds were so dense and the activities all about us so frenzied that we could scarcely push our way through to the entrance of the *medina* and thus to Christopher's house. Twice we were almost run down, first by the high, creaking wheels of a horse-drawn carriage, then by a motor bike zooming wildly in front of the horse. I thought it a miracle that we got to Christopher's house unscathed.

Christopher opened his brass-studded door onto a tiled patio: perfect taste was evident everywhere. In fact, it was so elegant—exquisitely hand-wrought iron bird cages, potted exotic plants, a small fountain—that Frances and I could not help reminding each other of the impoverished interior behind a similar door we had seen in the Hammamet *medina* in Tunisia. At Christopher's all was calm and serenity. As we sipped our Scotch, American fashion, in his modern, comfortable sitting room off the patio, we commented on the quiet here and the cacophony in the Place Jemaa el Fna nearby. "It's not always so quiet here," Christopher replied, and went on to tell us of his neighbors. He had never met them but had come to the conclusion that they were rich, because every few months there were unmistakable sounds of revelry coming from the house on the left, sometimes going on for two or three days and nights. Only a rich orthodox Muslim could afford all-night feasts, Christopher went on; the more elaborate of these followed the return from the long, expensive pilgrimage to Mecca, the birthplace of the Prophet Muhammad in faraway Saudi Arabia. By making the trip to Mecca, a Muslim not only is rewarded with the enviable title, "Hadji," but his way to heaven after death is assured. No amount of money is spared for the elaborate banquet called a *diffa* that celebrates a Muslim's return from his pilgrimage.

Christopher added that he was more immediately concerned with his own rather smaller *diffa* to celebrate our arrival; to do us even greater honor he had been working on it all day himself, with the assistance of his cook. He left us briefly, then returned to tell us that dinner was ready.

Our first course was the soup called *harira (Recipe Index),* made of lamb, a subtle spectrum of spices, and a lemon-and-cinnamon-flavored broth thickened with eggs. Christopher had made it so that we could taste one of Morocco's oldest, most inspired creations, and for another reason as well: it plays a dramatic role in Ramadan, Islam's great annual fast. For the 28 days of Ramadan, Muslims may not eat, drink or smoke from sunup to sundown. And because the Muslim calendar is based on the lunar year, the month of Ramadan is as likely to fall in midsummer as in winter. The end of each day's fast is announced by the firing of a cannon; at that instant, the first taste of food is always a spoonful of *harira,* the soup we were then eating. Christopher said—and quite seriously —that if we were to visit during Ramadan, we would hear at the crucial second before the first mouthful of *harira* a collective sigh of relief billowing throughout all Islam.

My respect for Christopher's gifts as a cook was increased when he served us a steamed chicken stuffed with nuts, raisins, and *couscous* flavored with honey *(Recipe Index).* The chicken was tender as a steamed chicken should be. And I was impressed that he had used the *couscous* as a stuffing, since it is more often served separately. The crisp, golden skin of the bird could only have been the result of its having been fried after the steaming. The Chinese often use this procedure and I know from experience that it takes considerable skill. With these two dishes, coming after those we had had in Casablanca and before that in Tunisia, I was beginning to discern a profile I had doubted I would find in North African cooking. By the time we departed for Fez, I found myself agreeing with Christopher's contention that North African cooking was one of the world's fine cuisines.

We drove north to Fez on the circuitous Middle Atlas mountain route. The trip through the mountains was, as everyone had promised, spectacular. We drove on a winding, climbing road past pink cliffs, sheer drops, lush gorges, and boulders of different shapes, sizes and colors—one on top of another as if carved and assembled into astonishing balance by a master contemporary sculptor. Valleys sloped toward the horizon and white-domed *kouba*—small shrines containing the remains of "wise men" —dotted the landscape like gleaming pearls. Not far from Fez we passed a thickly wooded forest. Grazing there was a large herd of inky-black goats, and nearby the goatherd stood leaning on a staff, his gaze aimed at the sky as he plaintively piped a flute.

The hotel Palais Jamai, once the palace of a grand vizier, stood at the entrance to the Ninth Century *medina* of old Fez. Our room, overlooking formal gardens, pools and fountains, had leather-covered walls with hidden oval doors that opened on to secret rooms sumptuously decorated with banquettes, cushions and rugs—an atmosphere exotic enough to provide endless fantasies. But there was no time to indulge in them now. As prearranged, we telephoned a tourist official named Mr. Aydi, who graciously came to visit us. While we sipped lemonade he told us he had planned a dinner that included a famed Fez specialty to be served to us in a former palace, now the finest restaurant in the heart of ancient Fez. He had also arranged that we have an English-speaking guide who would take us through the city's labyrinths.

As if Mr. Aydi had rubbed Aladdin's lamp, a tall, honey-colored young man, appropriately named Muhammad, appeared. He wore a white wool caftan flowing down to his white sandals, and as he strode ahead of us in the narrow, twisting alleys, his imposing presence cleared a path through the mobs of robed men, veiled women and ragged children.

Except for dim electric lights, the *medina* showed no signs of having been affected by any of the trappings of civilization as we know them. The walls were almost black with age, but sudden shafts of sunlight illuminated bearded, turbaned beggars huddled in dark corners, their skinny hands outstretched, and blind old men who tapped their staffs on the cobblestones, pressing quickly against the wall, as we did, for burdened mules to pass.

Out of darkness and into light again, we saw children bearing trays on their heads, bound for the communal bakery. Each tray was stacked with the family's unbaked bread, and each loaf was marked with the family's symbol. Deep within his cavelike shop, the baker reached into the glowing interior of a thick, stone-walled oven with a long paddle to slide in an unbaked loaf or pull a baked one out. "He has worked here for 50

years, and never has he mistaken one family's bread for another," Muhammad said. "Of this he is very proud."

We followed Muhammad like lambs—up, down, across and around old Fez. It may have been for this reason that the *souk*—alleys set apart for the sale of personal and household objects—seemed to intertwine with the food markets, unlike other Arab quarters we had visited where the market and the *souk* were entirely separate. When we reached our destination, we discovered that the ground floor of the restaurant, once a palace, was a continuation of the *souk*, with brass wares and rugs lining the marble, onyx and ornately designed mosaic walls. Once upstairs, we found we were to be the only diners; Muhammad explained that the restaurant was ordinarily closed on this day but that Mr. Aydi had ordered it to be opened especially for us. I took advantage of the fact that we were the only guests, and asked Muhammad to introduce me to the chef.

Like all other Muslim cooks I had met, this one was eager and amiable. He was making what looked like at least 50 very big *brik*. On the table was a layered mound of *malsouqua* pastry, and nearby was a covey of small braised birds—pigeons, I discovered. Muhammad, with a sweeping gesture that took in the other ingredients—parsley, coriander, onions, eggs, ginger, sugar, cinnamon, turmeric, cumin and bowls of butter and sauces—said, "He is making *bastila*." I recognized the name as the dish

Once a date market, the Souk Ablleuh in Marrakech now specializes in the pickled and preserved foods—especially lemons and olives—that Moroccans use in many dishes. The enameled basins contain pickled black, brown and green olives, or *mslalla,* and small, very hot red peppers. *Msir* lemons, preserved in brine, are kept in the glass jars lining the shelves.

169

we could have ordered anywhere we had been in Morocco but hadn't, because everyone had insisted that we must eat the best version of it, which could be found only in Fez.

Having seen the care it took to prepare the batter for *brik* in Tunisia, I knew how much time this towering heap of pastry must have taken to make. To assemble the *bastila* itself the cook started with a base of about 10 sheets of pastry piled one upon the other, sprinkled it with a mixture of chopped almonds, cinnamon and sugar, spread it with what looked like a scrambled-egg sauce, and scattered pieces of pigeon on top. After covering the pigeon with four or five (I soon lost count) rounds of pastry, he added successive layers of filling exactly as he had before, completing this pielike construction by enclosing it with all the remaining pastry. Frying a *brik* was child's play when compared with what followed. Although I watched the chef closely, I simply couldn't take in all at once how he managed in one or two movements to seal the open-ended layers of pastry together before placing the whole in a pan of hot oil, and frying it to a crisp golden brown on both sides.

When it appeared at our table, resplendent on its platter, it bore little resemblance to the *bastila* I had seen in the kitchen. It had been decorated with circles of cinnamon and sugar. Even before tasting it, I knew that this was the pinnacle of the Moroccan cuisine. I have since then evolved my own method of making a *bastila (Recipe Index),* and it tastes almost as good at home as it did in Fez, but nothing could recapture the pleasure Frances and I felt sharing it with Muhammad, all of us picking away at it with our fingers.

While we were drinking the inevitable three glasses of mint tea, Muhammad, to our surprise, shyly offered to sing for us. When we told him it would please us enormously, he lay back in the semireclining position I had been tempted to assume in Casablanca, and proceeded to sing mournful Arabic songs. Resting on one elbow, his long white caftan flowing down to the geometrically patterned rug, he brought to mind the greatest paintings of Matisse. The walls and ceilings, a mass of triangles, flower shapes and circles—all in blazing colors—were a proper setting for the food, for Muhammad himself, and his ravishing songs. We felt how much he belonged here, and were poignantly aware that we did not.

Muhammad escorted us to our car when we were ready to leave for Rabat, and on the way out of the *medina,* Frances touched his arm and made him stop. From a second floor somewhere near came sounds like nothing we had ever heard. "Music of the spheres," Frances said, and perhaps she was right. Muhammad told us that the sounds were the voices of very young children learning the verses of the Koran in a schoolroom overhead. We had to tear ourselves away from the haunting, hypnotically rhythmic sounds.

Before leaving Fez I telephoned Madame Becheton and, as good as her word, she had already done the marketing for dinner. We arrived that evening at her European-style apartment and met Monsieur Becheton, an amiable, soft-spoken man who owned a fashionable men's clothing store in the city. He offered us a drink of vodka—our first in Morocco—and then Madame Becheton invited me to join her in the kitchen.

Opposite: Sitting on the floor of a kitchen in Marrakech, a Moroccan cook applies the finishing touches to a *tajine* of chicken with lemons and olives *(Recipe Index),* which she has cooked in an earthenware *tajine slaoui.* Actually *tajine* applies to any dish cooked in a *tajine slaoui,* and it can be made with beef, mutton or pigeon as well as chicken. In its many variations, it is a favorite throughout North Africa.

Here was modern Moroccan cooking indeed. Although it seems scarcely possible to believe it now, she prepared a four-course dinner in precisely 40 minutes; and I know because I timed it.

I consider myself, if immodestly, one of the most efficient cooks around, but watching my hostess I realized I had met my match. She had everything ready to make her instant cooking possible—good work space, a four-burner stove, an oven and a refrigerator, equipment we take for granted at home but not often found in North Africa. It was not just the equipment, however, that made it all seem so simple but rather Madame Becheton's respect for the food she was cooking, her manual dexterity, and even more important to me, her knowing precisely what she was about. A large fish was scaled, cleaned and washed; a chicken singed, eviscerated, washed and dried; fresh parsley and coriander chopped to a powder; about 20 cloves of garlic quickly separated and counted; chunks of lamb taken from a marinade and strung on skewers to make kabobs, and finally, peaches skinned, bananas sliced, oranges peeled, strawberries hulled, and all the fruits placed in a bowl. In what seemed minutes the fish, stuffed with herbs, was baking in the oven; the chicken sizzling away in a *tajine;* the brazier on the terrace filled with burning charcoal, and the fruit mixed with kirsch and placed in the refrigerator.

At one point I had to ask our hostess to stop and tell me what she was doing. I had been intrigued from the start by whole lemons tightly packed in a jar. When she added the quartered lemons along with a handful of green olives to the browned chicken, she explained that the lemons—called *msir (Recipe Index)*—were a gift from her mother, who had pickled them in salt; they were indispensable, she said, to the making of this Moroccan *tajine (Recipe Index),* which, unlike the rapidly boiling Tunisian *tajine* Abdul had made for us in Tanya's kitchen, was allowed to simmer. The lemons, I discovered at dinner, provided brilliant accents of acidity—a perfect foil for the chicken.

The dining table shone with heavy silver, gleaming goblets and a charming centerpiece of fresh and fragrant flowers. As we proceeded from course to course, each one superb, I thought of our own so-called convenience foods—instant mashed potatoes, TV dinners and the like—and wished American women could see and taste what Madame Becheton had so quickly and creatively achieved. Here, indeed, was another facet of Moroccan cooking I had not expected to find. The speed of preparation had impressed me, but beyond that, this ancient cuisine was so basically sound that, like the French cuisine, it was flexible enough to keep its character despite such simplification.

Our farewell to the Bechetons was in a sense the beginning of our farewell to North Africa, made tolerable only by the prospect of spending a night and a day in Tangier before flying home.

There we stayed at the Hotel Minzah in the very heart of this busy city, where crowded buses, filled with passengers of all nationalities, were setting off on package tours. Chicly dressed Americans and Europeans mingled with Moroccans in garb even more varied and colorful than any we had seen thus far. The streets seemed as crowded and noisy as those of Paris or New York, everyone spoke what sounded like a different lan-

    Continued on page 180

A Moroccan Pie That Is a Work of Art

"There were so many dishes at the *diffa* Allah alone could count them." So may a Moroccan speak of a memorable meal. A ceremonial *diffa* held to celebrate a wedding, a pilgrimage to Mecca or simply a visit of friends may involve dozens of dishes, from a complex lamb *couscous* to a simple bowl of dates, nuts and raisins. But the Moroccan cuisine boasts more than mere amplitude; it is also highly refined, and one of its most elaborate creations is the *bastila (above; see Recipe Index),* which no first-rate *diffa* would fail to include. The *bastila* is a sort of Elysian pigeon pie that offers a subtle range of surprising tastes and textures. One recipe for it runs to 1,000 words, and its preparation can take hours *(next page).* But as anyone who has eaten *bastila* will attest, one taste is worth a thousand words—and all the effort as well.

In the rudimentary kitchen of the Mnebhi Palace in Fez, a professional cook named Rahma composes a *bastila* for a private luncheon being held by a Fez merchant. The palace is now a bazaar and restaurant, and Rahma, a member of the Fez Corporation of Cooks, has been hired for the occasion. At left she has already cooked the pigeons and now she prepares the rest of the pie filling in an earthenware pot called a *guedra*. The filling consists of eggs, butter, sugar, ginger, onions, saffron and a variety of other spices. The next step involves making the 40 or 50 paper-thin pastry circles that will be made into layers to enclose the pie and separate the different kinds of stuffing. Inverting a copper pan over the charcoal brazier, she first wipes it with a cloth dipped in olive oil *(right, top row)*, then repeatedly dabs the dough onto it to form a thin layer of pastry, which she peels from the hot surface almost at once. When she has enough pastry circles she turns the pan right side up and fits about eight circles into it *(second row)*, gluing them together with egg whites. Next comes stuffing, then more circles, then the pigeon meat, and finally, just before the last layers, nuts and brown sugar. The finished *bastila,* cooked golden-brown, is turned out of the pan *(bottom picture)*. It will be topped with sugar and cinnamon and, perhaps, almonds.

Overleaf: Pausing in a palace
doorway resplendent with fine
Moroccan mosaics and graceful
Moorish arches, a manservant takes
warm water, basin and soap to the
banqueting Fassis (as men of Fez
are called), who will afterward be
served the *bastila.* The washing of
hands before and after eating is a
ritual part of a Muslim meal.

After the preliminary hand washing comes the *bastila,* set on a low table in front of the guests *(left),* who eat it from the platter, using their hands and accompanying it with water (being Muslims, the Fassis do not drink alcohol). The *bastila* will be followed by a *couscous,* and then comes music and entertainment. First the orchestra—lute, violin, tambourine, finger cymbals and a drum called a *derbouka*—plays, and then a bearded dancer, who has made his entrance veiled as a female impersontor, performs a sinuous acrobatic dance with a tray of drinks perfectly balanced on his head.

guage, and the shop names along the boulevards were inscribed on the windows in Turkish, Portuguese, Spanish, German, French and, of course, in ornate calligraphic Arabic. Tangier is, in every sense of the word, an international city.

Stephen Hughes's thoughtful attentions had reached from Casablanca to Tangier, as indicated by a number of messages awaiting us at the hotel. Among them was one from Brion Gysin—a gifted American expatriate writer and painter whom we had heard much about from his publisher in New York—inviting us for dinner at his home that night. It was an invitation that was to provide a superb climax to our trip.

Meeting Brion was like meeting an old friend. Our shared involvement with food was only an introduction to a host of other mutual interests, among them the many artists and writers we both knew. We spoke the same language—in the deepest sense of the phrase—and we never stopped talking. To top it all, Brion was an authority on Moroccan cooking, having owned and run a restaurant where only the most exalted native food had been served. But like many artists he had in the end given up a successful business for painting and writing.

His hand had not lost its culinary skill, however, for of all the excellent food we had eaten in North Africa, Brion's was surely the most original. Although most of the courses were the traditional Moroccan ones we had had before, each dish had been so transformed by his inventiveness that they seemed entirely new to us. The *harira* was similar to the one we had had in Marrakech but it had been flavored with different herbs. The *bastila* that followed was not the large pigeon pie we had eaten in Fez; Brion had made individual pies and shaped them into triangles. The simple orange slices we had had in Casablanca came now embellished with shredded radishes. But the main course was the climax: the freshest of swordfish steaks covered with masses of sautéed pulverized almonds, the whole tartly flavored with lemon juice *(Recipe Index)*.

As a nightcap and farewell drink before saying goodbye to Brion and Tangier, we had some fine old cognac—the only un-African note in that wonderfully creative Moroccan feast.

It was while flying back to New York that I began slowly and objectively to assess North African cooking. I considered, for instance, the remarkable inventiveness with which lamb is prepared, and marveled at the number of sweet and savory ways it had been served to me. I thought of the dazzling virtuosity that goes into the Tunisian *brik* and the Moroccan *bastila* and other intricately constructed pastries, and I realized that North Africa's claim to a cuisine of its own is unquestionably true. While not so sophisticated and complex as the French cuisine nor so varied and subtle as the Chinese, the cooking of the Maghreb combines all those attributes in a way that makes it utterly distinctive.

I found myself thinking about it in musical terms, as I often do when deeply moved, and I still think of it that way: as a three-movement symphony held together by interlocking themes—Tunisia, a lively, fiery first movement, *allegro con brio;* pastoral Algeria, a slow *andante;* and Morocco, richest of all, a grand *finale maestoso.* Altogether a magnificent whole, not yet fully known or appreciated by the rest of the world.

Opposite: Taleb Ben Souda sells pastries door to door in Rabat's 12th Century casbah, or native quarter, whose alleys are not a great deal wider than his tray. Like most Moroccan pastries, Ben Souda's are based on honey and almonds. *Briwat,* the pastry at right, is a confection of almond paste, rice and honey wrapped in a delicate crust. The plain and powdered pastries in the center are *kab el ghzal,* or gazelle horns *(Recipe Index)*. The almond-topped delicacy in the foreground is *ghoriba,* a rich cookie made with flour, sugar and extravagant quantities of butter.

Brik bil Lahm *(Tunisia)*
GROUND LAMB TURNOVER

Combine the lamb, onions, parsley, salt and pepper in a deep bowl, and knead vigorously with both hands. Then beat with a wooden spoon until the mixture is smooth and fluffy. In a heavy skillet, melt 2 tablespoons of butter over moderate heat. When the foam subsides, add the lamb mixture and, mashing frequently with the back of a fork to break up lumps of meat as they form, cook until no trace of pink remains. Remove the skillet from the heat and stir in the cheese. Taste for seasoning.

To assemble with *malsouqua:* Spoon a quarter of the lamb filling onto the bottom half of 1 pastry round. Make a well in the mound of lamb and crack 1 egg directly into it, making certain that the egg remains intact. Fold the exposed half of the *malsouqua* over the egg and lamb; do not be concerned if the edges do not seal. Repeat to make three more *brik.* (If the rounds have holes in them you can, before filling, patch them with pieces torn from extra rounds that are imperfect.)

To assemble with *filo* pastry: Spread 1 sheet flat and brush the top with 1 tablespoon of the melted butter. Fold the sheet in quarters to create a rectangle 8 by 6 inches. Brush again with butter and fold in one of the 8-inch sides by 2 inches to make a perfect 6-inch square. Spoon a quarter of the lamb filling onto the center of one corner of the square, make a well in the mound of lamb, and crack an egg directly into it. Brush the edges of the square lightly with the beaten egg and fold the square in half diagonally to create a triangle, pressing the edges down firmly to seal them. Repeat the procedure to make three more *brik.*

To fry the *brik,* heat the olive oil in a heavy 8- to 9-inch skillet until it is very hot but not smoking. Slide two of the *brik* at a time into the hot oil and fry them for 2 to 3 minutes on each side, turning them carefully with a wide slotted spatula. When the *brik* are golden brown, transfer them to paper towels to drain while you fry the remaining two. Serve the *brik* while they are still hot, accompanied by the lemon quarters.

To make 4

½ pound lean ground lamb
¼ cup very finely chopped onions
2 tablespoons finely chopped fresh parsley
½ teaspoon salt
¼ teaspoon freshly ground black pepper
2 tablespoons unsalted butter
4 tablespoons unsalted butter, melted (only if using *filo* sheets)
2 teaspoons freshly grated imported Parmesan cheese
4 circles of *malsouqua (page 184),* or substitute 4 sheets *filo* pastry *(see Glossary),* each about 16 inches long and 12 inches wide, thoroughly defrosted if frozen
4 small eggs
1 egg, lightly beaten (only if using *filo* sheets)
⅓ cup olive oil
1 lemon, cut lengthwise into quarters

Pfepfel bar Labid *(Tunisia)*
CUCUMBER-AND-PEPPER RELISH

With a small, sharp knife, peel the cucumbers and slice them lengthwise into halves. Scoop out the seeds by running the tip of a teaspoon down the center of each half. Then cut the cucumbers into 2-inch lengths.

In a serving bowl, stir the lime juice and salt together until the salt dissolves. Drop in the cucumbers and peppers, and turn them about with a spoon. When they are evenly coated with the lime mixture, cover tightly with foil or plastic wrap and marinate at room temperature for at least 8 hours before serving. *Pfepfel bar labid* is traditionally served in Tunisia with *couscous (Recipe Index).*

To serve 4 to 6

2 medium-sized cucumbers
1 tablespoon strained fresh lime juice
1 teaspoon salt
2 green bell peppers, sliced lengthwise into halves, seeded, deribbed and cut into 2-inch squares

Tunisian artistry is expressed both in the filigreed bird cage and in the turnover tour de force called *brik.* Filled with a mixture of lamb and cheese and topped with an egg, the five *brik* on the left are made with packaged *filo* pastry, the others with homemade *malsouqua (page 184).*

183

The batter for *malsouqua* (1) falls in a fluid ribbon when lifted. Dabbing it onto the surface of a hot, inverted pan (2) and pulling it back again as you would a Yo-Yo, cover the pan with a film. Loosen the edges (3) with a knife and peel off the pastry (4).

To make about 12 rounds

½ cup olive oil
2 cups fine yellow semolina
⅛ teaspoon salt
1⅔ cups cold water

Malsouqua *(Tunisia)*
SEMOLINA PASTRY ROUNDS

"Malsouqua" are round, paper-thin pastries used to make Tunisian "brik" and Moroccan "bastila." Commercial "filo" pastry can be substituted very successfully, but the delicate crispness and flavor of "malsouqua" are preferred. Making them with predictable results can, however, require considerable practice and patience.

Fill a deep pot about 8 to 9 inches in diameter with enough water to come about ¾ of the way up the sides. Invert a heavy 10-inch skillet with a well-scrubbed unscratched bottom (or preferably a copper crêpes suzette pan) over the pot, and bring the water to a boil over high heat, thus allowing the surface of the inverted pan to become as hot as possible. Have a large kettle of water simmering on a nearby burner to replenish the water in the pot as it boils away, and place the following within easy reach: the olive oil, a pastry brush, a small mixing bowl filled with cold water, a thin-bladed knife, paper towels, a damp kitchen towel and two spread-out dry kitchen towels.

Now make the batter and fry the pastry in the following fashion: Pour the semolina into a cake pan 10 to 12 inches in diameter (or use a wide baking dish instead). Add the salt and ½ cup of the cold water. Begin stirring the mixture with your hand and continue to stir for about 5 minutes, or until the semolina has absorbed the water. Still stirring, slowly add ¼ cup more of the water; after that has been absorbed, stir in the remaining water in small amounts. When all the water has been used, the batter will begin to develop small bubbles on its surface as you stir. At this point, change your stirring motion to a clutching and releasing one and manipulate the batter in this manner until it becomes elastic and falls from your fingers in ribbonlike strands *(photograph 1)*. This process should take about 15 minutes from start to finish.

When the batter has reached the desired consistency, dip the pastry brush into the olive oil and very lightly and evenly brush the entire surface of the heated inverted pan. Wipe with a paper towel, leaving only the faintest film of oil on the pan. First dip your hand into the bowl of cold water, then, palm side down, scoop up a handful of the batter, continuously releasing and clutching the dough. With the same movements

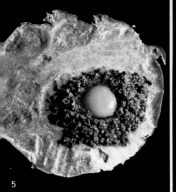 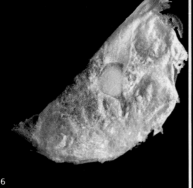  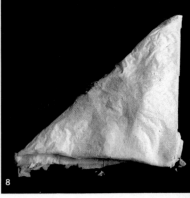

To shape a lamb *brik* with the *malsouqua:* Mound ¼ cup of the lamb-and-cheese mixture on one half of a circle of the pastry, and make a depression in the mound. Drop in a small egg (5), then fold the other half of the circle down over the filling (6).

To shape the *brik* with commercial *filo* pastry: Fold the *filo* in quarters, making a 6-by-8-inch rectangle. Fold in one end to make a square and place the filling and egg in one corner (7). Bring the opposite corner of *filo* over the filling, making a triangle (8).

—as if you were manipulating a Yo-Yo—first smear 2-inch-long streaks around the circumference of the pan. Then continue with similar dabbing movements all over the rest of the pan *(2)*.

As soon as the pan is entirely covered with the lightest, translucent film of batter, quickly wipe your batter-covered hand on the dampened towel and, before the *malsouqua* becomes the slightest bit dry, with your knife cut around the sides of the pan with small slashing motions until you have loosened the edges of the pastry *(3)*. Immediately slide the edge of the knife under the pastry and with both hands carefully and gently peel off the circle *(4)*. If at any point the pastry sticks to the pan, slide the knife under it to detach it. If there are any large holes in the pastry, replace the pastry round on the pan and with your index finger, dab some of the batter over the opening to patch it. Use the edge of the knife to lift the *malsouqua* off the pan again.

Lay the pastry on one of the dry kitchen towels and loosely cover it with the other towel. With a paper towel, clean the surface of the pan, brush it lightly with oil, and wipe as before. Make similar rounds of pastry with the remaining batter, and make a stack of the finished rounds. If one or more of the *malsouqua* are torn beyond repair, set them aside. They can be torn up and used to strengthen *brik (page 183)*.

You may use the *malsouqua* at once, or brush their edges lightly with oil, wrap in a towel, and then wrap in aluminum foil. Refrigerated, they will keep for 2 or 3 days.

Meh-lakh *(Tunisia)*
PICKLED VEGETABLES

Combine the vinegar and salt in a deep bowl and stir with a wooden spoon until the salt dissolves. Add the celery, carrots, turnips, zucchini and cauliflower, and turn them about to coat them well. With a slotted spoon, transfer the vegetables to two 1-quart canning jars, dividing the mixture evenly between them. Pour the brine into the jars, cover tightly with lids, and let the vegetables pickle at room temperature for 5 days before serving. They may then be kept for 2 or 3 weeks, either in the refrigerator or at room temperature. *Meh-lakh* is usually served as an accompaniment to apéritifs, especially *boukha* (fig brandy).

To make about 2 quarts

4 cups red or wine vinegar
¼ cup salt
3 medium-sized celery stalks, trimmed and with leaves removed, cut into strips about 1½ inches long and ¼ inch wide (1 cup)
2 medium-sized carrots, scraped and cut into strips 1½ inches long and ¼ inch wide (1 cup)
½ pound medium-sized white turnips, peeled and cut into strips 1½ inches long and ¼ inch wide (1 cup)
1 small zucchini (about ½ pound), peeled and cut into strips 1½ inches long and ¼ inch wide (1 cup)
½ pound cauliflower, separated into flowerets

7

6

A display of Moroccan specialties, distinctive for its diversity of sweet, spicy and tart foods, includes:

1 *Djeja m'qalia*—chicken with coriander and mint
2 *Qodban*—marinated lamb kabobs
3 *Shlada dyal fejjel ou lichine* —radish-and-orange salad
4 *Hut b'noua*—fish with almond paste
5 *Sucsu—Couscous* with lamb
6 *El lahm el m'qali*—lamb with olives and lemons
7 Mixed dates, nuts and raisins

To serve 4

½ cup olive oil
A pinch of ground ginger
¼ teaspoon pulverized saffron
    threads or ground saffron
1½ teaspoons salt
2 pounds boneless lamb shoulder,
    trimmed of excess fat and cut into
    1-inch cubes
2 cups finely chopped onions
¼ teaspoon finely chopped garlic
6 sprigs fresh coriander *(cilantro)*
2 salted lemons *(page 193)*,
    separated into quarters, or 2 fresh
    lemons, cut lengthwise into
    quarters and seeded
16 small green olives

To serve 4 to 6

4 large firm ripe tomatoes
3 large green bell peppers
3 tablespoons strained lemon juice
1½ teaspoons salt
Freshly ground black pepper
½ cup finely chopped onions
3 tablespoons olive oil
12 black olives, preferably the
    Mediterranean variety

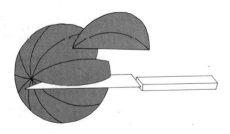

To serve 4 to 6

6 tablespoons strained lemon juice
2 tablespoons sugar
⅛ teaspoon salt
10 large firm red radishes, trimmed,
    washed and coarsely grated
4 medium-sized temple or navel
    oranges, peeled and with all the
    outside membranes removed

El Lahm el M'qali *(Morocco)*
LAMB WITH LEMONS AND OLIVES

In a heavy 12-inch sauté pan stir the olive oil, ginger, saffron and salt together. Add the lamb and turn the pieces about to coat them evenly. Pour in 3 cups of water, then add the onions, garlic, coriander and lemons. The liquid should almost cover the lamb; if necessary, add up to one more cup of water. Bring to a boil over high heat, then reduce the heat to low, cover tightly, and simmer for about 1 hour, or until the lamb is tender and shows no resistance when pierced with the point of a small knife. With a slotted spoon, transfer the lamb to a plate.

Bring the sauce remaining in the pan to a boil over high heat and cook briskly, uncovered, until it thickens slightly and is reduced to about 3 cups. Discard the coriander. Return the lamb and the liquid that has accumulated around it to the pan, add the olives and, stirring frequently, simmer for 4 to 5 minutes, until heated through. Taste for seasoning. Transfer the contents of the skillet to a heated bowl and serve at once.

Slata Mechouia *(Tunisia)*
ROASTED-TOMATO-AND-PEPPER SALAD

Preheat the oven to 400°. Place the tomatoes and peppers side by side on a large baking sheet and, turning them frequently so they color on all sides, roast in the middle of the oven for 20 minutes. Remove the tomatoes but continue roasting the peppers for about 20 minutes longer, turning them from time to time. Meanwhile, with a small, sharp knife, peel the tomatoes and slice them in half crosswise. Squeeze the halves gently to remove the seeds and juice and chop the tomatoes fine.

When the peppers are evenly colored, wrap them in a damp towel and let them rest for 5 minutes. Then rub the peppers with the towel until the skins slip off. Cut out the stems and white membranes, discard the seeds, and chop the peppers fine.

In a serving bowl, stir the lemon juice, salt and a few grindings of pepper together. Add the tomatoes, peppers and onions, and toss gently but thoroughly. Taste for seasoning. Then dribble the olive oil over the surface of the salad and scatter the black olives on top.

Slata mechouia is traditionally served as a first course, or as an accompaniment to *brik (page 183)* or to fried or broiled fish.

Shlada dyal Fejjel ou Lichine *(Morocco)*
RADISH-AND-ORANGE SALAD

To section an orange, use a small, very sharp knife and cut deeply into the peel near the stem. Cut the peel and all of the white membrane away from the orange, using short sawing motions. Now cut along each side of each membrane division to the core of the orange. As each orange section is freed, carefully lift it out. Combine the lemon juice, sugar and salt in a small serving bowl and stir vigorously until the sugar and salt dissolve. Add the radishes and oranges, and toss together gently but thoroughly. Serve at once, or refrigerate until ready to serve. Tightly covered and refrigerated, the salad can keep for 6 to 8 hours.

Qodban *(Morocco)*
MARINATED LAMB KABOBS

To serve 4

Combine the lemon juice, olive oil, coriander, garlic, parsley, ginger, turmeric, cumin and salt in a deep bowl and stir until all the ingredients are mixed. Drop in the lamb and turn the pieces about with a spoon to coat them well. Marinate at room temperature for at least 2 hours, or in the refrigerator for 6 hours, turning the lamb occasionally.

Light a layer of coals in a charcoal broiler and let them burn until a white ash appears on the surface, or preheat the broiler of your range to its highest point.

Remove the cubes of lamb and discard the marinade. Then, starting with a cube of suet and ending with one of lamb, thread the suet and lamb cubes alternately on six long skewers, pressing the suet and lamb firmly together.

Broil 4 inches from the heat, turning the skewers occasionally, until the lamb is done to your taste. For pink lamb, allow about 10 minutes; for the more traditionally Moroccan well-done lamb, broil the *qodban* for about 15 minutes.

Slide the lamb off the skewers onto a heated platter and discard the fat. *Qodban* will serve two or three as a main course or four as one of the dishes for a traditional Moroccan meal of many courses.

¼ cup strained fresh lemon juice
½ cup olive oil
2 tablespoons finely chopped fresh coriander *(cilantro)*
1 tablespoon finely chopped garlic
2 tablespoons finely chopped fresh parsley
1 teaspoon ground ginger
1 teaspoon turmeric
½ teaspoon ground cumin
1 teaspoon salt
2 pounds lean boneless lamb, preferably from the leg, trimmed of excess fat and cut into 1-inch cubes
3 pounds fresh beef suet, cut into 1-inch cubes

Djeja M'qalia *(Morocco)*
CHICKEN WITH CORIANDER AND MINT

To serve 4

In a small bowl combine the garlic, paprika, saffron, coriander, mint, cumin and 1 tablespoon of oil. With a wooden spoon, mix and mash the ingredients to a paste that is dense enough to hold its shape lightly in a spoon. If the paste seems too dry, stir in up to 1 tablespoon more of oil by the teaspoonful.

Pat the chicken completely dry with paper towels and sprinkle it inside and out with the salt and a few grindings of black pepper.

Preheat the oven to 375°. With your fingers, rub the entire surface of the chicken with the herb paste, patting and spreading it as evenly as possible. Place the chicken in a heavy 4- to 6-quart casserole, surround it with the chopped onions, and pour 1 cup of water down one side of the pot, without getting any water on the chicken.

Cover the casserole and bring to a boil over high heat. Then braise in the center of the oven for about 45 minutes. To test if the chicken is done, pierce a thigh with the point of a small, sharp knife. The juices that run out should be pale yellow; if the juices are pink, braise 10 to 15 minutes longer. Transfer the chicken from the casserole to a plate and keep the braising juices warm.

Preheat the broiler to its highest point, or light a layer of coals in a charcoal broiler and let them burn until a white ash appears on the surface. Broil the chicken 3 inches from the heat for about 6 to 8 minutes, turning it frequently with 2 wooden spoons, until it is richly and evenly browned on all sides.

Serve the chicken at once, accompanied by the heated braising sauce in a sauceboat or bowl.

2 teaspoons finely chopped garlic
1 tablespoon paprika
¼ teaspoon pulverized saffron threads or powdered saffron
¼ cup finely chopped fresh coriander *(cilantro)* leaves
¼ cup finely chopped fresh mint
½ teaspoon powdered cumin
1 to 2 tablespoons vegetable oil
A 3- to 3½-pound chicken
2 teaspoons salt
Freshly ground black pepper
1 cup coarsely chopped onions
1 cup water

Tunisian *yo-yo* are moist, orange-flavored doughnuts dipped into a lemony honey syrup and dusted with grated orange rind.

To make 10 doughnuts

2 large eggs
¼ cup vegetable oil, plus vegetable
  oil for deep frying
¼ cup strained fresh orange juice
2 teaspoons finely grated orange
  peel
2¼ cups sugar
2 to 3 cups all-purpose flour
1 tablespoon baking soda
2 cups cold water
2 tablespoons strained fresh lemon
  juice
½ cup honey

Yo-yo (Tunisia)
ORANGE-FLAVORED DOUGHNUTS DIPPED IN HONEY SYRUP

In a deep bowl, combine the eggs, ¼ cup vegetable oil, orange juice, 1 teaspoon of the orange peel and ¼ cup of sugar. Beat vigorously with a wire whisk or spoon until the mixture is smooth. Then, beating constantly with a spoon, sift in 2 cups of the flour and the tablespoon of baking soda, and continue to beat until the mixture is thick enough to fall from the spoon in a wide, slowly dissolving ribbon.

Cover the bowl with a towel and set the dough aside to rest for at least 30 minutes.

Meanwhile prepare the syrup in the following fashion: In a small, heavy saucepan, bring the remaining 2 cups of sugar, the water and lemon juice to a boil over high heat, stirring until the sugar dissolves. Cook briskly, uncovered and undisturbed, until the syrup reaches a temperature of 230° on a candy thermometer. Reduce the heat to low, add the ½ cup honey and the remaining teaspoon of orange peel and simmer for 5 minutes. Then remove the pan from the heat and cover to keep the syrup warm.

Pour vegetable oil into a deep fryer or large, heavy saucepan to a depth of 3 inches and heat until the oil reaches a temperature of 350° on a deep-frying thermometer.

Flouring your hands heavily, gather the dough into a ball and divide it into 10 equal parts. Shape each part into a 2-inch round ball, then flatten it slightly. Hold the round in the palm of one hand and punch a hole through the center with the floured index finger of your other hand.

Deep-fry the doughnuts, two or three at a time, for about 5 minutes, turning them about with a slotted spoon until they are golden brown on both sides. Transfer them to paper towels to drain, and fry and drain the remaining doughnuts similarly.

While the doughnuts are still warm, prick them in two or three places with the tines of a table fork. Then pick them up with tongs, dip them into the warm syrup, and serve at once.

Samsa *(Tunisia)*
ALMOND-AND-SESAME-SEED PASTRY

To make about 2 dozen pastries

2¾ cups (1 pound) blanched slivered almonds
1 pound (about 3 cups) white sesame seeds
1¼ pounds unsalted butter, melted and cooled
20 sheets *filo* pastry, each about 16 inches long and 12 inches wide, thoroughly defrosted if frozen *(see Glossary)*
1 cup sugar
1 cup water
2 tablespoons strained fresh lemon juice
1 tablespoon rose water *(see Glossary)*

Preheat the oven to 350°. Spread the almonds and sesame seeds evenly in a large shallow baking pan and brown them in the middle of the oven for about 10 minutes, stirring them from time to time so that they color evenly. A cup or so at a time, pulverize the almonds and sesame seeds in the jar of an electric blender. As they are pulverized, scrape the mixture into a deep bowl with a rubber spatula.

With a pastry brush, spread about 1 tablespoon of the melted butter over the bottom and sides of a 12-by-8-by-2-inch baking dish. Brush a sheet of *filo* pastry generously with butter and fold it in half making a 12-by-8-inch rectangle. Fit it into the dish and smooth out the pastry. Brush the top with butter and repeat with 4 more sheets of *filo,* buttering them, folding them, and placing one upon the other.

Spread the top sheet of *filo* evenly with 1 cup of almond-and-sesame-seed mixture, then add 5 sheets of *filo* as before. Spread another cup of the almonds and seeds over the pastry and cover with 5 more buttered and folded sheets of *filo.*

Spread any remaining almonds and sesame seeds over the top. Then cover them with the remaining 5 sheets of *filo,* buttering and folding the pastry as before. Brush the top with melted butter and, with a sharp knife, cut the pastry into 2-inch squares.

Bake the *samsa* in the middle of the oven for 30 minutes, lower the temperature to 300°, and bake for 30 minutes longer, or until the top is crisp and golden brown.

Meanwhile prepare the syrup in the following fashion: Combine the sugar and water in a small saucepan and bring to a boil over moderate heat, stirring until the sugar dissolves. Increase the heat to high and boil briskly, uncovered, for about 5 minutes, or until the syrup reaches a temperature of 220° on a candy thermometer. Pour the syrup into a bowl or pitcher and stir in the lemon juice and rose water. Cool the syrup to room temperature before using it.

When the pastry is done, and while it is still hot, pour the syrup evenly over the top. Cool to room temperature before serving.

Unusually mild for Algerian food, *sferia* subtly combines chicken with chick-peas and cheese-flavored croquettes.

Sferia *(Algeria)*
CHICKEN WITH CHICK-PEAS AND CHEESE CROQUETTES

In a heavy 3- to 4-quart casserole, combine the butter, chicken, onion, ½ teaspoon cinnamon, 1 teaspoon salt and several grindings of black pepper. Turning the chicken frequently, cook uncovered over high heat for about 15 minutes, or until it is golden on all sides. Add the chick-peas and water and, stirring constantly, bring to a boil over high heat. Reduce the heat to low and simmer covered for 1½ hours, or until the chicken is tender but not falling apart.

Meanwhile, preheat the oven to its lowest setting. Line a large shallow baking pan with a double thickness of paper towels and place it in the middle of the oven. Combine the bread and milk in a deep bowl, soak for 10 minutes, then squeeze the bread vigorously to rid it of all moisture. Discard the milk and return the bread to the bowl. Add the egg and egg yolk, and stir with a fork or spoon until the ingredients are well blended. Stir in the cheese, orange-blossom water, ¼ teaspoon cinnamon and ¼ teaspoon salt, and beat until the mixture is smooth. Taste for seasoning.

In a heavy 10-inch skillet warm the oil over high heat until a light haze forms above it. Moistening your hands frequently with cold water, shape the croquette mixture into about 2 dozen slightly flattened balls, each about 1 inch in diameter. Fry the croquettes 5 or 6 at a time in the hot oil for 1 or 2 minutes on each side, turning them with a slotted spatula. As they brown, transfer them to the paper-lined pan and keep them warm in the oven while you fry the rest in similar batches, adding more oil to the pan as necessary.

When the chicken is done, arrange the cheese croquettes in a ring around the edge of a large serving platter and place the pieces of chicken in another ring inside them. Remove the chick-peas from the casserole with a slotted spoon and mound them in the center. Drape the platter loosely with foil and return to the oven to keep warm while you make the sauce. Working quickly, beat the egg yolk and lemon juice together with a fork or whisk until they are well combined, beat in ½ cup of the sauce from the casserole, and then pour the egg mixture into the remaining sauce. Stirring constantly, cook over low heat until the sauce thickens lightly. Do not let it come to a boil or it will curdle. Taste for seasoning and pour the sauce over the chick-peas and chicken. Sprinkle the top with the parsley and serve at once.

Msir *(Morocco)*
SALTED LEMONS

With a small, sharp knife, slice each of the lemons lengthwise into quarters, cutting to within about ½ inch of the bottom so that the segments are not completely separated. Sprinkle the cut surfaces evenly with the salt and reassemble the lemons, pressing them gently into their original shape. Place the lemons in a canning jar large enough to hold them compactly, cover tightly with the lid, and marinate at room temperature for at least 2 weeks. Discard the juice that has accumulated in the jar and completely separate the lemons into quarters. The salted lemons are used in *tajine* such as *tajine msir zitum* and *el lahm el m'qali (Recipe Index)*.

To serve 4

2 tablespoons butter
A 3- to 3½-pound chicken, cut into 8 serving pieces
1 small onion, peeled and finely grated
½ teaspoon ground cinnamon
1 teaspoon salt
Freshly ground black pepper
1 cup dried chick-peas *(garbanzos)*, soaked 12 hours, drained, rinsed, simmered in water to cover for 1 hour and drained again, or substitute 2 cups drained canned chick-peas
1 cup water

CROQUETTES
1 small (½ pound) loaf fresh French- or Italian-type white bread, trimmed of all crusts and torn into ½-inch pieces
¼ cup milk
1 egg plus 1 egg yolk
1 cup freshly grated imported Gruyère cheese
1 teaspoon orange-blossom water *(see Glossary)*
¼ teaspoon ground cinnamon
¼ teaspoon salt
1 cup vegetable oil

SAUCE
1 egg yolk
1 tablespoon strained fresh lemon juice
2 tablespoons finely chopped fresh parsley

To make 4 preserved lemons

4 lemons
2 teaspoons salt

To serve 6

COUSCOUS

2 pounds *couscous (see Glossary)*

2½ teaspoons salt dissolved in
    2½ cups cold water

1 tablespoon olive oil

4 tablespoons unsalted butter, cut
    into bits

BEEF AND VEGETABLES

1 cup vegetable oil

2 pounds boneless chuck, cut into
    2-inch cubes and patted dry with
    paper towels

3 cups finely chopped onions

4 teaspoons *hrisa (opposite)*

⅛ teaspoon ground allspice

½ teaspoon salt

Freshly ground black pepper

4 medium-sized carrots, peeled and
    cut crosswise into 2-inch pieces

4 medium-sized turnips, peeled and
    cut into 2-inch pieces

½ cabbage, cored and cut into
    2-inch pieces

½ pound (about 1 cup) dried
    chick-peas *(garbanzos),* soaked
    for 12 hours, drained, rinsed,
    simmered in water to cover for 1
    hour and drained again, or
    substitute 2 cups drained canned
    chick-peas

3 medium-sized firm ripe tomatoes,
    quartered

3 cups cold water

6 medium-sized boiling potatoes,
    peeled

4 small unpeeled zucchini, cut into
    2-inch pieces

1 pound pumpkin, peeled and cut
    into 2-inch pieces

Kouski bil Lahm (Tunisia)
COUSCOUS WITH BEEF AND VEGETABLES

Spread the *couscous* evenly in a large shallow pan. Sprinkle it with 2 cups of the salted water, then dribble the tablespoon of oil over the top. Rub the moistened grains gently between your palms, dropping the *couscous* back into the pan until the water and oil have been completely absorbed. Cover with foil or plastic wrap and set aside at room temperature for 15 minutes; the pellets will swell slightly.

Meanwhile, in the lower part of a 4-quart *couscoussier* or in a deep 6-quart kettle or casserole, heat 1 cup of oil until a light haze forms above it. Add the cubes of meat and the onions, and sprinkle the meat with the *hrisa,* allspice, salt and a few grindings of black pepper. Fry uncovered over high heat for 6 to 8 minutes, turning the meat over frequently with tongs until it is golden brown on all sides. Add the carrots, turnips, cabbage, chick-peas and tomatoes, pour in 3 cups of cold water (or just enough to cover the meat and vegetables), and stir until the mixture comes to a boil. Reduce the heat to low.

Set the top part of the *couscoussier* in place. Or set a colander lined with cheesecloth into the kettle or casserole; it should not touch the food in the pot. Twist damp paper towels or kitchen towels into long narrow strips and wrap them around the rim of the *couscoussier* or kettle to seal the joint between the upper and lower parts.

Slowly add about 2 cups of the *couscous* to the upper pot or colander, rubbing the pellets between your palms as you drop them in, and letting them mound naturally. When steam begins to rise through the pellets, add another cup or so of *couscous* in the same manner. Repeat, letting steam appear after each addition. When all the *couscous* has been rubbed into the pot or colander, continue to steam uncovered and undisturbed for 20 minutes. Then remove the top part, return the *couscous* to the shallow pan again, spread it out with a wooden spoon, and set aside to dry.

As the vegetables and meat become tender, transfer them with a slotted spoon to a platter and drape foil over them to keep them warm. Add the potatoes, zucchini and pumpkin to the pot and, if necessary, pour in enough boiling water to cover the vegetables completely. Stirring occasionally, bring to a boil over high heat. Then reduce the heat to low, set the top pot or colander in place again, and let the vegetables cook while you complete the preparation of the *couscous.*

Sprinkle the remaining ½ cup of salted water and the butter bits over the *couscous* and rub the grains gently between your palms as before until the water and butter are completely absorbed.

Again seal the joint at the rim of the pot with the towel strips. Slowly add 2 cups of the *couscous* to the top pot or colander as you did before, rubbing the pellets between your palms as you drop them in, letting them mound naturally, and waiting for steam to appear before adding more. Steam uncovered and undisturbed for about 15 minutes, or until the zucchini is tender but not falling apart. Transfer it with a slotted spoon to the reserved meat and vegetables, then replace the top. Continue to steam the *couscous* undisturbed for another 10 or 15 minutes, or until it is soft but still somewhat resistant to the bite.

To serve, mound the *couscous* on a large heated platter. Return the meat and vegetables to the pot and cook over high heat for 2 to 3 minutes, until they are heated through. Moisten the *couscous* with about 1 cup of the sauce in the pot, and arrange the pieces of meat and vegetables around it. Pour the rest of the sauce into a bowl and stir in the remaining 3 teaspoons of *hrisa*. Serve at once, accompanied if you like by one or more of the traditional Tunisian relishes: potato salad *(below)*, turnip-and-lime-juice relish, or cucumber relish *(Recipe Index)*.

Hrisa *(Tunisia)*
RED PEPPER SPICE

Combine the red pepper, cumin and salt in a small bowl and stir until thoroughly blended. Pour the *hrisa* into an 8-ounce jar or bottle equipped with a tight-fitting lid. Cover and store in a cool place until ready to use.

To make about ¾ cup

½ cup ground hot red pepper (cayenne)
¼ cup ground cumin
2 teaspoons salt

Salatit Batata *(Tunisia)*
POTATO SALAD WITH CARAWAY

Drop the potatoes into enough lightly salted boiling water to cover them completely and cook briskly, uncovered, until they are tender but still intact. Drain off the water and, sliding the pan back and forth constantly, cook over low heat for a minute or so, until the potatoes are dry.

Meanwhile, in a heavy 10- to 12-inch skillet, warm the oil over moderate heat until a light haze forms above it. Add the lemon juice, the *hrisa*-water mixture, caraway and salt and, stirring constantly, cook until most of the liquid in the pan has evaporated. Remove from the heat, add the potatoes, and turn them about gently with a spoon until they are evenly coated with the seasoned oil. Taste for seasoning. Then transfer to a serving bowl and cool to room temperature before serving. *Salatit batata* is traditionally served in Tunisia as an accompaniment to *couscous (above)*.

To serve 4 to 6

4 medium-sized boiling potatoes, peeled and cut into ¼-inch dice
½ cup vegetable oil
2 tablespoons strained fresh lemon juice
1 teaspoon *hrisa (above)*, dissolved in 1 tablespoon water
1 teaspoon ground caraway seeds
1½ teaspoons salt

Lahm Lhalou *(Algeria)*
LAMB AND PRUNES WITH ALMONDS ("SWEET MEAT")

Pat the lamb dry with paper towels and sprinkle on all sides with the salt. In a heavy 3- to 4-quart casserole, melt the butter over moderate heat. When the foam subsides, add about half of the lamb and brown it in the hot fat, turning the cubes frequently with tongs or a slotted spatula. As they brown, transfer the cubes to a plate and brown the remaining lamb similarly. Add the water, cinnamon, almonds, sugar and orange-blossom water to the fat remaining in the casserole and, stirring constantly, bring to a boil over high heat. Return the lamb and the liquid that has accumulated around it to the casserole, reduce the heat to low and simmer covered for 45 minutes. Then add the prunes and turn them about to coat them with the cooking liquid. Simmer covered for 10 minutes longer, or until the lamb shows no resistance when pierced with a small knife.

Serve at once, mounded on a heated platter. Because this is an exceedingly rich dish, the Algerians never serve it as a main course but rather as one of the dishes in a multiple-course meal. It often precedes or follows chicken *couscous (Recipe Index)*.

To serve 6

2½ pounds boneless lamb shoulder, trimmed of excess fat and cut into 1½-inch cubes
½ teaspoon salt
2 tablespoons unsalted butter
1 cup water
1 cinnamon stick, broken into 1-inch lengths
1 cup whole blanched almonds
1 cup sugar
2 tablespoons orange-blossom water *(see Glossary)*
¾ pound pitted prunes

To serve 4 to 6

4 one-pound oven-ready pigeons,
    with wing tips removed, or
    substitute 4 one-pound squab
    chickens
Salt
Freshly ground black pepper
12 tablespoons (1½ quarter-
    pound sticks) unsalted butter
1 cup finely chopped onions
The pigeon or chicken hearts,
    gizzards and livers, finely
    chopped
2 tablespoons finely chopped fresh
    coriander *(cilantro)*
1 tablespoon finely chopped fresh
    parsley
1 teaspoon ground ginger
½ teaspoon ground cumin
½ teaspoon ground hot red pepper
    (cayenne)
¼ teaspoon turmeric
⅛ teaspoon crumbled saffron
    threads or ground saffron
⅛ teaspoon plus ½ teaspoon
    cinnamon
1 cup water
6 eggs plus 2 egg yolks
1½ cups blanched almonds
2 tablespoons sugar
18 *malsouqua (page 184)*, or
    substitute 10 sheets *filo* pastry
    (see Glossary), each about 16
    inches long and 12 inches wide,
    thoroughly defrosted if frozen
8 tablespoons (1 quarter-pound
    stick) unsalted butter, melted
3 tablespoons unsalted butter
    combined with 3 tablespoons
    vegetable oil
2 tablespoons confectioners' sugar
    combined with 1 tablespoon
    cinnamon

Bastila (Morocco)
FLAKY PIGEON PIE

Pat the birds thoroughly dry inside and out with paper towels and sprinkle the cavities and skin with ½ teaspoon of salt and a few grindings of pepper. In a heavy 12-inch skillet, melt 8 tablespoons of the butter over moderate heat. When the foam begins to subside, brown the pigeons in the hot fat, turning them frequently with tongs or a slotted spoon and regulating the heat so they color richly and evenly on all sides without burning. As they brown, transfer the birds to a plate.

Add the onions and the pigeon or chicken hearts, gizzards and livers to the fat remaining in the skillet and, stirring frequently, cook for about 5 minutes, or until the onions are soft and translucent but not brown. Stir in the coriander, parsley, ginger, cumin, red pepper, turmeric, saffron and ⅛ teaspoon of cinnamon. Add the cup of water and bring to a boil over high heat, stirring constantly. Then return the birds and the liquid that has accumulated around them to the skillet, and reduce the heat to low. Cover and simmer for about 1 hour, or until the birds are tender and show no resistance when a thigh is pierced deeply with the point of a small knife. Transfer the birds to a platter and, when they are cool enough to handle, with a sharp knife remove and discard the skin and bones. Cut the meat into strips about 2 inches long and 1 inch wide.

Pour 1½ cups of the sauce remaining in the skillet into a bowl and set aside. Bring the rest of the sauce to a boil over high heat and, stirring from time to time, cook briskly until it is reduced to about 4 tablespoons of glaze. As the fat rises to the surface of the boiling sauce, skim it off with a spoon and discard it. With a rubber spatula, scrape the glaze into a small bowl and return the reserved 1½ cups of sauce to the skillet.

Beat the eggs and egg yolks with a whisk or fork until they are combined, but do not overbeat them. Stirring the sauce in the skillet constantly, pour in the eggs and cook over moderate heat until the mixture forms soft, creamy curds. Remove the skillet from the heat and stir in the glaze. Taste for seasoning and set aside.

Melt 4 tablespoons of butter in a small skillet over moderate heat. When the foam begins to subside, add the almonds and, stirring frequently, fry them for about 5 minutes, or until they are lightly and evenly browned. Drain the almonds on paper towels, then chop them coarsely. In a small bowl, combine the chopped almonds, 2 tablespoons of sugar and ½ teaspoon of cinnamon.

To assemble the *bastila* with *malsouqua,* arrange 6 of the pastries on a flat surface, overlapping them in a large circle, then top with 6 more, overlapping as before. Stack 4 more pastries in the center. (To assemble the pie with *filo,* overlap 6 sheets of *filo* in a circle, fold 2 sheets in half and place them one atop the other in the center of the circle.) Sprinkle the almond-sugar-and-cinnamon mixture in a 9-inch-wide circle in the center of the pastry and spread it with half of the egg-sauce mixture. Top this with strips of pigeon or chicken meat arranged in one layer and cover with the remaining egg-sauce mixture. With a pastry brush, coat the exposed borders of the pastry lightly with the melted butter. One at a time, bring the 6 intermediate circles of *malsouqua* or 2 folded sheets of *filo* up over the filling, brushing each again with butter as you proceed. Top the center of the pie with 2 more circles of *malsouqua* or folded sheets of *filo,* and bring up the bottom layer of *malsouqua* or *filo* to enclose the pie.

In a heavy 10- to 12-inch skillet, melt the 3 tablespoons of butter and 3 tablespoons of oil over moderate heat. When the foam subsides, carefully slide in the *bastila* and fry it for 2 or 3 minutes, or until the bottom is golden brown. With the aid of a wide spatula, slide the *bastila* onto a plate. Place a second plate upside down over the *bastila* and, grasping both plates firmly together, invert them. Slide the *bastila* back into the skillet and brown the other side for 2 or 3 minutes.

Transfer the *bastila* to a heated platter and sprinkle it with the sugar-and-cinnamon mixture. Cut it into wedges and serve at once.

Makroud el Louse (*Algeria*)
SOFT ALMOND COOKIES

To make about 6 dozen cookies

Preheat the oven to 350°. In a deep bowl, stir the almonds, 2 cups of the sugar and the lemon peel together until they are well blended. Make a well in the center, drop in the eggs and, with a wooden spoon, slowly stir the ingredients together. Continue to stir until the mixture is smooth.

Divide the mixture into quarters. On a heavily floured surface, roll each quarter with the palms of your hands into a cylinder about 18 inches long and 1½ inches in diameter. Flour your hands constantly as you roll the dough to prevent it from sticking to your fingers.

Flatten each cylinder into an oblong about 2 inches wide and, holding a sharp knife at a 45-degree angle, cut each cylinder diagonally into 1½-inch-thick slices. Dust the slices with flour, place them about 1 inch apart on ungreased baking sheets, and bake in the middle of the oven for about 15 minutes, or until the cookies just begin to color. Dust off any excess flour with a pastry brush and transfer the cookies to wire racks to cool.

Meanwhile, prepare the syrup in the following fashion: Combine the remaining ½ cup of sugar and the water in a small saucepan and bring to a boil over high heat, stirring with a wooden spoon until the sugar dissolves. Cook briskly, uncovered and undisturbed, for 15 minutes. Pour the syrup into a shallow bowl and when it has cooled to room temperature, stir in the tablespoon of orange-blossom water.

Spread the confectioners' sugar in a large shallow pan or on paper towels. Dip the cookies one at a time into the syrup and, when they are coated on both sides, roll them in the confectioners' sugar. Set the cookies aside on paper towels to dry. In tightly covered jars or tins, the cookies can be kept for several months.

2½ pounds blanched whole almonds, finely pulverized in a nut grinder or with a mortar and pestle (6 cups)
2½ cups sugar
2 tablespoons finely grated lemon peel
4 eggs
2 cups cold water
1 tablespoon orange-blossom water (*see Glossary*)
4 cups confectioners' sugar

Torshi (*Tunisia*)
TURNIP-AND-LIME-JUICE RELISH

To serve 4 to 6

In a serving bowl, stir the lime juice and salt together until the salt is dissolved. Drop in the turnips and turn them about with a spoon. When they are evenly coated with the lime mixture, cover tightly with foil or plastic wrap and marinate at room temperature for at least 3 hours. Just before serving, stir in the *hrisa. Torshi* is traditionally served in Tunisia as an accompaniment to *couscous (Recipe Index).*

1 tablespoon strained fresh lime juice
1 teaspoon salt
4 medium-sized white turnips, peeled and cut crosswise into ⅛-inch-thick rounds
1 teaspoon *hrisa (page 195)*

Glossary

À L'ESCAVÈCHE (Belgium): Fish or poultry cooked and then pickled in a marinade and served hot or cold. A typically Spanish method of preparing certain popular Belgian dishes.

BABKA (Poland): A pastry that takes its name from "grandmother" or "old lady" because its round shape is reminiscent of elderly peasant women in their shawls and long skirts.

BAKLAVA (North Africa): A sweet cake made with layers of thin pastry (FILO) interspersed with nuts and spices and covered with syrup. It is common throughout North Africa, the Middle East and the Balkans.

BANITSA (Bulgaria): A pielike construction of light flaky pastry (FILO) filled with cheese or vegetables.

BARSZCZ (Poland): A soup with a base of beets.

BASTILA (Morocco): A multilayered pie with a filling of pigeon or chicken, nuts, cinnamon and egg sauce. *See malsouqua.*

BEDOUIN (North Africa): A nomadic Arab of the desert.

BERBERS (North Africa): An indigenous North African race older than recorded history. Including several branches and constituting a large portion of the North African population, the Berbers are distinguished from the nomadic Arab population (BEDOUIN) by deep attachment to their towns and land.

BOUKHA (Tunisia): A fig brandy.

BRIK (Tunisia): A turnover consisting of thin pastry (MALSOUQUA) with a filling of various ingredients that almost always include a whole egg.

BRIWAT (Tunisia): A confection of almond paste, rice and honey.

BRYNZA (Romania): A brined white sheep's-milk cheese resembling Greek FETA. Available in cheese stores.

BÜNDNERFLEISCH (Switzerland): Air-cured beef. The name comes from Graubunden, the German name for the canton of Grisons, where much of the best quality of this dried meat originates.

CEAUN (Romania): A large heavy pot, usually of cast iron.

CHAKCHOUKA (Tunisia): A spicy vegetable mixture used as a base in soups or TOUAJEN.

CHRUST (Poland): A type of sugar-coated biscuit.

CIORBA (Romania and Bulgaria): A sour soup that may include any combination of vegetables, meats or fish, and herbs. The Bulgarian version is less highly seasoned than the Romanian.

CITRIC, OR SOUR, SALT: A crystalline product extracted from lemons and limes that imparts an acidulous taste, and is used to flavor the jelly that is part of *karp po żydowsku,* Poland's sweet-and-sour carp dish.

CIUBRITSA (Bulgaria): An herb resembling tarragon; also a combination of spices into which bread is dipped.

COUSCOUS (North Africa): Tiny pastalike pellets usually made with semolina and water. Also the cooked dish of steamed *couscous* with sauce, or other accompaniment.

COUSCOUSSIER (North Africa): A pot like a double boiler with openings like a sieve in the bottom of the top pot. COUSCOUS grains steam uncovered in the top pot, while the accompanying sauce or stew simmers in the bottom pot. Available in specialty cookware stores.

DIFFA (Morocco): A festive meal to which guests are invited.

EDAM (Netherlands): A mild buttery cheese made from partially skimmed milk and shaped into grapefruit-sized balls. Those exported to the United States have a bright red covering. Also made in the United States. Aged Edams, which are rare in the United States, have a harder texture and stronger and more interesting flavor than the young variety.

ÉGRAINAGE (Belgium): A pruning, cutting-back procedure that allows fruit such as Belgian hothouse grapes to develop to a large and uniform size.

EMMENTALER (Switzerland): The best known of all Swiss cheeses, widely imitated in other countries as "Swiss cheese." Made from whole fresh milk and named for the Emmental Valley in the canton of Bern, it is distinguished by its large holes and mild flavor.

FENDANT (Switzerland): A fruity white wine produced in the canton of Valais from the Fendant grape.

FETA: A Greek cheese. Made from sheep's or goat's milk, it is white and pleasantly pungent. Available in Greek or specialty shops in the United States, it may be substituted for BRYNZA and SIRENE.

FILO: Tissue-thin sheets of pastry that can be purchased fresh or frozen by the pound in Greek or specialty shops. It is used in making BANITSA and may be used as a substitute for MALSOUQUA in BRIK and BASTILA. Should be kept refrigerated. As *filo* dries out instantly, the sheets should be kept covered with a damp towel while being used.

FONDUE (Switzerland): From the French word for melted. The classic Swiss fondue combines melted cheese with wine and is served with cubes of bread for dunking.

GHIVECIU (Romania), **GHIVETCH** (Bulgaria): A mélange of vegetables and meat cooked in a large earthenware pot. The Bulgarian version is spicier and often has a topping of yoghurt and eggs. Both are named after the Turkish pot called a *güveç.*

GOLDWASSER (Poland): A liqueur made in Gdańsk, flavored with aniseed and caraway. Flakes of gold are suspended in it.

GOUDA (Netherlands): A smooth, mellow cheese made from whole milk, similar in taste and texture to EDAM. Also made in the United States.

GRAPPA (Switzerland): The Italian name for a strong drink distilled from grape husks, served as a brandy. Called *marc* in French.

GRUYÈRE (Switzerland): A firm natural cheese with small holes and a piquant flavor. Also a processed cheese with a milder flavor and creamier texture. Named for a town (Gruyères) and valley (Gruyère) in Fribourg.

HADJI (North Africa): The title conferred on one who has made a pilgrimage to Mecca.

HARIRA (North Africa): A meat-and-vegetable soup flavored with HRISA, and traditionally served to break the fasting of RAMADAN.

HRISA (North Africa): A combination of spices, predominantly crushed red pepper, used to flavor and season almost anything except desserts.

HUTSPOT (Netherlands), **HOCHEPOT** (Belgium): A stew of meat and various vegetables. The English word hodgepodge derives from the name of this stew.

JENEVER (Netherlands): A Dutch gin that bears little resemblance to gin in the United States, though it is also flavored with JUNIPER berries. Not suitable for mixed drinks, it is traditionally drunk cold and straight.

JUG (Romania): Yoke, used to refer to the centuries of Turkish domination.

JUNIPER BERRIES: The fruit of the juniper tree, about the size of peppercorns, they are available dried. They have a warm, pungent flavor and are widely used in Belgian cooking.

KAAKI (Tunisia): Pretzellike snacks made from salt, flour and water sold by street vendors.

KABANOS (Poland): A very thin, dried pork sausage.

KASHKAVAL (Romania, Bulgaria): A mild, yellowish table cheese, also used for grating, made from sheep's milk. Available in cheese stores. Provolone or sweet Münster can be substituted.

KEBABCHA (Bulgaria): Skinless sausages of ground meat mixed with spices and grilled on skewers.

KESRA (North Africa): A type of Arab bread.

KIEŁBASA (Poland): Polish word for many kinds of sausage. In the United States *kiełbasa* is almost always a highly spiced mixture of beef and pork.

KIRSCH (Switzerland): A brandy distilled from cherries. Imported brands have a more delicate flavor than domestic United States types.

KRUPNIK (Poland): A honey liqueur, served hot; also the name of a barley soup.

KURBAN (Bulgaria): A thick soup with a meat base plus vegetables such as tomatoes and peppers, it often symbolizes a ritual offering, and is served on festive occasions.

LOUKANKA (Bulgaria): A type of hard sausage resembling salami.

MAGHREB (North Africa): The "west"; Arabic designation for North Africa, between Suez and the Atlantic, the Sahara and the Mediterranean.

MALSOUQUA (Tunisia and Morocco): Paper-thin semolina pastry used to make BRIK and BASTILA. FILO may be substituted.

MAMALIGA (Romania): A staple of Romanian peasants, resembling Italian *polenta* or cornmeal mush. It often takes the place of bread.

MAVROUD (Bulgaria): A dark red wine.

MAZURKA (Poland): A cake from the Mazur region, which also gives its name to the dance on which some of the piano pieces of Chopin are based.

MEAD: A fermented drink based on honey and water, popular in Poland where it is called *miôd.*

MECHOUI (North Africa): A whole roast lamb, the main meat dish of Algerian desert cooking.

MEDINA (North Africa): The Arabic word for city, it indicates the old section of any city built by the Muslims before the arrival of Europeans.

MEKENE (Bulgaria): A tavern.

MERGUEZ (Tunisia): Hot sausages made of ground meat mixed with lamb's-tail fat and spices. They are deep-fried and preserved.

MESOLCINA (Switzerland): Thin slices of air-cured ham from the Mesolcina Valley.

MEZELICURI (Romania): Hors d'oeuvre or snacks.

MITITEI (Romania): Tiny highly spiced grilled sausages of ground beef, often served as an appetizer.

MSIR (Morocco): Salted lemons preserved in jars and used as a flavoring agent in TOUAJEN.

MSLALLA (Morocco): Pickled olives.

MUNARA: A tool for coring squash. Available in some stores carrying Middle Eastern products.

MUST (Romania): Unfermented grape juice produced when the new grapes are pressed.

MUSTĂRII (Romania): Rustic, open-air taverns that, in season, dispense MUST and lightly fermented grape juice, usually accompanied by MITITEI.

NEUCHÂTEL (Switzerland):
A light, sparkling wine from
northern Switzerland. Widely
exported.

ORANGE-BLOSSOM WATER
(North Africa): An extract of
orange blossoms used as a
flavoring agent. Available in
Middle Eastern or specialty
stores.
ORZO: Tiny oval-shaped pasta
resembling grains of rice in
appearance.
OSCYPKI (Poland): A ewe's-milk
cheese made, with variations, in
the mountainous regions of most
Slavic countries.

PASTERMÁ (Bulgaria),
PASTRAMĂ (Romania):
Preserved meat that is salted and
sometimes smoked, made of pork,
lamb, beef, goose or goat. Some
varieties are highly spiced. It is
usually cooked by grilling.
PIED-NOIRS (Algeria): Europeans,
particularly Frenchmen, living in
Algeria, now mostly repatriated.
PIORA (Switzerland): A soft
delicate cheese made in the
Italian-speaking Ticinese region
of Switzerland.
PITA (North Africa): A flat Arab
bread.
POD IGATO (Bulgaria): "Under
the yoke"; refers to the years of
Turkish domination.
POLDER (Netherlands): A region
of land below sea level that has
been reclaimed from the sea by
means of dikes and dams.
PRIMEURS (Belgium): Tiny
flavorful vegetables picked when
they attain their first growth.
Available in the United States in
jars.

QUETSCH (Luxembourg): A
kind of plum used in pastry
fillings and to make a liqueur
called Quetsch.

RACLETTE (Switzerland): A
melted-cheese dish; also the name
of a cheese for making it that is
exported to the United States.
RAMADAN (North Africa): The
ninth month of the Muhammadan
year, in which Muslims fast from
sunrise to sunset.
RIJSTTAFEL (Netherlands): A
"rice table." Originating in
Indonesia, formerly a Dutch
possession, it is an elaborate meal
consisting of rice served with
numerous side dishes and
condiments. It is very popular in
the Netherlands.
ROSE WATER (North Africa): A
sweet liquid flavoring distilled
from rose petals; the petals are
often imported from Bulgaria.
Available in Middle Eastern
stores or specialty shops.
RÖSTI (Switzerland): A dish
made of cooked cold potatoes that
are first grated and then sautéed
so that they form a cake.

SALTPETER: A curing agent;
used in making KIEŁBASA.
Available in drugstores.

SALUMERIA (Switzerland): The
name for a sausage shop both in
Italy proper and in the Italian-
speaking Ticinese region.
SARMALE (Romania): Fermented
cabbage leaves filled with ground
meat and seasonings and shaped
into balls.
SBRINZ (Switzerland): A hard
cheese similar to Parmesan used
for grating when mature, but
suitable as a table cheese when
young.
SHAFFISER (Switzerland): A
lively white wine from the Lake
Bienne region of Neuchâtel.
SEMOLINA: Finely granulated
meal made from the branless inner
kernels of durum wheat grains. It
is used in the manufacture of
pasta and COUSCOUS. Available in
Middle Eastern or specialty
stores.
SHOPSKA SALATA (Bulgaria): A
simple salad of tomatoes,
cucumbers and SIRENE cheese.
SIRENE (Bulgaria): A pickled
white sheep's-milk cheese
resembling Greek FETA and
Romanian BRYNZA.
SLIVOVA (Bulgaria): Plum
brandy.
SMEN (North Africa): Aged or
rancid butter made from sheep's
or cow's milk.
SOUK (North Africa): A market
or, in larger cities, a street or
quarter devoted to buying and
selling.
STUICA (Romania): A pike, often
used in making fish CIORBA.

TAJINE, plural TOUAJEN
(North Africa): A one-pot dish
combining meat, fish or fowl with
broth, vegetables and seasonings.
Also the name of the earthenware
pot in which it cooks. A TAJINE
SLAOUI is a pot made in the town
of Salé in Morocco.
TEXEL (Netherlands): An island
off the coast of Holland famous
for its marsh-fed sheep, which
yield a superior, slightly salty
meat.
TUICA (Romania): Plum brandy.
TURBEREL (Romania): A lightly
fermented grape juice served in
MUSTARII.

USZKA (Poland): Little
packets of dough filled with meat
or mushrooms and added to
soups.

WÄHEN (Switzerland): Large
round, open tarts that are filled
with vegetables, cheese or
fruit.
WATERZOOI (Belgium): A
souplike stew of poultry or fish in
a thickened broth.
WITLOOF (Belgium): Flemish for
endive. Called *chicorée de
bruxelles* by French-speaking
Belgians.
WLOSZCZYZNA (Poland): "Italian
commodities," or green
vegetables.

ŻUBRÓWKA (Poland): A
vodka lightly flavored with
buffalo grass.

Mail-Order Sources

The following stores, grouped by
region, accept mail orders for
foods called for in this book. Unless the name of the store is self-
explanatory, those places that carry
cheeses only are so indicated; all
other stores listed carry a variety
of canned and dried products; a
few will ship fresh ones. Because
policies differ and managements
change, check with the store in
question to determine what it has
in stock, the current prices, and
how best to buy the items you
want. Be as specific as possible
when inquiring. Some stores require a minimum amount on mail
orders, ranging from $2.50 to $25.

East
George Malko
185 Atlantic Ave.
Brooklyn, N.Y. 11201

Sahadi Importing Co., Inc.
187 Atlantic Ave.
Brooklyn, N.Y. 11201

Kalustyan Orient Export Trading
Corp.
123 Lexington Ave.
New York, N.Y. 10016

European Grocery Store
520 Court Pl.
Pittsburgh, Pa. 15219

Stamoolis Bros. Grocery
2020 Penn Ave.
Pittsburgh, Pa. 15222

Cheese & Wine Cellar
Montgomery Mall
Bethesda, Md. 20034

Wine & Cheese Shop
1413 Wisconsin Ave., N.W.
Washington, D.C. 20007

Acropolis Food Market
1206 Underwood St., N.W.
Washington, D.C. 20015

Magruder's Grocers
5626 Connecticut Ave., N.W.
Washington, D.C. 20015

South
Hickory Farms Inc. (cheeses)
2030 Lawrenceville Highway
Decatur, Ga. 30033

Antone's Import Co.
P.O. Box 3352
(807 Taft St.)
Houston, Tex. 77019

Barzizza Brothers International
Trade Center
351 So. Front St.
Memphis, Tenn. 38103

Bert's Groceteria
3464 Main Highway
Miami, Fla. 33133

Progress Grocery
915 Decatur St.
New Orleans, La. 70116

Ideal Bakery (*filo*)
2436 Ursulines Ave.
New Orleans, La. 70119

Midwest
Swiss Colony
Lindale Plaza
Cedar Rapids, Iowa 52402

Conte-Di-Savoia
555 W. Roosevelt Rd.
Chicago, Ill. 60607

Shiekh Grocery (cheeses)
652 Bolivar Rd.
Cleveland, Ohio 44115

Samos Wholesale Grocery
(cheeses)
727 Bolivar Rd.
Cleveland, Ohio 44115

Demmas Shish-Ke-Bob
5806 Hampton Ave.
St. Louis, Mo. 63109

Heidi's Around the World Food
Shop
1149 So. Brentwood Blvd.
St. Louis, Mo. 63117

Paul's Cheese Stall
116 Union Market
St. Louis, Mo. 63101

West
Economy Domestic and Imported
Grocery
973 Broadway
Denver, Colo. 80203

C & K Importing Co.
2771 West Pico Blvd.
Los Angeles, Calif. 90006

Haig's
441 Clement St.
San Francisco, Calif. 94118

Vern Anderson's Delicatessen
9575 S.W. Beaverton Highway
Beaverton, Ore. 97005

De Laurenti Importing
Stall 5, Lower Pike Place Market
Seattle, Wash. 98101

Canada
Main Importing Co., Inc.
1188 St. Lawrence
Montreal 126, Quebec

Cooke's Fine Foods
5961 Brock St.
Kingston, Ontario

The Cheese Shop
258 Laurier Ave. West
Ottawa 4, Ontario

Recipe Index: English

NOTE: An R preceding a page refers to the Recipe Booklet. Size, weight and material are specified for pans in the recipes because they affect cooking results. A pan should be just large enough to hold its contents comfortably. Heavy pans heat slowly and cook food at a constant rate. Aluminum and cast iron conduct heat well but may discolor foods containing egg yolks, wine, vinegar or lemon. Enamelware is a fairly poor conductor of heat. Many recipes therefore recommend stainless steel or enameled cast iron, which do not have these faults.

Recipe Index: Foreign

General Index
Numerals in italics indicate a photograph or drawing of the subject mentioned.

Credits and Acknowledgments

Sources for illustrations in this book are shown below. All photographs by Sheldon Cotler except those by: Richard Jeffery, pages 14, 15, 31, 34, 55, 60, 67, 68, 72, 73, 75, 82, 99, 102, 103, 113, 135, 139, 140, 142, 173, 182, 184, 185, 186, 187, 190, 192. Eliot Elisofon, pages 76, 80, 81, 84, 85, 86, 88, 89, 92, 93, 94, 95, 96, 97. Other photographs: page 4: Walter Daran, top; Susan Wood, bottom left; Monica Suder, bottom right. Page 105: Fred Eng. Drawings by Gloria duBouchet, pages 11, 39, 79, 109, 147, 188.

The following people contributed some of the recipes in this book or assisted in testing them in the FOODS OF THE WORLD kitchen: Bernard Koten, Director of the Russian Library at New York University, contributed to the chapters dealing with Poland, Romania and Bulgaria. Also for Poland, Mrs. Stanislawa Sokolowska; for Switzerland, Erwin Herger, Head Chef, Chalet Suisse Restaurant; for Belgium, Bruno Caravaggi and Gino Robusti, co-owners of the Quo Vadis Restaurant, all of New York City. Also for Belgium, Mr. and Mrs. Lucien Redemans, L'Abreuvoir Restaurant, Brussels. For the Netherlands, Hugh Jans, food columnist, *Vrij Nederland* magazine, Amsterdam, and Marianna Swan, New Milford, Conn.; for North Africa, Bada Hlia and Touraia Sharouria, Moroccan Mission to the United Nations; Fatma and Sahbi Overtani; Aicha Hanafi, Manouche Halfon; and Paula Wolfert, all of New York; Christopher Wanklyn of Marrakech.

For their help in the production of this book the author, co-author, editors and staff wish to thank the following: *in Switzerland:* Georges Hangartner, Director, Dolder Grand Hotel; Fred Birman, Press Chief, Swiss National Tourist Office; Rudolf Kieni, Director, Swiss Dining-Car Company; Mrs. H. Zumsteg, Kronenhalle Restaurant; Fernand Barbey, Treasurer, Wine-Growers' Association; Roland Pecorini, Hotel Des Mayens; Rehane Repond; Joseph Farner and Willi Bühlmann, Swiss Union of Cheese-Makers; René Vallelian; René Kramer; Roger Beuchat, Director, Neuchâtel Tourism Office; René Berner, Director, Continental Hotel; Paul Barraud, École Hôtelière; Mrs. Lydia Meyer-Liechti, Gasthaus Zum Schiff Restaurant; Jean-Jacques Monnard, Director, Canton of Vaud Tourism Office; *in Belgium:* Jacques Champion; Mr. and Mrs. Jacques Bolle; Mr. and Mrs. Robert de Clercq; José Géal, Toone Theatre; Jean Haesaerts; Mr. and Mrs. Robert Halewijn; Mr. and Mrs. Frédéric Hayez; Mireille Henrard, Commissioner General, Belgian Tourism; Mr. and Mrs. Marcel Kreush, Villa Lorraine Restaurant; Norbert Lauwers; Honoré Loones, Hotel Gauquie; Mr. and Mrs. J. P. Maas; Armand Vanbillemont; Willy Van De Vivjer, Hotel Duc de Bourgogne; Frans Vromann, École d'Art Saint Luc; Henri Wittamer; *in the Netherlands:* Restaurant de Gravemoeln; School Voor Banketbakkers; *in Poland:* Jan Kalkowski, *Przekroj* magazine; Edward Kaminski; Jerzy Blikle; Kazimierz Bilanow, Polish Interpress Agency; Dr. Tadeusz Przypkowski, Director, Museum of the Przypkowski Family; Antoni Reczajski, Deputy Director, Ministry of Internal Trade; Mrs. Wanda Jostowa, Curator, Museum Tatrzanskie; Edward Szot, Director, Wierzynek Restaurant; *in Romania:* Nadejda Ciobanu and Veronica Brote, National Tourist Office; Julian Vintila, Director, Athenée Palace Hotel; Constantin Priboi, Commercial Director, Athenée Palace Hotel; Serban Andrescu, Director of Hotels and Restaurants, Brasov area; George Oprea, Director, Hotel Delta; *in Bulgaria:* Dimitar Vlaytschev, Balkan Tourist Restaurants; Radoslav Radoulov, Committee for Tourism; Christo Marinov Ivanov and Penko Bonev, Balkan Tourist Office, Sofia; *in Tunisia:* Tanya Matthews; Ali Chelbi, Le Malouf Restaurant; Houssein Talha and Mohamed El Hedi, M'Rabet Restaurant; Paul Albrecht and Habib Ben Salah, Dar Zarrouk Restaurant; Jalel Ben Abdallah; *in Morocco:* Brion Gysin; Robert Eliot; Lea Becheton; Marie-Louise Guinaudeau; *in Washington, D.C.:* Embassy of the Polish People's Republic; Bistrakapka Genova; *in New York City:* Jan Aaron; Pierre Artigue, Executive Secretary, Belgian American Chamber of Commerce in the U.S.; Mme. Aicha Benhima, Moroccan Mission to the U.N.; Eveline Boon, Netherlands National Tourist Office; Jadwiga Daniec; Hedi Drissi, Tunisian Mission to the U.N.; Evelyn Farlin; Lucille Gordon; Simone Gossner; Elzbieta Halberstam; Heinz Hofer, Switzerland Cheese Association; Esther Isaacs; Irene Lupu, Romanian National Tourist Office; Guenadi Pankin, Director, Bulgarian Tourist Office; Anna Rosenblum; Betty Vreeland and Liliane Wilcox.

In New York City the following shops and galleries also contributed to the production of this book: Michael Bertolini Antiques; Bloomingdale's; Richard Camp Antiques; Richard Carleton, Ltd.; Cepelia Corp.; Compass Antiques Co.; Connoisseur East; George Cothran Flowers; Country Floors, Inc.; Cross Keys Antiques; Decorative Accents; Decorative Resale, Inc.; Efendi East Arts and Fashion; Four Seasons Antiques; Globe-Trotter Antiques; H. J. Kratzer, Inc.; La Cuisiniere, Inc.; Le Tree Art; Lord & Taylor; Robert Lustig, Objects of Art; Ann Mandel, Ltd.; Meuniers; A. Morjikian Co., Inc.; Patina Antiques; Putting Antiques Corp.; Romanian National Tourist Office; C. Timothy Schwab; Henrietta C. Stern, Inc.; F. Palmer Weber Associates, Inc.; The Window Shop, Inc.

Sources consulted in the production of this book include: *Bulgaria Today,* William Cary; *Polish Cookbook,* Zofia Czerny; *All the Best in Belgium and Luxembourg,* Sidney Clark; *A Belgian Cookbook,* Juliette Elkon; *Grandes Recettes de la Cuisine Algérienne,* Youcef Ferhi; *Fez: Traditional Moroccan Cooking,* Z. Guinaudeau; *The Swiss Cookbook,* Nika Standen Hazelton; *La Cuisine Tunisienne,* Mohamed Kouki; *Cooking the Polish Way,* Lila Kowalska; *Encyclopedia of Wines and Spirits,* Alexis Lichine; *Polish Cookery,* Marja Ochorowicz-Monatowa; *North Africa,* Doré Ogrizek, ed.; *Rice, Spice and Bitter Oranges,* Lila Perl; *A History of Modern Poland,* Hans Roose; *The Romanian Cook Book,* Anisoara Stan; *The Art of Dutch Cooking,* C. Countess van Limburg Stirum.